CRETE RECLAIMED
A feminist exploration of bronze age Crete

Susan Evasdaughter

Illustrated by Billie Walker-John
Foreword by Rodney Castleden

Heart of Albion Press

CRETE RECLAIMED
A feminist exploration of bronze age Crete

Susan Evasdaughter

CRETE RECLAIMED
A Feminist Exploration of Bronze Age Crete

SUSAN EVASDAUGHTER

Illustrated by Billie Walker-John

ISBN 1 872883 44 3

© Text copyright Susan Evasdaughter 1996
© Foreword copyright Rodney Castleden 1996
© Illustrations copyright Billie Walker-John 1996
© Maps copyright Bob Trubshaw 1996

The moral right of the author has been asserted.

All rights reserved. No part of this book may be reproduced in any form or by any means without prior written permission from Heart of Albion Press, except for brief passages quoted in reviews.

British Library Cataloguing in Publication Data
A catalogue record for this book is available from the British Library.

Printed in England by DAR Printing

HEART OF ALBION PRESS
2 Cross Hill Close, Wymeswold,
Loughborough, LE12 6UJ

*Artist's impression of sacred activities of a Cretan priestess.
Based on scenes from the Ayia Triada sarcophagus.*

Acknowledgements

A special note of thanks is due to Roberta Wedge without whom this book would not have come into being. I am grateful for initial encouragement, for finding a publisher and for her guidance, questioning and conscientious and detailed comments on the text.

I should also like to thank Billie John for her commitment and patience through all the drawing and redrawing of the illustrations to my (sometimes stringent) requirements.

Bob Trubshaw's guidance and support in the writing of this book has also been invaluable. He has directed me to sources I would otherwise have missed and helped me to refine my arguments.

Grateful thanks are also due to the many academics who sent information despite their busy schedules.

The assistance and earnest efforts of the staff of the library at Hebden Bridge in acquiring the most obscure texts for me must not go unmentioned.

Finally, I should like to thank all the readers of the first two booklets who wrote to me expressing their gratitude to me for writing them. It is their encouragement that has spurred me on over the past four years to write this book and it companion volume, *Journey through the Labyrinth*, which is due for publication next year.

Contents

Preface	ix
Critical Phases in Cretan History	x
Chronological Table	xi
Foreword by Rodney Castleden	xiv
Introduction: An Island with a Sacred Past	1
1. Daily Life on Bronze Age Crete	7

In The Beginning . . ., The Golden Age, social organisation, the potential of pacifism, overseas settlements, overseas trade, literacy and sealstones, industry, technology and the legal system, medical knowledge, diet.

2. The Meaning of Sacred Art	44

The early prehistoric background, Cretan art: stonework, pottery, faience and ivory, metalwork, frescoes and textiles.

3. Gender Roles	65

A prehistoric perspective, women as the natural leaders of society, physical build, the prevalence of matriarchy, linguistic evidence, the origins of patriarchy, the devaluation of women, matrilineal endogamy, evidence recorded by the classical Greeks, the Greek mainland and the Aegean, the attitude of the classical Greeks to matriarchy, the Amazons, the women of ancient Crete, the problem of ethnocentricity, the archaeological evidence, the men of ancient Crete.

4. Religion: The Goddess and Her Symbols 115

The Goddess tradition, centres of celebration, public and private rituals, different stages in the development of religious ideas, the role of the godling in Cretan religion, attitudes to death and burial practices.

5. Not with a Whimper 168

The fall, invasion or immigration? - the arrival of the Mycenaeans, life after the generalised destruction, the fall of Knossos, the final loss - the Dorian invasion, Gazi and Karphi, escape and emigration, the jewel in the empire builder's crown.

6. The New Religion 188

Zeus and the overthrow of the Goddess, the new Goddesses

7. Conclusion 202

Glossary 204

Sources and Further Reading 206

Notes on Text 211

Index 220

Preface

While I was a student a friend, Jenny Donald, visited Crete. On her return she was full of the wonders of the island's past but incensed by the way she felt it was being misrepresented. Years later, when I first encountered the wonders displayed in Iraklion's Archaeological museum, Knossos and the sacred caves, I was similarly concerned. I determined to find out more about what lay behind these wondrous remnants and discovered a glorious, flourishing, contented society, at peace with itself and the world for over two thousand years.

The most fundamental characteristic of this bronze age culture, its gynocentricity, is immediately apparent from the surviving artefacts. Its god was a woman, its religious leaders were women and all the important people depicted on artefacts and discovered in stately burials were, without exception, women. Despite the abundance of archaeological remains, the interpretations of many scholars remain misleading. It is the desire to present a truer picture of ancient Crete that prompted the writing of this book.

My first visit to Crete in 1983 led to the publication of two booklets, *A Sacred Island* and *The Home of the Labyris*. Since then there have been two major international seminars on "Minoan" Crete and we have lost, through premature death, some important contributors to the field, Marija Gimbutas, Mark Cameron and Spyridon Marinatos. Sadly, despite the revalatory work of these and other dedicated scholars, little has changed in the way the male dominated discipline of archaeology marginalises the role of women in prehistory.

This book is an attempt to draw aside the curtain of androcentric [1] prejudice and explore the evidence of ancient Crete. If a more balanced view of the past results through such research, this will foster a sense of pride in the great achievements of our foremothers. It is hoped that this will imbue us with courage in the present and hope for the future.

Critical Phases in Cretan History

Neolithic (pre-bronze age) From 6000-3000 BC (pre-ceramic). Goddess figures found in neolithic tell on the Kephala hill (site of Knossos).
Towns (pre-Temple Palaces) 2600-2300 BC: Vasiliki pottery. From 2400: common civilization, coastal settlements. By 2200 BC 75,000 people in over 100 settlements.
Early Temple Palaces 1900-1700 BC: Knossos built c.1930. No rivalry between the settlements.
New Temple Palaces 1700-1450 BC: Better constructed buildings replaced the old ones on the same sites with no break in the evolution of civilisation after the destruction (probably by earthquake). Ayia Triada built.
Eruption of Thera 1760-1500 BC: Disagreement between scholars as to date and whether it was implicated in the generalised destruction on Crete.
General Destruction Around 1450 BC: Most of the Temple Palaces destroyed, probably by fire. Evidence shows Knossos not destroyed until 1375 or even 1150. The surrounding cities continued to be inhabited. No evidence of loss of life due to the destruction. Mycenaean settlement on Crete apparent from their militarism, burial systems and arts but the cultural base of the island remains matrifocal and Cretan. Decrease in Cretan exports.
Iron Age
Began around 1200 BC and established in mainland Greece and Italy c.1000 BC. Iron began to replace bronze allowing for the production of powerful weapons.
Dorian Invasion
In 1200 all major towns on the Greek mainland, except Athens, were taken over by the Dorians. Around 1100 BC Crete was also invaded and subjugated by Dorians.
Classical Greece
500 BC is recognised as the peak of this era which was noted for its architectural, political, social, artistic and literary achievements. All of these were the remnants of earlier Cretan and Aegean cultures appropriated by the new patriarchy. The Greek states of the classical period were underpinned by marriage, the male-dominated nuclear family, private property, slavery and the disfranchisement of women.

Official Dating Systems

Platon	Approximate dates (all BC)	Evans
Pre-Palatial	3000–2600	Early Minoan I
	2600–2200	Early Minoan II
	2200–2050	Early Minoan III
	2050–1700	Middle Minoan I
First Palatial	1900–1700	Middle Minoan II
Second Palatial	1700–1450	Middle Minoan III
Post-Palatial	1450–1425	Late Minoan I
	1425–1250	Late Minoan II
	1250–1100	Late Minoan III

Note:

Prehistoric systems of dating are, by their very nature, open to challenge and refinement. The above systems are still broadly used though some scholars have made their own amendments. Peter Warren, the British archaeologist who has excavated on and written about Crete for many years, for example, places the beginning of Early Minoan I well back into the 4th millenium BC at around 3500 and scholars continue to dispute the date of the final fall of Knossos.

Given the context of this book, neither of the above sytems of dating are linguistically appropriate. The great Cretan edifices were not 'palaces' and Arthur Evans' identification of this culture with King Minos was inappropriate. As these terms are still used widely by scholars, however, I have found it necessary to use the Evans sytem of dating.

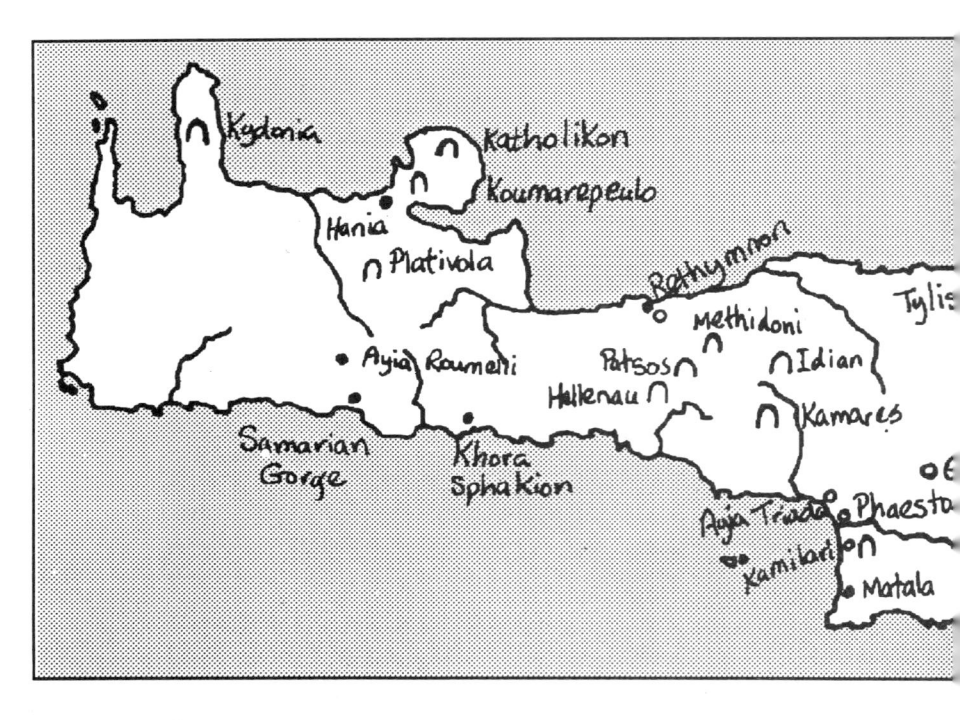

⋂   Sacred caves (E = Eileithyian Cave)
○   Temple Palaces or Country House shrines
☐   Mt Juktas mountain top sanctuary
●   Modern tourist locations

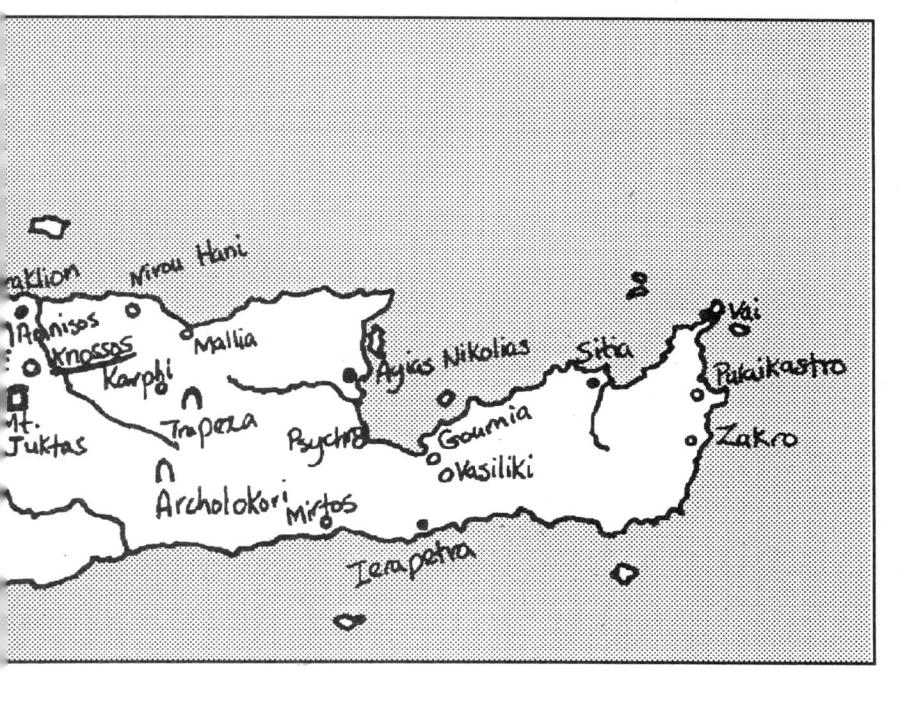

Crete - the sacred sites

Foreword

Between about 3000 and 1400 BC the Minoans built one of the world's great civilizations on the island of Crete. In the human story that has ebbed and flowed for the last 40,000 years, the era of *Homo sapiens sapiens*, is a swelling sea, there have been just a score of occasions when the energies of that ocean have gathered together into towering waves of achievement, glittering brilliantly for a short time only as they topple, break and collapse. Each of these cultural *tsunamis* seems to represent the highest level of human achievement, a model, a paradigm of what it is possible for us to aspire to. Each has something to tell us about the way we might live our lives now and in time to come. Each must be explored. Their differing flavours or textures result from differing ideologies; each civilization was gripped by a distinctive set of fundamental beliefs and this released an archetype from the collective unconscious. Jung argued that in the 1930s and 40s the German people were possessed by Wotan, the North European god of storm and war, and that Adolf Hitler worked, as a completely unconscious shaman, to unleash this dangerous archetype. A kind of psychological plague, a *furor teutonicus*, spread and threw the German nation into a frenzy of aggression and destruction.

The Minoans too were possessed, but by an archetype of a different stripe. They were possessed by their Great Goddess, who was later known as Rhea and Hera, and it was their priestesses who worked to reinforce this possession with elaborate religious rituals; the result was what I have called a *euphoria minoica*, a Minoan ecstasy. And it is there to see in every vibrant fresco image.

The leading characteristic of the Minoan civilization was not militarism, as it was in Nazi Germany or the Roman Empire or a dozen other, earlier cultures, but something more constructive and more life-enhancing and, to most of us, infinitely more attractive. The other thing that is distinctive about the Minoan civilization and, I think, unique is that it was dominated by an élite of women. At a time in the West when the long-suffered, traditional role of women in society as subjugated subordinates has been challenged and the bars of gender-bias have been severely shaken and cracked, it is particularly useful to look back at this other society, that of bronze age Crete, and see just what sort of civilization was built upon 'feminine' values.

It is just a hundred years after Sir Arthur Evans' dig at Knossos began and there has been a century of discoveries about the nature of the Minoan civilization. The time is ripe to look at it again and try for a new synthesis. Others, like Hans Wunderlich and myself, have looked at the great 'palaces' unearthed at Knossos, Phaistos and Mallia and concluded that Evans was wrong to see them as primarily royal residences. The so-called 'palaces' make better sense interpreted as temple-complexes run by powerful elites of priestesses. Susan Evasdaughter takes this idea and develops it with commitment right through to the time when the priestesses' deity, the Great Goddess, was finally supplanted by a god, Zeus. There seems to be an echoing memory of this time, back in the fourteenth and fifteenth centuries BC, in the Greek myths in which Zeus and Hera are at odds with each other. It is made to appear like an engaging tiff, a mere domestic marital squabble, but it is a serious backward reference to the earlier power struggle between two different belief systems. The Greek myths show that there was an uneasy marriage between the old and the new religious principles.

Susan Evasdaughter bravely reconstructs that older principle, seeing it as the foundation stone of a golden age in ancient Europe, and she writes of it with a rare passion. There is a wealth of fine detail in her book about the everyday lives of the people of ancient Crete and about all of the wonderful Minoan sites that are still there to be visited on Crete. This is a book not just for the academics, but for visitors to Crete and for those interested in ancient religions.

The archaeological work continues, at Knossos itself and at other sites, and more pieces of the complicated Minoan jigsaw are being added every year. Since 1970, spectacular finds of frescoes, more complete than those at Knossos, have been found at Akrotiri on Santorini. The new finds there add more fuel to the flames of Susan Evasdaughter's ideas. They give us scene after scene of elaborate religious ceremony, usually dominated by women, and one shows in breathtaking detail exactly how the bronze age Minoans living on Santorini imagined the Great Goddess looked. She is of course incomparably impressive and beautiful: I can see that in spite of the culture gap and in spite of the time gap that separates her from me. It looks as if Susan Evasdaughter will be proved substantially right by the accumulating evidence of archaeology.

Susan Evasdaughter's Crete Reclaimed is a painstaking work of careful reconstruction. We are presented with an incredibly rich evocation of life on ancient Crete, and many different aspects of its culture. All the evidence for a matrilineal and matriarchal society is assembled and offered in a powerful and overwhelmingly convincing statement about the role of women in ancient societies.

Her study is wide ranging in its references - from Crete to Egypt, Turkey to Greece, Sicily to Britain and back to Malta - and the result is a kaleidoscopic treatment of ancient mythology that carries an important message. Religion in the ancient world developed (Susan Evasdaughter would certainly not let us say progressed!) from Supreme Universal Monotheism involving worship of the Great Goddess, through Monotheism involving the Great Goddess and her year-godling consort, to Polytheism involving a diminishing number of goddesses and some gods who were growing in importance. At the end is the Patriarchal Monotheism that Europeans seem to have been stuck with mostly since that time. Susan Evasdaughter asserts that the Minoan pantheon was completely free of male deities. There she and I differ. But it is her role, her destiny, to take up this admittedly strong position and hold it uncompromisingly, and she will, I believe, be widely respected for it. She has a refreshing irreverence towards the orthodoxies, the holy cows of archaeology and it is sometimes out of such situations that new perspectives emerge. Susan Evasdaughter is Jacob wrestling with the angel.

Her idea of 'eracentricity' is one that is very close to my own heart. Like her, I believe that we too often see the world around us and the worlds that have gone before us through the distorting lenses of our own concerns, our own values, our own totems and prejudices; too often this prevents us from seeing reality as it is and was. And the danger implicit in this is that we are also preventing ourselves from seeing the future, the reality that will be, for what it will be.

Trying to see the past for what it was is not merely a question of academic honesty; it is a question of being honest about where we are and where we might be going.

Rodney Castleden
Brighton 1995

© copyright Rodney Castleden

Introduction

An Island with a Sacred Past

Long before the emergence of classical Greece, from which our own western European culture claims to have derived so much, a great civilisation flourished in the Aegean for over 2,000 years. It was from this advanced culture that the Greeks derived the political, philosophical, legal, mathematical, medical and scientific systems that they are credited with inventing.

The era in Cretan prehistory which this book deals with is approximately 2600-1200 BC, which corresponds roughly to the bronze age. This period was inappropriately designated as 'Minoan' by Arthur Evans, the British archaeologist who excavated Knossos. He derived the term from classical Greek legends where the title Minos is used. This epithet is a generic term similar to Pharaoh (ruler); Ariadne, the Minos of Crete, or Phasiphae (Ariadne's mother) the 17th Minos.

The Minos of Greek legend, post-dates the origins of what Evans called the 'Minoan' civilisation of Crete by around two thousand years. The generic term has become associated with the father of Ariadne, the princess who, in the mythical tale, assisted the Athenean prince Theseus in his escape from the labyrinth after he had slain the minotaur (half-man half-bull, son of Queen Pasiphae).

It is unfortunate that this association has been made between Minos and bronze age Crete. False extrapolations have subsequently led a number of modern writers to refer to the ruler of this sophisticated culture as a King Minos. The evidence for there being a king of Crete at Knossos or anywhere else on the island or territories during what is known as the 'Minoan' period is less than there is for there being a minotaur to whom young innocents were sacrificed. As I hope to establish in this book, there is a good deal of evidence to suggest that bronze age Crete, with its Goddess religion, was a matriarchal culture [1]. It was organised around queens who combined religious and secular roles in the guidance of their people. For this reason I have attempted to avoid the misleading term 'Minoan'.

Crete Reclaimed

The physical focus of this artistically advanced and learned culture was the Temple Palace. These religious and administrative centres, which have been found both in great cities like Knossos and small towns like Gournia, were an expression of the pinnacle of Cretan achievement. The advanced techniques used in their construction demonstrate the Cretan capacity for the practical, while the vast range of exquisite artefacts they contained illustrates this people's refinement.

The one uniting factor in all examples of bronze age Cretan genius is that they were motivated by devotion to a female deity, the Great Goddess. Her sacred imagery and symbols are ubiquitous throughout the architecture and artefacts of the period. A similar cultural focus was used by many other peoples which preceded bronze age Crete and were contemporaneous with it. A female deity was celebrated in many parts of Europe, north Africa and the Near East until Her replacement by the male gods of the Indo-Europeans. These invaders from northern peripheral areas swept through vast areas of what is now central Europe, the Aegean and Turkey, sacking the ancient Goddess-oriented cultures. Crete survived longer than most of her neighbours because of the geographic isolation of the island and the impression that its culture made on the Mycenaeans, the northern invaders who settled in the Peleponnese area of mainland Greece.

Around 1450 BC, the Cretan priestess-queens, anticipating the inevitability of invasion and domination by barbaric Indo-European forces, laid waste their great Temple Palaces thereby returning them, together with the sacred treasures they still contained, to the sanctity of the earth. Only Knossos, Arkhanes and Hania in the west, continued as large centres for religion and administration. Around 1100 BC these expectations were fulfilled and this great culture was finally eclipsed with the invasion of the Dorian Greeks.

Bronze age Crete stands out amongst its contemporaries for many reasons. Its great achievements in the fields of art, architecture and construction are superbly documented by the artefacts which have survived and, due to their island's relative geographical isolation, the Cretans were able to continue, far later than most other regions, in the old religious tradition which focussed exclusively on a female deity.

It was the Cretans fierce commitment to their deity that caused the island to feature so strongly in the Greek epics and in some of the surviving work of classical Greek historians [2]. These legends and records highlight the pivotal role of Crete in the ideological overthrow of the Goddess tradition and gynocentricity.

We know from historical records and cross-cultural studies of the tradition of gynocentricity (matriarchy) and how this was gradually

Introduction

usurped by men culminating in the establishment of patriarchy. James Mellaart, the British archaeologist responsible for the excavation of the highly-developed neolithic settlements at Catal Huyuk and Hacilar, was left in no doubt by his findings at these sites, of the pre-eminence of women in these cultures. It is from this area that the first settlers on Crete are thought to have originated.

The vast majority of cultures which once had a different social organisational base from those of the west have been contaminated by external influences through colonisation, missionaries, the mass media and various methods of financial exploitation. It is now, therefore, virtually impossible to refer to other contemporary cultures which are organised on a matrifocal rather than a patrifocal basis [3]. Economic and social development has allowed for a relative redistribution of wealth in the west. Women have been allowed access to education and consequently many are able to express dissatisfaction with the secondary place they are allotted in male defined culture. One of the most recent demands of women has been the insistence that they have access to religious authority in the Church of England.

Because we are unable to point to many contemporary societies where matriarchy is the norm, scholars who wish to explore a non-patriarchal social organisation must look to the past. This has been done in a dedicated and scholarly manner by a small number of researchers; Elizabeth Gould Davis, Merlin Stone and, more recently, Riane Eisler and Elinor Gadon, all of whose work will be refered to in the ensuing pages.

It is unfortunate that more of the ancient matriarchal civilisations which existed throughout the rest of the world are not as beautifully and clearly documented as that of bronze age Crete. Despite the abundance of archaeological evidence, the modern androcentric mind has great difficulty in accepting even the possibility of matriarchy, let alone its postulated near-universality in the ancient world. The evidence is overwhelming and indisputable, yet difficult for us to comprehend and assimilate.

The Cretan remains offer not only a potted history of that culture but can also be seen as a show case of the near ubiquitous matriarchal culture of the ancient world. In all the areas that were inhabited in the prehistoric period, the evidence, if somewhat scattered, is still quite clear. It comes from all continents, although the best documented sites are in Anatolia (now Turkey), Old Europe (of which Crete is a part) and Malta.

Much of the evidence comes from the artifacts (see figs 1, 3, 13, 14 and 15) that demonstrate that these cultures were organised around a female religious principal. Although there can be no automatic acceptance of a direct relationship between this and a matriarchal social structure, there are strong indications that this was the case.

It could be argued that the driving force behind the move to patriarchy was competition and the emphasis on the individual rather than the group or one group against another, leading to greed and the concept of personal wealth. Patriarchy began with the disintegration of the matrilineal clan system and was sustained by the development of an ideology which, through mythology, religion and a redefinition of the taboo system, gave the basis for new legal systems. Monogamous marriage was developed in order to facilitate male property inheritance and the concept of individual (male) ownership grew to encompass women and children as chattels of men. Laws, which were given religious sanction, were developed to discriminate against women and girls in favour of men and boys. Women, who had once owned the land and headed the clans, became disinherited and disenfranchised. Men began representing their wives in public office and finally took over from them, dismissing women to the nursery, kitchen and bed.

One of the major limiting factors of most academic disciplines in the past has been the gender of its practitioners. Archaeology is no exception, it is a shining example of a male bastion. This factor, coupled with the nature of the society from which archaeologists are derived, has inevitably coloured both their expectations in relation to excavation work and their conclusions. Given Evans' solidly middle class English background and the constraints of Victorian archaeology, we should be amazed at the degree of open-mindedness he achieved in relation to ancient Cretan culture.

With the gradual changes taking place in present day society which are permeating into the academic world there are now a small number of women scholars and even fewer men who are prepared to move away from the more usual ethnocentric views. In 1991 anthropologists Joan Gero and Margaret Conkey edited a collection of papers concerned with gender bias in archaeology. Philosophical archaeologists Shanks and Tilly (1992) and Julian Thomas (1991) are questioning the entrenched precepts of their discipline and appeal to colleagues to be more sensitive to the inherent 'otherness' of the subject matter.

The present book makes no apologies in its attempt to introduce an alternative perspective by describing, through slightly less ethnocentric eyes, the matrifocal nature of ancient Cretan culture. An enormous metaphysical leap over millennia of gender

Introduction

indoctrination is necessary in order to hypothesise about anything other than a male-dominated world. It is what we have all grown up with and what our history lessons were full of. My culture offers me no preconceptions about the pre-eminence of women in all things so in that sense I do not approach archaeological remains in the same way a male scholar would. My feminist sensibilities assure me that there is no reason why women should not have been pre-eminent but it is the material remains from Crete (and many other cultures) that must be allowed to tell the story for themselves. By using this archaeological evidence I will attempt to show that ancient Crete was a theocracy with a woman centred social structure which included sacred alliances of priestesses and a ruling Queen or Queens who was so revered that she was seen to represent the Goddess on earth.

Nothing we do or say can undo the misogyny, cruelty and calculated oppression of women that is the history of the world. In Europe women were tortured and murdered (many of them burnt alive), for over four centuries (from 14th to 17th) [4]. Rape, suttee, female infanticide, foot binding and genital mutilation are adjuncts to the patriarchal organisation of society. Although we are unable to change the past we can make it visible and learn from it. This new knowledge can encourage us to make changes in the present and the future. I believe that a better understanding of our matriarchal heritage will give us all inspiration and offer both genders a new, more appropriate, sense of self.

1
Daily Life on Bronze Age Crete

In the Beginning . . .

The story of Crete begins around 6000 BC when the first settlers arrived on the island, probably from Anatolia (now a province of Turkey). Finds of jewellery and vases from this time show a strong Anatolian and North African influence. The round *tholos* tombs (large, circular, dome-shaped, sometimes known as 'beehive tombs') seen in central Anatolia were also popular on Crete at this time.

In the early 1960s the British archaeologist James Mellaart excavated part of the village of Catal Huyuk (inhabited between 6250-5400 BC) and neighbouring Hacilar (5700-5000 BC) in Anatolia. In Mellaart's view both sites revealed unequivocal evidence of the primacy of the female principle in religion and society. The Catal Huyuk birthing Goddess, Her power emphasised by Her large proportions and leopard throne (fig. 1) crystalises this people's belief system. The culture was focussed around and motivated by its communally-held belief in a female deity. Women were also the heads of households [1]. One of the many other factors that this culture had in common with Crete was that there was no sign of disturbance caused by warfare for over 1500 years.

Different levels exposed by archaeological digs represent the remains of successive generations of habitation. Remains from some of the levels of Catal Huyuk are contemporary with those discovered in the neolithic (new stone age) levels on Crete. Place-names from Crete have similarities with those of Anatolia and the sacred symbols of the Cretan religion derive from there. The pillar (a structure with which their Goddess is interchangeable in later artistic representations of Her), the *labyris* and the Horns of Consecration all have their antecedents in Anatolia. This is also true of many of the Cretan Goddess' attributes: the serpent, dove and bull. The sacred sign of the *labyris* was found painted

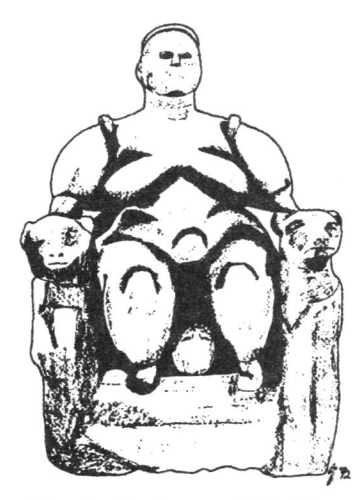

Fig. 1 Enthroned Birthing Goddess from Catal Huyuk 5750 BC. This figure was found in a grain bin. Her power is represented not through Her actual size but by Her proportions, the throne and the leopards which flank Her.

on shrine walls at Catal Huyuk. Indeed this symbol survived in Caria (in Anatolia) long after it fell from symbolic use on Crete.

Together with evidence of similarities between the two communities, the knowledge that the two matriarchal societies of neolithic Catal Huyuk and Crete existed simultaneously has led some archaeologists to consider the possibility that they were both off-shoots of the same culture. Arthur Evans supported this view. Most scholars, however, prefer to leave the field a little more open and say that the original inhabitants of Crete arrived from the east; possibly western Anatolia, Syria or Palastine. The waistcoat, codpiece and figure-of-eight shields, which are evident in Cretan artefacts from 1700 BC, have parallels in Lybia and pre-dynastic Egypt.

One avenue of exploration in the quest for the origins of the early Cretans is their language. It was believed, until as late as the 19th century, that all ancient cultures were illiterate. Bronze age Crete however tells a very different story. The earliest form of writing found on Crete was of the hieroglyphic type, called 'pictographic' by Evans. This dates from the Middle Minoan IA period of c.2000 BC. It has similarities with the scripts used by Hittite and Anatolian peoples, leading scholars to believe that they were all derived from a much older form of language.

A later form of Cretan script is known as Linear A and similarities have been claimed with the contemporary language of Lybia. Much excitement was focussed around the symbols which correspond to the Hittite for Mistress or My Lady which were inscribed on a Cretan libation table designating it as being for the deity. In later times the foremost Goddess of the Hittites, Ishtar (a descendant of the Great Goddess) was known or addressed by this title [2].

George Thompson, a specialist scholar of the prehistoric Aegean, noted that the 'Minoans' had affinities with other matriarchal peoples of the Aegean including the Carians, Leleges and Lycians (see fig 2), some of whom originated in Anatolia [3]. An image of a thriving Anatolian

Fig.2 Map of Aegean.

province that sent out satellite groups from around 7000 BC onwards to settle in different parts of the Aegean including Crete suggests itself. Although the consensus amongst most archaeologists is that there is not enough evidence from this period to say what caused these first spreads to occur it is possible that there may have been the pressure of external threat. Mellaart found evidence that some neolithic communities in Anatolia suffered from periods of disturbance and upheaval caused by patriarchally-organised warring tribes (Kurgans) from the north but not until around 5000 BC [4].

Each of the ten levels of neolithic debris found on the Kephala Hill, which was later to become the site of Knossos, corresponds to an approximately 300 year period, giving valuable evidence about life on Crete at this time. This, along with other archaeological evidence, reveals that the neolithic Cretans lived on hill tops and in caves. They were the equivalent of peasant farmers who cultivated crops and bred cattle, sheep and goats. They spun their own wool, wove their own cloth and played music using whistles made from the toe bones of animals.

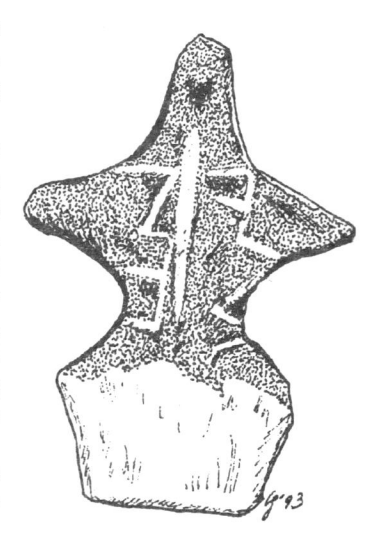

Fig.3 Late Neolithic Goddess with chalk-filled incised markings 5000-3100 BC from the Kephala Hill tell.

Their spirituality is attested to by the remnants of around twenty Goddess figures of fired clay which were found in the neolithic levels of the Kephala Hill. Some were incised and the marks filled with chalk (fig.3) in the style of finds from Catal Huyuk and they usually had long necks, a feature common to similar figures found throughout Old Europe [5].

Largely because of the dramatic development that Crete underwent during this period, some theorists argue that these first neolithic settlers were joined in the Early Minoan period by new immigrants, possibly from Lower (northern) Egypt, who increased the population, developing settlements into townships. The language of this second wave of settlers in the bronze age is thought to have been either semitic or derived from Asia Minor (Anatolia). They are thought to have brought the knowledge of how to work copper, bronze (an alloy of copper and tin), silver and gold. The culture which developed these skills had evolved in the Middle

East at a very early date and gradually spread over Western Asia and Europe. It is generally known as the bronze age because of the metals used at that time for making tools, jewellery, ritual apparatus and weapons. As Rodney Castleden, a geographer and geomorphologist by training who has been researching prehistory for the past 30 years, points out however:

> the idea of new people to explain new ideas is itself old and suspect. A newer view is that a society may evolve gradually for a certain period, but when any one of its sub systems is taken across a threshold, stresses are created, sending a whole sequence of changes rapidly through the whole society like a chain reaction. [6]

Whether change was stimulated by internal development, perhaps informed by external contact, or by immigration, archaeological evidence shows that the Cretans developed and advanced very rapidly during the period from around 3000 BC.

Communal dwelling arrangements and burials show that the matrilineal clan was still the main social unit. Towards the end of the Early Minoan I period (c.2600 BC) what is as yet the only identified forerunner of the Temple Palace, a large building known as the House on the Hill, was constructed at Vasiliki.

The Golden Age

Perhaps this Aegean civilisation was the mysterious Atlantis and doubtless if it had been allowed to continue the history of the entire area and perhaps of the world would have been very different [7].

Although the archaeological evidence, particularly the frescoes and other artefacts suggests that the whole tenor of bronze age Cretan society was idyllic, it was no pipe dream. As this matriarchal culture developed, it was to produce Europe's first civil engineers, who built networks of paved roads, aqueducts, viaducts, irrigation channels, drainage systems and harbour installations. A well more than 17 metres deep, dating from 3000 BC, is evidence that these engineering skills were developed early.

Nicholas Platon, who was Director of Antiquities on Crete for many years, has written extensively on the subject. He points out that a great deal of effort was expended in improving the living standards of the islanders through the use of communal wealth or public money. This was a caring society. We can imagine that the priestess-queens and their deputies would have been responsible for commissioning and

Crete Reclaimed

administering the building of the network of public roads which criss-crossed the island from end to end, for the water supply and drainage installations at all the main urban centres and the building and maintenance of burial complexes.

This was a culture that was both innovative and practical. Their magnificent and sophisticated design of Temple Palaces has not been seen anywhere else in the world. The level of artistic achievement in all areas is astonishingly high and the prevalence of widespread literacy is evinced by the discovery of Linear A (Europe's earliest system of writing) at 27 sites.

Finds from elsewhere in the Aegean dating from this period show that 3000 BC onwards was generally a time of great prosperity. This early Cretan culture developed into one which is considered highly advanced even by modern western standards. The quality of life seems to have been very high and there is nothing to suggest that this was not shared by the whole population. From 1900 BC the large surplus of food and luxury goods is attested to by the vast areas given over to storage in communal buildings like the Temple Palaces and so-called 'Country Houses' and the Cretans' activities as prolific traders. From 1700 onwards they were expanding to inhabit other islands. A wide area of the south Aegean, reaching from as far as Samos to the north-east and Aegina to the north-west, and including coastal areas of what is now Turkey, shows evidence of Cretan settlements. Scholars have proposed that life on Crete until around 1500 BC was little short of perfect.

Despite the mythical horrors of human sacrifice, the folk memories that the classical Greeks inherited of ancient Crete were quite different. Homer, writing in AD 64, stressed the idyllic character of life on the island, which jars with the notion of a blood-thirsty minotaur.

> Out in the wine dark sea there is a land called Crete. A rich and lovely land, washed by the sea on every side; and in it are many peoples and ninety cities. There, one language mingles with another. In it are Achaeans, great hearted native Cretans, Kydonians and Dorians in three tribes and noble Pelasgians.
> Homer *Odyssey* Book 19

Similarly, the Athenian, Plato (427-347 BC), in his *Republic*, stated that Crete was the home of an advanced culture and the centre of 'a great and wonderful empire'. Archaeological finds continue to corroborate these accounts with persistent regularity.

Daily Life

Perhaps Crete was the lost Atlantis, the land of milk and honey that the scholars of the classical age remembered in their legends with such reverence and regret. Until recently it was believed that this could not be possible because Plato's calculations in plotting the geographical location of Atlantis did not support this theory. Subsequently scholars have shown that all the calculations are out by a uniform factor of ten, something which could be accounted for by an error of translation [8]. If this is taken into account the location and size of the island match Crete.

The description of Atlantis, as recorded by Plato in *Critias*, can be traced back to Solon, a friend of his great grandfather who heard the story from Egyptian priest/esses when he was there in 590 BC. Part of the legend is that Atlantis was a sacred island of great wealth that was sunk by an earthquake. Thera (now Santorini), the volcanic island 70 miles to the north of Crete erupted some time before the massive destructions which occurred on Crete around 1450 BC. Evidence from the excavations at Akrotiri, a town on Thera, show that the island was certainly a Cretan province [9]. It seems that in the Egyptian folk memory of Atlantis, the actual eruption and virtual disappearance of the island of Thera to its present crescent shape, has been compounded with the destruction of many religious centres on Crete, the beginning of the demise of ancient Cretan culture. The legend may have represented Crete, Thera, or Cretan settlements generally. In any event the paradisaical way of life epitomized by bronze age Cretan culture disappeared from existence (immediately on Thera and gradually elsewhere in the Aegean) and the catalyst for this was remembered as a great catastrophe that caused an island to be subsumed by the ocean.

An island paradise was the legend but what was life really like for the ancient Cretans, at home and in settlements on the neighbouring islands? Was it really the halcyon Garden of Eden that Plato's vision of the lost Atlantis suggests? There is little to contradict this view. As well as a surfeit of raw materials and the right climate for successful agriculture, Cretans developed the knowledge and skills needed to become a refined and prosperous trading nation. The climate of peace that pervaded the Aegean at this time must have been a major contributor to their success.

The primary prosperity of the early Cretans came from the agricultural surplus that accrued because of the unique geography of the island. The peaks of the Cretan mountain ranges retain their snowy covering throughout most of the year providing a welcome series of streams and underground water courses. This, combined with the range of mild climates, from upland plains to low lying valleys, made ideal conditions for the proliferation of crops. These pre-requisites combined with the agricultural skills that the neolithic settlers brought with them, provided a stable, reliable and prolific food supply which allowed for the development of a highly sophisticated culture.

> we have to admit that the 'first civilisation of Europe' was also one of the most accomplished and inventive that the world has ever known. [10]

Crete's secondary wealth grew from the artistic ingenuity and skills of its people in the design, production and decoration of ceramics and the manufacture of fine textiles, aromatic oils and medications. Many of these products were exported. There would have been a surplus of food products (raisins, wine, olives, olive oil, honey, nuts) and timber which could also have been exported.

Underpinning this material success was the Cretans' religion and social organisation, which decreed that the community, or clan, came first. It was this philosophy that allowed for the cooperative effort required for the construction of the great Temple Palaces or labyrinths, the sacred centres designed for collective and private religious practices, administration and the storage and distribution of the district's surplus wealth.

Each of the major religious centres that have been fully excavated – Knossos in the north, Phaistos and Ayia Triada in the south and Mallia and Zakro to the west – had enormous storage capacity (usually identified as 'magazines' on site guides). These 'magazines' are usually located close to a complex of rooms that were clearly designed for ritual purposes. The sacredness of the storerooms was further emphasised by the *labyris* carved on their walls and mounted on a pole (fig. 4) supported by pyramidal bases which stood outside them. Such bases can still be seen outside the 'magazines' at Knossos. These associations suggests that the wealth of Crete

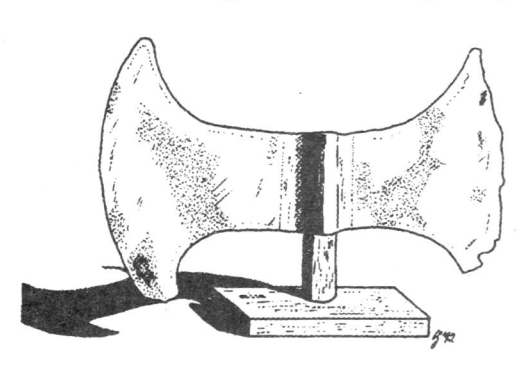

Fig.4 Pillar-mounted bronze votive labyris 1700-1500 BC

was, in the minds of its people, inextricably linked with their belief in the Great Goddess (who's principle symbol is the *labyris*). She was seen as the beneficent provider of all things.

Social Organisation

According to George Thompson, an expert on social organisation in the prehistoric Aegean, the societies that were prevalent there in the bronze age were matriarchal and based around matrilineal clans. The basic social organisation consisted of a clan elder and her multigenerational family in the female line.

The archaeological evidence from Crete – remains of settlements, burials, the depiction of women and men in frescoes and other artefacts – tell us something of their social relationships. The arrangement of dwellings and the popularity of communal *tholos* tombs for example, suggest a clan based social organisation and fresco evidence establishes the pre-eminence of women.

Supporting this there is a battery of indirect evidence. Matrifocal societies that survived into the historical period practised exogamy for reproduction, together with what Thompson refers to as group marriage. Marriage as we understand the term did not exist on bronze age Crete. It was not invented until the Greek City State system introduced monogamy to ensure patrilineal succession rights and the subjugation of women. Thompson uses the term 'marriage' to refer to the temporary sexual arrangement that existed for the procreation of children, where women would choose one or more of the men from another clan (exogamy) [11]. He documents this with reference to a wide range of cultures and refers us to the works of many classical chroniclers who studied social organisation in neighbouring countries. These early historians emphasise that, in these cultures, the paternity of children was irrelevant as their name, identity and succession rights were derived from their mother's clan. This evidence is explored in Chapter 3.

We can only speculate about the social relationships among the women and men of Crete, but in doing so we must be careful to avoid inappropriate modern western concepts. There is nothing to suggest the same exaggerated class and gender differentiation and the outlawing of homosexual relationships for example. That certain distinctions between the sexes were important can be seen from the Grandstand, Grove Dance and other frescoes found at Knossos. Yet the frescoes, Linear B tablets and other artefacts also suggest that there may have been few roles that were exclusive to one sex or the other. The frescoes also reveal women in intimate association with each other and men who clearly took great pride in their personal appearance.

Villages and Houses

At Fournou Korifi, a village dating from the Early Minoan II period (c.2600–2200), around 120 people are thought to have lived in the 90 adjoining rooms that formed the settlement. Peter Warren, the British archaeologist who excavated the site, believed that the occupants continued in the same communal or clan based way of living throughout the settlement's long history. Other archaeologists, however, have interpreted the same evidence as indicating that these buildings were the mansion of a chief [12] and eight separate households [13]. The later, Middle Minoan to Late Minoan period (c.1700-1450), small town of Gournia consisted of small houses packed tightly together on the hillside. These were clustered around a miniature Temple Palace which indicates the strong communal focus of the inhabitants.

Findings at both these sites concur with those of Marija Gimbutas who was professor of archaeology at UCLA in America until her recent, untimely death. Gimbutas brought a radically new approach to her subject through her extensive knowledge of folklore and mythology. She specialised in the study of the prehistoric cultures of Old Europe, a large geographical area reaching from southern Poland and the western Ukrane to as far south as Sicily and Crete. She found that in these cultures housing arrangements showed no sign of the differences in social class that became so important in later patriarchal societies [14].

On Crete the larger conurbations show a high degree of versatility. Ayia Triada is thought to have included a row of shops, and excavations at many settlements have revealed fine houses. The Town Mosaic from Knossos, a collection of small house fronts made by a ceramic process called faience and thought to be the remnants of a board game, is a useful source of information about the houses of Cretan cities at this time. They show semi-detached villas of up to four floors including an attic. Such houses were not lacking in sophistication as, for example, there is evidence that windows were fully glazed. A clay model of a two-storey house with verandas, a balcony and a flat roof was found at Arkhanes.

Country House Shrines

As well as the Temple Palaces and the houses of the small villages, towns and great cities, another building which had central importance was what has become known as the Country House or villa although these were, as much as anything else, religious complexes. They were built throughout the island in the New Temple Palace period of Middle Minoan III and the beginning of Late Minoan I. Many were repaired and

Daily Life

rebuilt during their lifetime which, for most of them, ended with the fires of 1450. They were designed in the palatial style with a high standard of architecture, fixtures and fittings, though they had no central court. Some were as large as a Mycenaean palace. They usually had storerooms for farm produce and a large proportion of their rooms were reserved for religious use. They were located alone about 7-10 miles apart, near to a water supply and overlooking a naturally defined area of countryside. Examples include Tylissos, Sklavokampos, Amnissos, Prasa (near Amnissos), Vathypetro and Apodoulou (south of Rethymnon). House A at Tylissos is built to a similar design but, unusually, it was an integral part of the town there. Linear A tablets were found at several Country House Shrines as were sealings made by the same seals as those excavated at the Temple Palaces. This information together with the large volume of seals recovered from these sites suggest that they were also important administrative centres.

Given their obvious religious, storage and administrative functions, they had much in common with the Temple Palaces although there were clearly significant differences in overall design and size.

The Temple Palaces

The first or 'Old' Temple Palaces were built at Knossos, Phaistos, Mallia and Zakro around 1900 BC. They were outstanding architectural achievements, the focus and pinnacle of ancient Cretan sophistication. They all conformed to a basic design though some were larger than others. Knossos, which was built on five floors, connected by magnificent staircases, contained around 1500 rooms and Zakro, one of the smallest, consisted of 250-300 rooms spread over two or three storeys.

Each was arranged in a similar way and shared similar features. All had elegant, luxurious interiors in which gypsum and timber were used to excess. Frescoes in both delicate and dramatic style and lavish textiles in the form of drapes and upholstery would have decorated many of the rooms, corridors and stairwells. A special feature of bronze age Cretan sacred design was the downward tapering wooden columns which were oval or circular in cross section. Sacred pillar crypts, storerooms packed with *pithoi* (enormous clay storage jars), monumental staircases, lightwells, glazed sash windows, porticoed (roofed) gardens, lustral chambers (ritual cleansing areas) and full plumbing were also common to all the great centres. The fresh water supply was delivered through a sophisticated system of terracotta pipes which were tapered at one end to fit into a collar, and organised so that the flow of water would create a pressure and prevent sediment collecting. Some of the underground drainage pipes were as high as a woman.

Crete Reclaimed

The architectural design and incorporation of this specific combination of features was unique to Crete, so it was clearly not learnt or copied from anywhere else in the world. On the contrary, it seems that Crete's great neighbour to the south, Egypt, was not above emulating the designers of the great labyrinths. Rodney Castleden, who has made a studied reappraisal of the function of Knossos, presents a good case for the now-lost labyrinth of Hawara, built in Egypt in about 1800 BC, having been based on the design of Knossos. It had many chambers, colonnaded courtyards and winding passages. Even when Herodotus visited, around 1400 years after it was built, this was still hallowed ground, only its official attendants being allowed to descend to the level where the mummified crocodiles had been placed so many centuries before.

At each of the sites where Old Temple Palaces have been excavated there is evidence of destruction by fire in 1700 BC. These great fires, which heralded the end of the Early Minoan II period, are thought to have been caused by a severe earthquake which left the first series of labyrinthine centres in ruins. These were, however, quickly replaced by new ones, into which an ingenious structural elasticity was built to help withstand any further natural onslaughts.

The sacred walkways and theatral areas of the Temple Palaces were designed for the ritual dances and processions that were performed in honour of the deity. Small images of Her in terracotta and faience would have stood in niches in passageways and on the bench like altars of ritual rooms and at least one monumental statue of Her in wood is thought to have stood in a sanctuary hall in the east wing of Knossos. All the symbols that are clearly associated with the Goddess on sealstones, rings, vases and other artefacts, were incorporated into the decor of Knossos, and by implication the other Temple Palaces, most of which did not survive the 1450 destructions. The *labyris* which were carved on pillars, featured in frescoes, decorated vessels, stood on long poles in pyramidal stands or were set between Horns of Consecration in every part of these labyrinths defined them as sacred to the Goddess.

Only the larger complexes at Knossos, Phaistos, Mallia, Zakro and, more recently, Ayia Triada are usually given the epithet 'Palace'. It was the veteran Cretan archaeologist and former director of the British School at Athens, Sinclair Hood, who pointed out that the village of Gournia had, at the centre, its own small scale version of a labyrinth. It covers 1200 square metres making it half the size of Zakro and one-third the size of Mallia but its design and layout closely correspond to the larger Temple Palaces. The name palace conjures up the idea of a royal presence but it is difficult to image that a royal court existed in the midst

Daily Life

of this industrial town, though this could certainly have been a sacred centre used for storage, administration and the performance of both private and public religious ritual. The existence of this complex at Gournia raises questions as to the function of its larger, sister complexes.

Apart from storage and sacred celebration, what were these magnificent and seemingly eccentric edifices really used for? Archaeologists and other scholars are generally in agreement that a large proportion of their rooms, usually at least the whole of the west wing, where the storerooms are also often located, were designated as sacred and devoted to purely ritual use. The naming of many of the other rooms, however, is the source of some disagreement. Evans designated areas in the east wing of Knossos as 'domestic quarters' and claimed that the rooms located on the upper floors were 'public rooms'. Although many scholars have questioned the details of Evans' reconstructions at Knossos they remain in broad agreement about the designated function of the different parts of the complex. Evans' nomenclature has led to inferences being drawn at other Temple Palaces. At Phaistos for example the excavators labelled three sets of rooms as royal apartments. The extra set being for the 'prince'!

In 1976 Hans Wunderlich, a German geologist, wrote a book called *The Secret of Crete*. Although his arguments, which are more notable for their ethnocentric prejudice than their accuracy, have now been discredited, he does raise some interesting questions about the Temple Palaces. His contentious critique is refreshing because of the different angle from which he approaches the subject. The anomalies that Wunderlich draws our attention to certainly exist. As Castleden puts it, 'Wunderlich's negative arguments, against Evans' theories, are more plausible than his own proposals of an alternative explanation.'

In his questioning of the acceptability of Evans' designations of the use of the various rooms of the Temple Palaces, Wunderlich is arguing that they were great funereal complexes for the regeneration of the dead. He is influenced in this opinion by the *pithoi* which were found in profusion in each of the centres. But – although *pithoi* were used for burials as well as for the storage of foodstuffs, wine and oil – no human remains were discovered in any of those found at the Temple Palaces. They contained only the remnants of agricultural produce: peas, barley and broad beans for example.

Wunderlich claimed that the general belief in any extensive secular use of the Temple Palaces is probably mistaken and provides a convincing catalogue of evidence to support this view. He points out that their layout is somewhat bizarre if they are to be considered as the thriving power centres of a royal court. There is no direct access at Knossos to different parts of the complex as one would expect in a secular palace. It is not possible to pass between the North-South Corridor and the East Parallel Corridor. The Knossos Throne Room is clearly one of the main focal points in the whole complex yet it is, without doubt, a religious room.

Another point Wunderlich makes is that gypsum, used extensively at Knossos, is a very soft stone which wears quickly with excess usage and would be a poor choice for the most important royal palace. The original stones show very little sign of wear, indicating to Wunderlich a lack of the daily activity that might be expected from a thriving palace and retinue. As a religious building, however, Knossos would only have been in full use for the festivals that were the highlight of the Cretan religious calender: the spring planting, harvest and bull festivals for example.

Arguing in the same vein, Castleden uses the 1160 BC Egyptian labyrinth of Medinet Habu, which was the mortuary temple of Rameses III, and the temples of ancient Sumeria as possible parallels for the Cretan labyrinths. Only a small religious elite would normally reside in these extensive sacred complexes. Further support for this view comes from Catal Huyuk where it was the practice of the neolithic people to bury their dead under the sleeping platforms of dwellings. Here Mellaart found that many of the houses, which were also religious shrines, had few burials in relation to the time period that they had been in service. In one, for example, the remains of only six people were found in a building which had been used for over 120 years. This average of one per 40 years makes sense if we imagine that it represented the lifespan of a succession of priestesses or other religious officiants.

When considering the lack of wear and tear on the labyrinths it is important to remember that there are different types of gypsum and, as Ann Brown of the Ashmolean museum in Oxford notes [15], the type that was used in, for example, the Throne Room at Knossos, was resistant to water and wear and tear, whereas the type which was available locally is highly water soluble. Also, in acknowledging that the labyrinths were complexes of sacred shrines, it can be assumed that people trod with reverence in the presence of the deity. Frescoes show figures barefoot or wearing soft leather slippers.

The Cretans' practice of using plaster to cover many of the flooring areas would also have offered protection. There is clear evidence of this at Phaistos and at Mallia. In the latter case the Central Court, which was comprised of beaten earth with some paved sections, was almost completely covered by several layers of white plaster. For the Cretans' ancestors at Catal Huyuk in Anatolia, the use of plaster as a covering had

Daily Life

important religious significance. Some of the ritual objects discovered there were enveloped in about 40 layers of it.

Another of Wunderlich's points relates to the scarcity of windows in these luxuriant buildings when the Cretans were able to build the equivalent of modern glazed sash windows. Parts of the interiors of the Temple Palaces, he notes, were like caves. Only a religious designation of the buildings would explain this.

In support of his claim that these great structures were ritual centres, Wunderlich points out that the three large 'palaces' (Knossos, Mallia and Phaistos) all have four entrances, one for each cardinal direction. The length and breadth of their central courts conform to the same rectangular design, they are in striking agreement of almost exactly two-to-one proportion and all have a ten degree deviation from a strict north-to-south layout. The same arrangement can be observed in the religious monuments built by neolithic peoples. The direction of the rows of megaliths at Carnac in Brittany, France, for example was determined by the rising and setting of the sun on a particular day of the year.

The locations of these great centres, claims Wunderlich, were poorly chosen with regard to water supply, an important consideration if they really were residential palaces. Having fresh spring water piped from cisterns high up on hills close to Knossos and Phaistos can be explained only if it was determined by religious rather than practical reasons.

There is also the anomaly of the juxtaposition of work rooms and so called 'Residential Areas' at both Knossos and Phaistos. At Phaistos it is difficult to explain why the supposed forge is only twenty metres and the stone mason's workshop barely ten metres away from the 'Royal Apartments'. At Knossos workrooms are situated across a corridor from the Hall of the Double Axes. Such arrangements make sense if we postulate that it was accepted Cretan practice for craftspeople creating objects for use in religious ritual to do so in a sacred setting.

Much has been made of the presence of the fully flushing lavatories found at the Temple Palaces. Such a high standard of hygiene was not to be seen in England until the end of the 19th century. These toilets present a further problem however. Since the Cretans were so demonstrably capable of providing full and efficient plumbing, why would there have been so few toilets in the whole of Knossos if it were, as Evans claims (and other archaeologists seem to accept), a residential palace. In his drawing reconstructing the first floor of the east wing of Knossos Castleden has identified three toilets in the south-west corner. These are in addition to the room designated as a toilet by Evans in the so called Queen's Rooms. Surely the principal Cretan 'palace' would be replete with such amenities.

It is beyond doubt that the Temple Palaces were packed with cult rooms, altars, sacred repositories, lustral basins, votive offerings and pillar crypts. They, and the so-called Country Houses were, above all else, religious centres. It is only the degree to which these buildings were used for secular purposes which is in question. But is this an appropriate question to ask or does it pose a false dichotomy? All the evience suggests that in ancient Cretan society religious and secular activities were one and the same.

The layout of these great centres only fails to make sense if we assume the presence of a large secular court possibly including a nuclear or extended royal family. But there is no archaeological evidence to support this. Such a concept is a product of ethnocentricism. Julian Thomas is one of the new school of archaeologist who are more sensitive to the issues raised by ethnocentricity. A more apt description of his concerns, if I might be allowed to invent a new word, would be 'eracenticity', or the influence that who we are, in the era in which we live, has on the very different period in the past that we are claiming to understand and explain. We must all cast aside our preconceptions and open our minds to alternative ways of social organisation and religious practice.

There is no evidence to support Wunderlich's contention that these magnificent edifices were temples for the (male) dead. They were, rather, designed to facilitate the religious practices of the bronze age Cretans to whom the omnipotent Great Goddess was the creator and provider of all things.

The Potential of Pacifism

> An air of tender humanity permeated the culture of the matriarchal world, that primordial race of women with whom all peace vanished from the earth . . . Matriarchal states were famed for their freedom from strife and conflict . . . matriarchal peoples assigned special culpability to the physical injury of any living creature, even of animals. [16]

Although these comments, made by early religious historian J.J. Bachofen, may appear rather romantic, archaeologists have been surprised by the lack of any evidence of defensive measures on Crete during the bronze age. No great walls like those of the citadels of the Mycenaeans or impenetrable harbours, approximating to those of the later Byzantine invaders of Crete, were found even though the area around Knossos alone is estimated as having had 20,000 inhabitants and

Daily Life

extreme wealth by any standards. Wunderlich noted with amazement that 'the entire area around Knossos was open to attack from all directions'. Nowhere have military weapons, or evidence of Cretan uniforms or armour been found. The anomalous warrior graves (discussed in Chapter 5), where soldiers were buried with full armour and weapons date from after the time of the great disaster of 1450 and are associated with a small elite of foreigners, possibly Mycenaeans. The swords found at Mallia and Archolochori were too long and fragile for use in battle. The war sword with its strong blade and solid handle was a Helladic invention and reached Crete late, probably at the time of the arrival of the Mycenaeans, around 1450 BC. Although more efficient weapons could be made once iron came into widespread use, the Cretans' lack of weaponry was certainly not due to lack of technology. They were more advanced than most others of their time in the skills required to produce such implements.

In sharp contrast to their near neighbours the Mycenaeans, no scenes of battle are depicted in the wide range of artists' subjects that have survived. The Cretan artist concerned herself with sacred symbolism and with the natural world. There are however, many examples of scenes of battles, conquests, chariots, weapons and other military regalia that were produced for Mycenaeans by Cretan artists. Scenes depicting Cretan gatherings recorded in miniature frescoes are distinctly non-military. The Temple fresco, the Sacred Grove Dance, the Theran harbour scenes and two scenes from Tylissos are all associated with ceremonial and festive occasions rather than the gore or glory of battle.

Cretan shields depicted in the Knossos frescoes were symbolic rather than defensive. Although the western Etruscans used similar 'Figure of Eight' shields to guard the body of the Royal Lady against any evil influences, this was not the symbolic role of the shield on Crete [17]. The 'Adoration of the Shield' painting on a limestone tablet from Mycenae suggests that the shield represented the Goddess Herself [18].

The chariot, which among the Mycenaeans and others was a vehicle of war, was for the matrifocal Cretans a sacred conveyance. It is depicted on sealstones (small gemstones carved with a scene usually of religious significance) and the painted sarcophagus from Ayia Triada in this role, usually with two female figures sharing a chariot pulled by griffons, goats or horses.

Despite the complete lack of any evidence for militarism on Crete, misleading titles are often given on site plans. Chambers have been designated as 'guardrooms' at Phaistos and Knossos, niches at Phaistos are assumed to be for sentries and a keep has been falsely identified at Knossos. In a similar vein it has been claimed that a fresco known as the

Captain of the Blacks is evidence of the use of slave troops or mercenaries on Crete. As restored it shows a Cretan man in front of (assumed to be leading and in control of) a group of darker skinned men running at the double. In the original fresco fragment however the black figures are represented only by one knee set against a blue ground and the back of one head against white. As Jacquetta Hawkes, a specialist in Aegean archaeology, points out, this is not sufficient evidence, as some scholars suggest it to be, for the presence of Nubian mercenaries on Crete.

The total lack of fortification and militarism on Crete during the bronze age is taken by many writers to indicate naval supremacy but this seems unlikely given the complete absence of military subjects (even at sea) in Cretan art. The Cretans' seafaring skills would, through travelling and trading, have kept them well abreast of affairs in the Aegean. Their own philosophy may have reflected the climate of non-aggression in the surrounding area. Once the Achaeans (invading tribes from the north that later became the Mycenaeans) had settled in the Peleponnese, it is probable that there was a generalised lack of aggressive intent in the Aegean until the 15th or even as late as the 12th century BC. There are a number of reasons why it would have been possible for the whole region of the Aegean to have shared in an informal non-aggression pact. Thomson presents convincing evidence of a shared ancestry and therefore a similar religion and ideology. The Cretans and other Aegean settlers are thought to have originated from the culture that inhabited Catal Huyuk, in Anatolia, of whom it was said that,

> There had been no wars for a thousand years, there was an ordered pattern of society. [19]

The evidence of anthropologist Peter Ucko supports the theory of a common ancestry. In his extensive study of neolithic figurines he noted similarities between those of Crete and the Greek mainland [20].

The philosophy of clan based matrifocal societies was one of working together for the benefit of the group rather than for individual wealth. Because of our own patriarchal history we look for reasons why peoples did not express aggressive intent against each other rather than accepting that the 'great hearted' native Cretans, as Homer refered to them, had no philosophy of aggression in their social vocabulary.

During the bronze age the whole of the Aegean and countries surrounding Crete were affluent and contented with each area

Daily Life

benefitting from the flow of trade. The aggression that struck these lands came from outside, from the far borders of civilisation, from men who were not socialised into a system of peace and cooperation in a land of plenty, but into a struggle for survival in a barren wilderness. Problems arose when these much less developed cultures, finding themselves with inadequate resources, developed a patriarchal ideology and social structure. The deity their society was focussed around was not a goddess of giving but a god of war. These were the Indo-Europeans. Unable to subsist in their own poorly endowed geographical areas they organised themselves into raiding parties against wealthier, more civilised, cultures. This is the pattern of events that Gimbutas has traced to the devastating invasions by the peoples she calls the Kurgans in the 5th, 4th and 3rd millennia BC. Her findings are corroborated by those of James Mellaart. The Kurgans were patriarchal warloving pastoralists who originated in the Eurasian Steppes to the north of the Black Sea. They overwhelmed the peace-loving matrilineal peoples of Old Europe and destroyed their culture, massacring the men and forcing the women into sexual slavery.

In the remnants of Cretan culture, which survived earlier invasions because of its island location, we have a picture of how the matrifocal cultures of the whole of Old Europe might have evolved had they been left in peace.

In her visionary book, *The Chalice and the Blade* (1987), Riane Eisler, a highly respected American scholar in the field of peace and equality issues, contrasts the different philosophies of what she calls the 'gylanic' or more egalitarian (matriarchal) cultures and the 'androcratic' or dominator (patriarchal) cultures. She describes Marija Gimbutas' evidence that the people of Old Europe were peace-loving agriculturalists with no philosophy of war. Not until the first wave of invasions from peripherally-located patriarchal cultures (the Indo-Europeans) did the neolithic and early bronze age peoples had any need of defence against aggressive attack. Although these attacks had reached as near as the Cyclades, defensive walls were found on this circle of island to the north of Crete, they did not afflict Crete until around 1100 BC with the invasion of the Dorians.

Overseas Settlements

Evidence of bronze age Cretan colonies has been found on a number of Aegean Islands, the Greek mainland and at Miletos on the northern Turkish coast. It is difficult to say what prompted these settlements. Was it trade, to relieve over population, a desire to protect Cretan interests, or just a healthy expansion of a successful culture into welcoming surrounding regions made possible by the common origins of many of the peoples of the Aegean?

The neolithic settlers who arrived on Crete around the sixth millenium were from the same area of Asia Minor as the peoples who settled in other parts of the Aegean. The earliest inhabitants of the Cycladic islands, the circle of islands to the north of Crete, are thought to have come from the east (Anatolia) and the south, (perhaps Crete) and were familiar with the use of copper. This culture developed under Cretan influence in the Early Cycladic period then, early in 3000 BC, these tribes spread to the Peloponnese and on to central Greece and southern Thessaly in the Early Helladic period. George Thompson suggests that this culture was spread by the Carians and the Leleges, both known matriarchal tribes. He demonstrates that the Cretans had affinities with these peoples and the Lycians (another matrifocal Aegean culture), all of whom may have originated in Anatolia.

The Cretan spread into the surrounding area took place at the end of the Early Minoan period, long before 1900 BC, the time that the first Temple Palaces were built. Archaeological evidence shows that the culture of the indigenous population of the islands and that of the Cretans existed side by side. This suggests that there was probably a free and easy movement between the islands and that such settlements in no way indicated a desire on the part of the Cretans to dominate or colonise other lands.

Some theorists however believe that the Cretans probably ruled Thera, Melos, Naxos, Paros, Andros, Mykonos and Delos and had political control over the Aegean in the Late Minoan IA period (1550-1500) when Cycladic pottery closely imitated the Cretan styles. The types of clay, loom weights, shapes of lamps and fire boxes of these islands showed so much cultural transformation that it is attributed to the influence of the Cretan settlers. There were certainly established Cretan towns on these islands and others in the Aegean: Trianda on Rhodes, Akrotiri on Thera, Phylakopi on Melos, Kastri on Kythera, Ayia Irini on Kea and Miletos on the south-west coast of Anatolia (fig. 2). Most of these settlements were deserted rather than destroyed or they may have been absorbed into mainstream or later cultures. The demise

Daily Life

of these Cretan outposts appears to have been linked to the island-wide devastation on Crete itself in 1450. The settlements on Kastri and Kythera were abandoned and Ayia Irini on Kea was destroyed by fire a few years after 1450. The date at which Akrotiri, the Cretan town on Thera, the volcanic island between Crete and the Cyclades, was deserted has recently become the subject of contention. Most theorists believe the date to have been between 1470 and 1500 although Christos Doumas argues that it was no later than 1759 BC [21].

At the settlement on Kea all the features of bronze age Cretan town planning and architecture are evident including paved roads with gutters and stone staircases in solidly-constructed houses. A special kind of building, a sanctuary, was also excavated. It lay close to the eastern gate and comprised an anteroom, shrine, inner chamber and other apartments where the priestesses may have lived.

Another of these colonies, at Kastri on Kythera, an island just off the southern-most tip of the Greek mainland, was excavated in 1932 by the English archaeologist Sylvia Benton. The site is the location of a city which in classical times was known as Skandeia. Benton found evidence of a Cretan colony which flourished for over 800 years from 2300 to around 1500–1450 BC, at which time it was deserted but not destroyed. Perhaps the ex-patriots were summoned home for the fall of the great Temple Palaces or the danger of volcanic eruption may have been deemed too great in this part of the Aegean. The area was not inhabited again until the sixth century AD.

Some of the best finds from this settlement belong to the 1550–1500 period and include a conical greenstone bowl, two silver cups and gold beads, all imports from Crete. Other legacies of Cretan influence may be the religion of the Kytheran Aphrodite which, like the Paphian Aphrodite on Cyprus was closely related to that of the Cretan Goddess.

On mainland Greece, although the legends say nothing definite about Cretan settlements in these areas, sacred myths referring to Crete were associated with the most important mainland sanctuaries: Delphi, Olympia and Eleusis.

There are also many indications that settlements at Caria and Lycia in Asia Minor had close connections with Crete. This has been borne out by excavations at Miletos and Iasos. Similarly, in Phoenician territory, especially at Ugarit, Cretan settlements which had begun as trading stations had expanded into proper colonies [22].

On Thera, the volcanic island just one day's sail (120 kilometres) north of Crete, a Cretan settlement was discovered in 1870 at

Akrotiri. The buildings had been buried in pumice and ash but no human skeletons were found and clearly the area was deserted well before Thera erupted.

A wide array of frescoes which had been preserved by the pumice from the eruption was found at the settlement. In just one room, Room 5

Fig. 5
The Crocus Picker from Xestes 3, Thera. 1759 BC or earlier. Part of a scene set in a hilly landscape where two elegantly dressed women (priestesses) collect saffron. She wears something similar to a Sacral Knot at the back of her belt and her bodice is decorated with tassels resembling labyris/waz lily shapes and bordered by forms also encountered in the lower border of the Throne Room, Knossos. In another scene from Room 3a (first floor) the crocuses are heaped at the feet of the Goddess.

Daily Life

of one large house (the West House) there were scenes from the religious, ceremonial and daily life of the community. A priestess holding a censer is painted on the door jamb, perhaps to indicate that this room or the adjoining one (room 4) had been purified for ritual usage. The fabric of her dress has a lozenge pattern and a snake adorns her head. The other frescoes are of fishers and there is a continuous miniature sea and landscape fresco, part of which is thought to have depicted the island before the eruption. The scenes of this fresco depict ships leaving from one port (perhaps on Crete or the Greek mainland) and arriving at another (almost certainly Akrotiri). Harbours which show similar features to those in the fresco have been excavated on the two islands. Some of the passengers on the boats have helmets painted above their heads, showing them to be Mycenaean military. Boar's tooth helmets which exactly mirror these representations have been recovered from Mycenaean sites. The soldiers are passively seated and clearly travelling in peace, perhaps as envoys.

The pre-eminence of women is clearly evident in this and the many other Theran frescoes. Priestesses and other important women in lavish gowns are the main subjects. From one of the other buildings on Thera (Xeste 3), we have the only extant example of a painting of the Great Goddess. She is seated on a raised area with a griffon in attendance and women collecting and heaping crocuses from a bucket into a large basket at her feet. The figure on the dias is around four times as large as Her attendants. The designs on the fabrics of the women's attire and in the decorative background have much in common with sacred Cretan symbols. The bodice of one of the priestesses in the scene of the crocus pickers (fig. 5) is edged with the same design that we see in the Throne Room at Knossos. The decorative jewellery or fabric which hang from her sleeves are reminiscent of the lily/*labyris* shape which is so familiar in Knossian symbolism. Her pony-tail and the decoration at the back of her waist call to mind the sacral knot worn by the Knossian priestess queen La Parisienne (fig. 6).

One of the town's buildings is known as the House of the Ladies because its wall paintings depict a range of clearly important women (fig. 7). Frescoes of men and boys show them engaged in fishing, boxing and, as we see them in Knossian frescoes, carrying vessels.

Lyvia Morgan who has made an intensive study of the miniature frescoes of Thera, sums up the Aegean situation thus:

> a pattern is emerging in which each of the major
> settlements on the islands (Thera, Melos, Kea, Kythera)
> almost certainly in mutual contact with one another,

flourished at a time of unsurpassed wealth, of artistic and technological innovation and of mercantile expansion: the period of the richest Mycenae Shaft Graves and the height of the Minoan palatial system. [23]

The evidence suggests a picture of a wealthy, peaceful Aegean where its peoples shared a common origin and held similar cultural views. This was a time of plenty which, combined with the clan philosophy of shared wealth and a belief in the beneficence of the Great Goddess, made it also a time of peace. Crete, perhaps because of its greater size and available resources was the centre-piece of this Aegean culture leading, though not overshadowing, her neighbours in the fields of artistic achievement and technological innovation.

Fig. 6 La Parisienne, Knossos, 1400 bc 46 A fragment from the Camp Stool fresco showing a priestess of Knossos. She is double the size of the other figures in the fresco (as restored) and wears a very large sacral knot.

Overseas Trade

The bronze age Cretans were practised traders. Their surplus of raw materials and skills in textiles and the arts was much sought after by their neighbours. Between 2000 and 1500 BC they are known to have exported woollen cloth and painted pottery to the Aegean, Cyprus, Syria and Egypt, together with oil and wood of which they would have had a large surplus. Their import requirements of stone for bowls and seals would have come from the Peleponnese, their gold and silver from the Cyclades or Asia Minor and other precious goods like ivory from Afghanistan and Syria and small quantities of tin from Anatolia.

Established sea routes existed to the west with southern Italy and Sicily, to the north with the Cyclades and Attica, to the east with Rhodes, Cyprus, Asia Minor and the Levant (now Lebanon, Syria and

Israel) and to the south with Egypt.

There is only meagre evidence on Crete of anything which could have been taken in exchange for the mass of exported Cretan wares. The monkeys kept as pets by Cretans, antelopes and palms are likely candidates, as is papyrus (used for writing on), all of which would have long since perished. Excavated examples include about twenty Egyptian scarab seals found in Middle Minoan I and II deposits; a number of single carved objects; and an ivory sphinx found in a Mallia house dating from the 17th century BC which is thought to have been a gift from one of the Pharaohs. Trade would not have been limited to direct exchange with one country. An excess of monkeys taken in trade with Egypt for example, could have been exchanged for goods elsewhere on route home.

Fig. 7 Theran Priestess 1759 BC or earlier. One of a group of important women from the House Shrine of the House of the Ladies. The original is set in a lozenge-star background. The difference between the hairstyles of this figure and fig. 5 may signify differences in role, status or age.

Unfortunately little of the Cretan pottery found in Egypt, for example the Kamares ware from Fayum, was in well-dated contexts. Embassies from Crete to Egypt are however known to have taken place during the reign of Queen Hatshepsut (1473-1458 BC) a Pharaoh who brought great wealth to her people through trade and peace. She reigned in the XVIIIth dynasty, just after the establishment of the New Kingdom. In a scene depicted on the walls of an Egyptian tomb in which Cretans feature, the envoys carry flagons, large jars and graceful cups. Jacquetta Hawkes, an eminent archaeologist who has succeeded in bringing gender issues into her discipline in a most scholarly manner, suggests that these goods may have been sent to celebrate the enthroning of Hatshepsut.

The title Keftiou may have distinguished the Cretans from other overseas visitors although this name could also have been used to refer to the people of the islands of the Aegean generally. Aegean islanders, including Cretan community exported their own goods. The principle export of the Cretan colony on Kyrene, for example, was the plant silphium. Wall paintings of visitors named as Keftiou appear in five tombs of high officials at Thebes, the capital of Egypt throughout the earlier part of the XVIIIth dynasty. One such fresco, in the tomb of Rekhmire, Vizier to Thotmes III (1504–1450 BC), shows figures wearing decorated skirts which are similar to those depicted in the 'Processional Fresco' from Knossos. These emissaries carry wares that are of Cretan quality and style.

In the 1950s it was discovered that this painting had been altered by overpainting around 1460–1450 BC. As originally painted the figures had been wearing cod-pieces and the short stiff skirts upturned at the back, associated with bronze age Crete. The newer version shows longer skirts with the cod-pieces less evident. The amendments are seen by some scholars as indicating that there was a distinct change of style in Cretan dress which was caused by the Mycenaean domination of Crete from around 1450 and that the Egyptians were eager to make a diplomatic acknowledgement of this. But this seems a dubious assumption. Would the foreign envoys be expected to see that they had been appropriately represented on paintings in a tomb? Also, as Hood pointed out, the longer skirt for men had been worn on Crete before this time and, like so many other aspects of Cretan culture was later adopted on the mainland. He further notes that the 'earlier' short stiff skirt with pronounced cod-piece is depicted in a wall painting from the Mycenaean palace of Pylos which dates from as late as the 14th or 13th century BC. So it seems that fashion then, as now, was reasonably flexible. Given that the name Keftiou could also refer to other Aegean islanders, the alterations may have been made after a visit by another group of Keftiou who favoured this fashion or following a return visit by the Egyptians. The reason behind the recording of the difference may have been due to the pedantry of a particular artist or regional official or a comment made by any international trader on a visit to the tomb.

It is difficult to say whether the Keftiou of the frescoes were women or men since many aspects of the dress and hairstyles of bronze age Cretans were common to both sexes. The Egyptian artist has translated their appearance to fit with local convention. The hair and stance is very stylised with only a hint of the long separate tresses that characterised

Daily Life

Cretan coiffure and no jewellery is evident. The Egyptians distinguished the sexes by different colours but it seems that representational conventions cannot always be relied upon in instances where there was a deviation from Egyptian norms. The great pharaoh Hatshepsut, for example, had busts made of herself sporting the pharaonic beard.

Following the settlement of Mycenaeans on Crete around 1450 BC, the two groups maintained their own identity and both Mycenaean and Cretan pottery were imported to Egypt and Western Asia side by side. This cooperation in the facilitation of trading implies a positive relationship between the two great powers of Crete and Mycenae and suggests that neither culture had subjugated the other.

Thompson points out that it was the militarism of the Mycenaeans that eventually cost them the riches of international commerce. When Egypt was raided by Menalaus, the pharaohs ceased trading with the Greeks for two hundred years. Perhaps, he continues, it was to compensate for the income lost by this that the Mycenaeans went on to ravage the wealth of Troy. One thing is clear, the days of peaceful trading and prosperity of all the nations in the area came to an end when the *labyris*, the butterfly of peace, was replaced by the sword, the weapon of greed.

Literacy and Sealstones

Archaeological evidence from Knossos, Ayia Triada and many other sites reveals that the bronze age Cretans were literate, used a decimal system for numbering and had an exact system of weights. They clearly had need of formal numeracy systems from early on in their development. Signs for units, tens, thousands and so on are evident in hieroglyphic and linear scripts.

The first written languages were invented and developed in a religious context by matrifocal societies. What is probably the earliest example of a script comes from Gimbutas' excavations of settlements at Vinca, 14 miles east of Belgrade in what is now Serbia, which was occupied between 5300–4000 BC. Groups of marks forming the script appear on small figures and vessels. Like the Cretans, the people of Vinca may have used clay tablets or other degradable materials for recording text but none have survived.

The bronze age Cretans were responsible for the invention, transmission and adaptation of their own scripts. Their first form of writing was similar to Egyptian hieroglyphics. The earliest full surviving example dates from about 1900 BC though the germs of a script with pictorial characters can be seen on seals from the end of the third millennium. These symbols, 'pictographs' as Evans called them, were found on seals, seal impressions, tablets and labels at Knossos, Phaistos and Mallia. They continued in use up to about 1600 BC and were, therefore, contemporaneous with later forms of script.

A linear development of this hieroglyphic script was used on what are thought to have been labels for boxes and chests which had been secured with lumps of clay stamped with seals. These probably contained documents written on more perishable materials such as parchment, papyrus or palm leaves. Archaeologists are led to this conclusion because such 'labels' were usually found with large numbers of sealings or other stamped impressions which had probably been used to authenticate the missing (degraded) documents. Some of the sealings had vegetable matter adhering to them, indicating that they were attached to documents or texts written on some form of more perishable material.

Further evidence that the mass of Cretan texts would have been written on something akin to paper comes from the nature of the handwriting that survived on more durable materials. The scribes' style became more and more cursive as time went on, leading to a script that was more proto-linear than hieroglyphic. This change is seen to indicate that the bulk of writing would have been in ink [24].

The next development was Linear A. Gimbutas found similarities between this script and others from Old Europe, leading her to believe that the Cretan script may have its roots in a much older written language which was used by the neolithic peoples of Asia Minor, from which they both probably originated. Pictographs appear on Linear A tablets, perhaps to help anyone unfamiliar with the new symbols, and continued to be used in religious contexts. Many Linear A tablets were actual texts rather than just labels for lost works.

Evans believed Linear A texts to be trade records and accounts, though the examples from Zakro are clearly sanctuary archives. One of the tablets appears to be a list of *labyris*. Other evidence of the religious use of the script is evident in the four or five syllabic signs said to make up the name Asasara and Asasarame, which are thought to be attributive epithets of the Great Goddess. The symbols on the silver and gold *labyris* recovered from Archolochori have been interpreted as Da Ma or Mother Earth.

There are a number of reasons to suppose that literacy may have been widespread in the Cretan population.

1. Finds of writing have been widely distributed on sites throughout the island and not confined to the Temple Palace dignitaries. Examples have been discovered at what Evans refered to as 'quite a modest house', the House of the

Daily Life

Frescoes in the vicinity of Knossos. He saw the evidence of Linear A and the elegant frescoes here as indicative of 'the wide diffusion of culture among all classes'. While it is unlikely that this particular building, or indeed any of those which abut onto Knossos were for the exclusive use of one family, the presence of written script here may indicate that it was not exclusively reserved for a religious elite.

2. The samples that have survived have so far been discovered on just about everything including metal, stone, walls, rings, vases and of course tablets. It is unlikely that all these texts were written by and for the consumption of a restricted group.

3. If there was widespread literacy on the island we might reasonably ask why there were not even more evidence of this. As already noted there are clear indications that most of the writing was done with ink on some form of paper. Further support for this theory comes from finds at Knossos and Ayia Triada. At Knossos a jar and cups were found to have been written on with dark sepia (from cuttlefish) ink and a soft reed pen [25]. The script that survived on the inside of the cups takes the same spiral form as the printing on the Phaistos disc. Also, at Ayia Triada, a sphinx made from serpentine was found to have been written on with ink. Its design incorporates a hollowed out section which could have been used as an inkwell. These finds coupled with the knowledge that the Egyptians used papyrus extensively for writing, suggests that the Cretans produced much more written material which did not survive because biodegradable date palm leaves, papyrus or parchment was used. Some of the Linear B tablets from Pylos were shaped in a leaf form which may recall the use of 'leaf' paper.

4. Castleden cites evidence of a Cretan who was either a resident of, or visitor to, Egypt, who used written text to advertise their skills at foretelling the future. There is also the instance of an exorcism for disease written in the 14th century BC in the language of the Keftiou which survives on Egyptian papyrus [26].

Around 1450 BC Linear B was introduced for record keeping at Knossos. It also came to form the basis of the script of the mainland. Many people contributed to the dicipherment of this script, including Alice Kober who was the first person to recognise declension changes and gender endings. It was however Michael Ventris, a British architect, who finally decoded Linear B.

Many scholars remain sceptical about the decipherment which they claim is still hypothetical; others accept that Linear B was developed from Linear A. One theorist, Furumark, has suggested that it was derived from the Cretan hieroglyphic script as some of its signs are topologically closer to these symbols [27].

Linear B was initially thought to be limited to Knossos itself but examples have now been found at Hania and other sites to the west of the island. The Linear B tablets that survived at Knossos did so only because of the fires that raged on its destruction. We could therefore, reasonably expect that any other buildings that were subsumed by flames would have yielded Linear B remnants had any been present at the time of their destruction in 1450. As the other Temple Palaces revealed only Linear A tablets we may conclude that Linear B was a later development and therefore came into use between the generalised destructions and the fall of Knossos. It would however be difficult to say just when Linear B was introduced because the tablets which preceded those preserved in the fire at Knossos would have disintegrated or been reused.

The contents of the Knossos tablets are so complex and minutely detailed that it is thought impossible that the script could have been brought by the Mycenaeans who arrived in large numbers around 1450, the earliest time that the script could have been developed. The Knossian Civil Servants must therefore have developed the script and then worked on its content, perhaps in cooperation with Mycenaeans. Castleden agrees with Professor John Chadwick, who has worked on the decipherment of Linear B for over 40 years, that many of the tablets are examples of practice exercises [28]. This is particularly true of those whose subjects, like chariot groups, were previously alien to Knossos. Close analysis has revealed several different hands each copying one original script and the many deletions and errors suggest that these are new symbols being tried out.

In 1939 the Linear B tablets which were so helpful to Ventris were uncovered in the ruins of the Mycenaean palace at Pylos on the south western tip of the Peloponnese. They are identical in writing and style to those from Knossos. Archaeologist Spyridon Marinatos, who made the study of Cretan and Mycenaean cultures his life's work and conveyed his

Daily Life

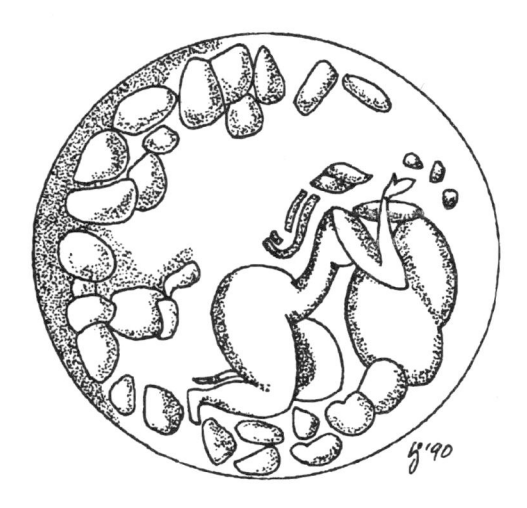

Fig. 8 Goddess with Rocks sealstone Knossos 1600-1500 BC. This rare depiction of the Cretan Goddess naked (Her large proportions identify Her) may be intended to emphasise Her close association with the rocks.

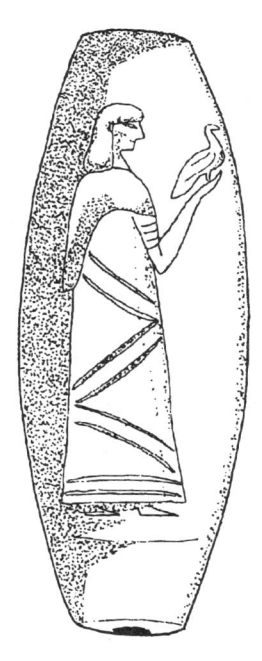

Fig. 9 Priestess with Dove. Sealstone in green jasper.

enthusiasm for Aegean archaeology to his daughter Nanno, believed that these Pylos tablets were written by scribes from Knossos even though they have been dated as late as 1200 BC. It is improbable, given the turmoil and rapid cultural change of those times, that over 200 years could separate these two sets of tablets. This theory adds to the mounting evidence that Evans' date for the abandonment and destruction of Knossos (1375) is much too early.

Despite the loss of much of Crete's writings and our inability to translate Linear A, the ancients' influence on language lives on. Words like labyrinth, hyacinth and cypress date from bronze age times as do the occasional place name; Knossos, Amnissos, Phaistos, Tylissos and Zominthos, the name still used for a spring in the Ida mountains.

Although sealstones were not directly associated with script they were clearly central to Cretan commerce and administration. Arthur Evans' interest in Crete was first prompted by sealstones. There is no general agreement on their function but at the time of Evans' arrival on the island at the turn of the twentieth century, women were using them as charms to stimulate lactation. Indeed collectors know them as *galopetrai* or milk stones. At that time white stones were particularly prized because of their milky colour. For the bronze age Cretans they could simply have been a constant personal reminder of the power and beneficence of the Goddess, a sophisticated equivalent of the christian rosary or Saint Christopher pendant perhaps. The way that they were used to seal bottles and jars however, also indicates an economic function. Many surving seal impressions show the marks of several strands of string on their reverse side, suggesting perhaps that they had been used to seal scrolls with string wound around them.

No two sealstones of the thousands that have been found were exactly the same though many shared similar themes. Most of them had a religious topic (fig. 8). Some depict dramatic scenes while others are more formal and less expressive like the amygdaloid (almond shaped) green jasper depicting a priestess, with a dove (fig. 9). Perhaps they represented an early form of identity or payment/barter card which took the place of currency and consequently could not be passed from one generation to the next. Evans pointed to a number of instances in which sealings have been over stamped or 'counter signed'. If they were personal identity tags this would indicate the sophistication of the activities of Cretan commerce. Their uniqueness is attested to by the practice of burying them with their erstwhile owners. This emphasis on individuality shows that people were still valued for themselves even within such a strongly community-based society.

Industry, Technology and the Legal System

The archaeological remains on Crete astounded the world as they revealed the nature and structure of an extremely advanced and sophisticated society. Bronze age Crete was seen to have produced Europe's first civil engineers who built complex high rise buildings, extensive networks of paved roads, aqueducts, viaducts, irrigation channels, flushing toilets, drainage systems, harbour installations and magnificent ships.

Cretan society was composed of architects, designers, builders, sanitation and plumbing engineers, agricultural and horticultural specialists, boat builders, dyers, spinners, weavers, textile and clothes designers, carpenters, tanners, potters, experts in ceramic design and production, stone carvers, gold and silversmiths, miniature sealstone carvers and fresco painters, oil and wine manufacturers, distillers,

Daily Life

pharmacists, scientists, medical practitioners, scribes as part of a vast civil service, priestesses and ruling Queens.

Given the social organisation around matrilineal clans it is clear that women played an important part in the industrial and technological development of bronze age Crete. The spinning and weaving of woollen cloth had been an important part of Cretan industry from very early in the development of their culture right through to its close. Loom weights and spindle whorls (dating from 4000 BC) were found in the neolithic mound on the Kephala hill and sheep were included in the lists on Linear B tablets from Knossos. Although there is nothing to suggest that men were not involved in these crafts, spinning and weaving are in most ancient mythologies associated with women and with female deities. Arachne, the spider Goddess is said to have spun the world and the Greek Fates (all female) were believed to spin destinies. In the Temple Palace at Arkhanes, semi-precious loom weights were found which may indicate that the priestesses themselves wove certain sacred garments, perhaps those used to adorn the Goddess impersonator (see Chapter 4).

Scholars like Briffault and Neumann, through extensive research into early mythology, concluded that pottery was invented by women. Cross-cultural anthropological studies reveal that women were often the sex that practised this craft. Marija Gimbutas believes that the most sophisticated creations of Old Europe (in which Crete is included) - the most exquisite vases now extant - were 'women's work'.

Something else which is also apparent from anthropological studies is that in the primarily agricultural economies of developing nations, the cultivation of the soil is, to the present day, primarily in the hands of women [29]. As Thompson put it, given their role in the initiation and development of agriculture, it is not surprising to learn that women were in control of this fundamental contribution to the wealth of Crete.

> There is no need to insist on the supreme importance of agriculture. The point is that this mode of production was initiated by women, who thus played the decisive part in the origin of civilisation. [30]

Even into the classical period Greek women were traditionally the owners of land, a convention that was reflected in Greek mythology in which the earth is identified with the Goddess. This association stretched far beyond the Aegean. Many religions explicitly attribute the invention of agriculture to the Goddess. Isis is repeatedly mentioned as the inventor of agriculture in Egyptian texts and in Mesopotamian tablets the Goddess Ninlil is revered for teaching her people to farm.

Religious associations between women and agriculture span many thousands of years; from Catal Huyuk, where the small statue of the Goddess (fig. 1)was found in a grain bin and offerings of grain were made in Her shrines, to classical Greece where ears of wheat were carved on the temple at Eleusis and such offerings were made to Demeter and Hera. Indeed, the lack of vegetation in winter was attributed to Demeter's sorrow at the loss of her daughter Persephone.

This is not to say that men were not involved in agricultural activities. It is clear from the Harvesters Vase and other artefacts that they were, but the evidence suggests that it may have been women, as part of their role as heads of clans, who were seen as the guardians or 'owners' of the land (see Chapter 3).

As representatives of the Goddess on earth, women as priestesses were also the arbiters of religion and as a consequence would have been responsible for the way their society was ordered and organised, for a legal framework and judgements. Again there are mythical associations. Maat is the Egyptian Goddess of justice and as Eisler points out:

> 'Even after male domination was imposed . . . Isis and the Greek Goddess Demeter were both still known as lawgivers and sages dispensing righteous wisdom, counsel and justice. Archaeological records of the Middle Eastern city of Nimrod, where the already martial Ishtar was worshipped, show that even then some women still served as judges and magistrates in courts of law.' [31]

In Ireland the Celts celebrated Cerridwen as the Goddess of intelligence and knowledge. Both the Greek Fates who enforced law and the Muses who inspired creativity were female and Sophia's association with wisdom prevailed into medieval Christian times.

The persistence of female oracles, who transmitted the word of the gods to the people well into the classical Greek era, suggests that the indigenous Aegean population was more comfortable with women in the role of law-giver or guide in important issues. Had there been no tradition of women as intermediaries between the deity and humanity the invading Indo-Europeans would not have tolerated such a challenge to their explicitly-stated belief in the inferiority of women.

It seems reasonable then to assume that women on Crete, in the role of priestesses, acted as guides and law-givers to their people, interpreting the word of the Goddess for them. This kind of sacred guidance or leadership is not suggestive of a monarch or ruler. The role

Daily Life

of the priestesses of Crete would seem to be more akin to a that of a prime minister or abbess.

The extent of women's involvement in Cretan culture should be remembered when considering the many magnificent achievements of the bronze age Cretans.

We should of course avoid the assumption that the mothers of young children were bound by childcare ties. Anthropological evidence from a wide range of other cultures shows that the needs of infants would be met through extended families and clan networks. There would be an abundance of older children and ageing adults to assume responsibility for their nurture, education and training. Eleanor Leacock's review of women in egalitarian societies, using examples ranging from the San in south-west Africa to the Inuits of the Antarctic and native Americans, has shown that in these cultures the whole social group shared responsibility for children. For a discussion of this arrangement in the present-day stone age culture of the Yequana Indians of Venezuela, see Jean Liedloff's book, *The Continuum Concept* (1986). Older children would also be engaged in learning and refining their future chosen or inherited roles and skills. Swedish archaeologist Paul Åström has noted the palm prints of children on Linear B tablets, indicating that they would have worked on preparing them for use.

Linear B scripts date from the period following the generalised destruction (around 1450) which is considered by some scholars to be the beginning of an era of transition towards a different way of life on Crete. Despite their late date however these texts, along with the frescoes and royal burials dating from this time (which will be discussed later), indicate that women still took the lead in Cretan society. Evans found the inscriptions to make numerous references to women in all the different professions that had made the culture such a success. Just one example however illustrates how vulnerable these ancient texts are to misinterpretation. The job title Barley Reaper, has also been construed as Clothworker or Wardress. While there may be confusion as to the exact occupations, the sign for women is unequivocal. Women are clearly listed as road builders at one extreme and as belonging to Associations of Priestesses at the other.

Castleden is convinced of the power held by the priestesses of Knossos. Amongst his evidence for this he cites the frescoes and the role of *klawiphoroi* or key bearer, a religious post specified in the tablets. It was held exclusively by women and undoubtedly involved important secular responsibilities.

Medical Knowledge

Texts found in Egypt record the particular renown of the healing and pharmaceutical skills of the Cretans and mention the medicinal properties of a certain Cretan bean that was widely prescribed and taken. Their knowledge of medicine is demonstrated by their ability to extract opium from the poppy, indicated by the cuts in pods on the head of the Poppy Goddess from Gazi (fig.10). They also used herbs like dittany for medicinal purposes. Mythology supports anthropological and historical evidence that in many cultures medicine was the exclusive province of women [32]. In the *Odyssey*, the classical heroine Helen gives a draft to her companions which seems to be an opiate. Its effect was calming and induced a feeling of well-being. The Poppy Goddess expresses the link between healing and mysticism evident in older cultures. This is further confirmed by the many hundreds of scorched models of clay limbs that were recovered from peak sanctuaries. Such practices suggest a link between healing and religion which may indicate the involvement of priestesses.

Fig. 10 Poppy Goddess from the sanctuary at Gazi near Iraklion. 1350-1200 BC.

Diet

[At Catal Huyuk] there were no human or animal sacrifices; pets were kept and cherished. Vegetarianism prevailed, for domestic animals were kept for milk and wool not meat . . . There is no evidence of violent deaths. [33]

This quote, by Elizabeth Gould Davis, from the work of James Mellaart, supports the findings of Bachofen a hundred years earlier, who stated that '. . . the early matriarchies being for the most part non-meat eaters'.

Daily Life

Indeed in his description of the different ages of humanity, one of Hesiod's negative defining characteristics of the peoples who succeeded the older cultures, the war-loving 'race of bronze', is their preference for flesh, 'they ate no grain, but hearts of flint were theirs . . .'

Animal bones have, however, been found at a number of religious sites which may indicate that meat was eaten on special festive occasions. The ancient Cretans clearly had a plentiful and varied range of foods other than meat at their disposal. The remains of oil, grains, peas, bitter vetch (a kind of pea), beans and other legumes have been found in *pithoi*. We also know that they grew chickpeas, pigeon peas, sesame, hemp, flax and castor oil plants. Grape presses from a number of sites indicate the early use of wine, and grapes were dried to make raisins for winter food and as a possible export. Olive presses and separators found at Gournia are of the type still used today, demonstrating that as early as the Middle Minoan period the Cretans had invented a process for extracting olive oil still effective enough to meet modern standards. Linear B tablets show that bees were kept for honey allowing for large surpluses which would have ben exported or made into mead.

2
The Meaning of Sacred Art

The Early Prehistoric Background

> The universal desire of mankind to depict Her and worship Her image heralded the birth of art.
>
> Between 9000 and 7000 BC art makes its appearance in the Near East in the form of statuettes of the supreme deity, the Great Goddess.
>
> James Mellaart [1]

Early in human social cognition a sense of wonderment and reverence must have grown around what appeared to be the magical properties of nature. Rain falls from the skies providing the water on which all life depends. Plants and trees offer food and materials for shelter and flowers blossom providing exquisite beauty and perfume to the delight of all who encountered them. It seems inevitable then that our early ancestors, who were so much more aware of their dependence on the forces of nature than we are, should deify and celebrate this magical essence. Their sense of reverence was defined, recorded and transmitted through folk memories and the use of symbols; images in sand, earth and clay, carvings and paintings on cave walls, the fashioning of rocks into different shapes, the use of shells and colour and later through the building of massive earthworks and standing stone complexes.

The pinnacle of this wonderment and reverence that our earliest ancestors had for nature was focussed around the female who creates life directly from her own body and sustains it with milk from her breasts.

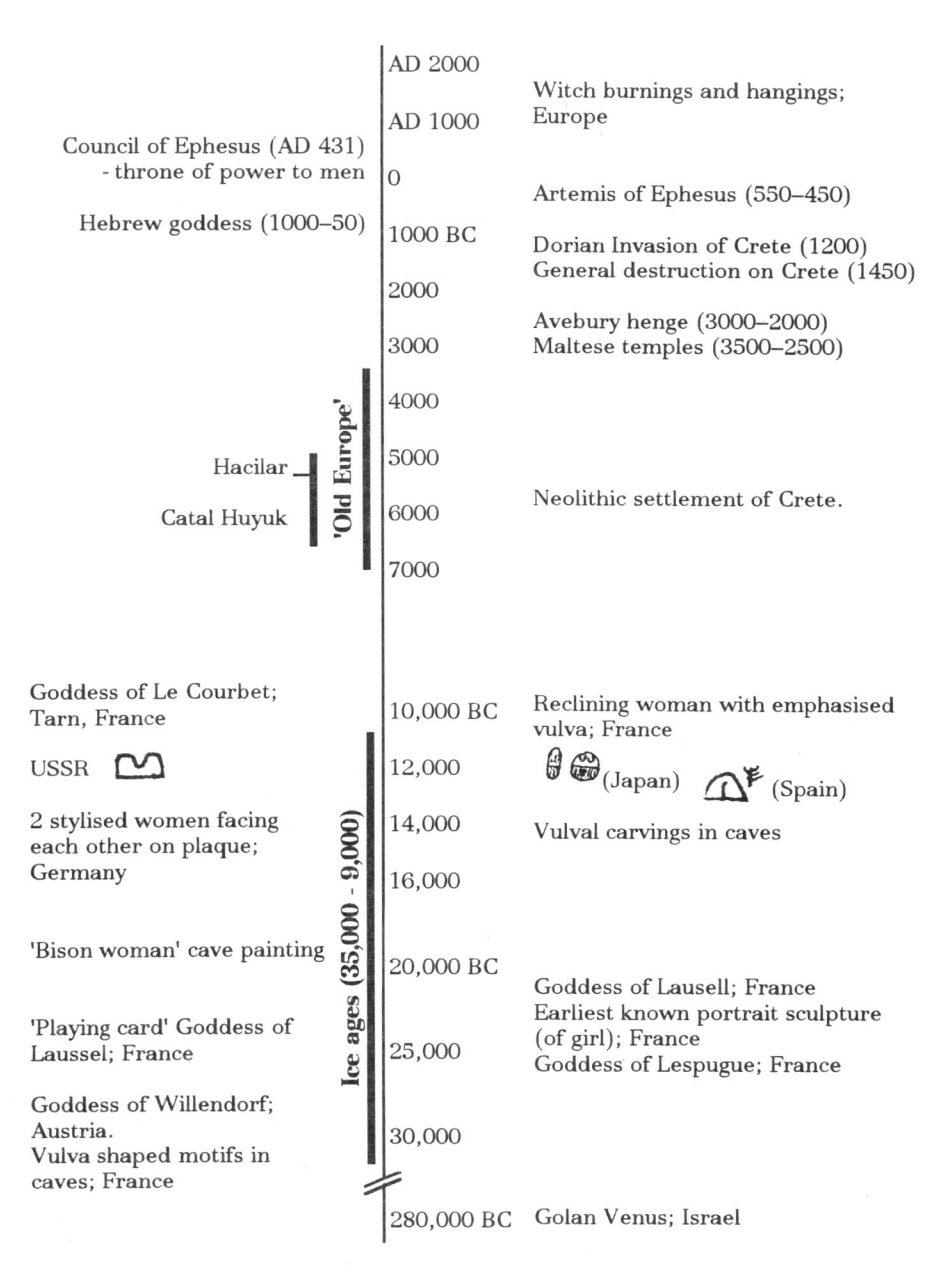

Left	Timeline	Right
	AD 2000	
		Witch burnings and hangings; Europe
	AD 1000	
Council of Ephesus (AD 431) - throne of power to men	0	
		Artemis of Ephesus (550–450)
Hebrew goddess (1000–50)	1000 BC	
		Dorian Invasion of Crete (1200)
	2000	General destruction on Crete (1450)
		Avebury henge (3000–2000)
	3000	Maltese temples (3500–2500)
	4000	
Hacilar	5000 'Old Europe'	
Catal Huyuk	6000	Neolithic settlement of Crete.
	7000	
Goddess of Le Courbet; Tarn, France	10,000 BC	Reclining woman with emphasised vulva; France
USSR	12,000	(Japan) (Spain)
2 stylised women facing each other on plaque; Germany	14,000	Vulval carvings in caves
	16,000	
'Bison woman' cave painting	20,000 BC	
		Goddess of Lausell; France
'Playing card' Goddess of Laussel; France	25,000	Earliest known portrait sculpture (of girl); France
		Goddess of Lespugue; France
Goddess of Willendorf; Austria. Vulva shaped motifs in caves; France	30,000	
	280,000 BC	Golan Venus; Israel

Ice ages (35,000 - 9,000)

'Time line'. All dates are approximate; archaeologists continually ammend dating in the light of new evidence.

Nature itself, encompassing all creation, is to the present day personified as female.

In Europe evidence concerning the beliefs of our early ancestors begins around 40,000 years ago in the upper paleolithic when the first Cro-Magnon peoples entered Europe. The funereal rites of a burial at Les Eyzies in France, the earliest human burial so far discovered, involved the placing of vulva-shaped cowrie shells on the skeletal remains. The first clearly religious icons were figures whose female proportions were emphasised, often to the point of being wildly exaggerated. Many such figures were found to have been stained with red ochre pigment. Skeletons were similarly coloured. Religious historian E.O. James believed that both the cowrie shell and the red ochre were symbols for the female. The latter was 'still in later traditions the surrogate of the life giving or menstrual blood of women' [2].

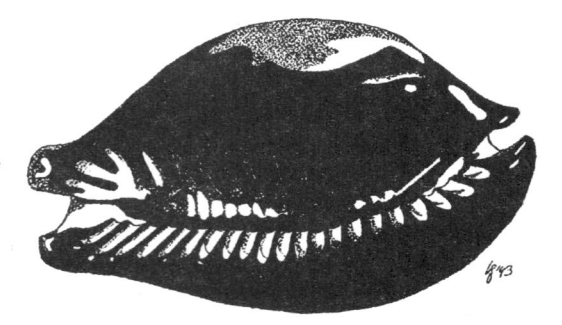

Fig. 12 Vulva-shaped cowrie shell.

This association of the divine with the female continued throughout the ice age (fig. 11) with paintings and the carving of vulval shapes on cave walls and the fashioning of Goddess figures. Some well-known examples come from Willendorf (fig. 13), Vestonice, Lespugue, Laussel (fig. 14), England (fig. 15) and Catal Huyuk (fig. 1). These beliefs endured throughout the neolithic in most areas of Europe and the Near East and possibly much further afield and on an increasingly restricted basis, into the bronze age.

Peter Ucko's extensive study of the neolithic figurines of Egypt, the Aegean and Near East led him to the tentative conclusion that prehistoric figurines were produced for a variety of reasons. Although he argues that only early historical material should be used to help determine the function of these figures, he uses very late ethnographic evidence as the basis for his assertion that many of them may have been children's dolls. In this study he never states explicitly what an identifying characteristic of a deity would be but is wary of accepting any figure in this role. Given what we know of Cretan religious practices, however, he gives an inappropriately restricted definition to the Great Goddess, assuming Her to have been associated exclusively with fertility and the earth. His view that not all early figurines can be taken as

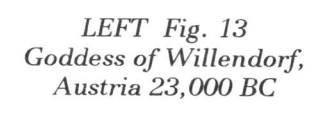

LEFT Fig. 13
Goddess of Willendorf,
Austria 23,000 BC

BOTTOM LEFT Fig. 14
Goddess carved above a
cave entrance, Lausel
(Dordogne, France)
22,000 BC. She hold a
crescent moon-shaped
horn.

BELOW Fig. 15
Grimes Graves Goddess,
Norfolk, England. 2200
BC. 107 mm high.

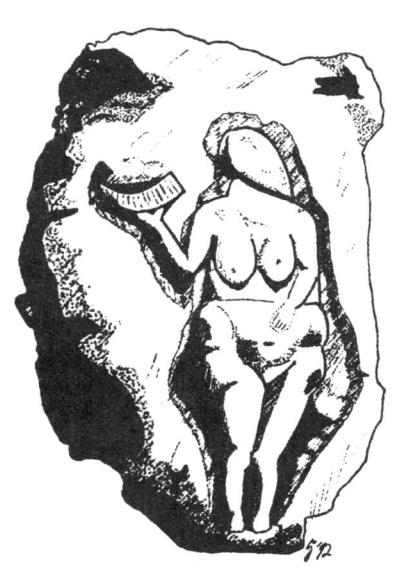

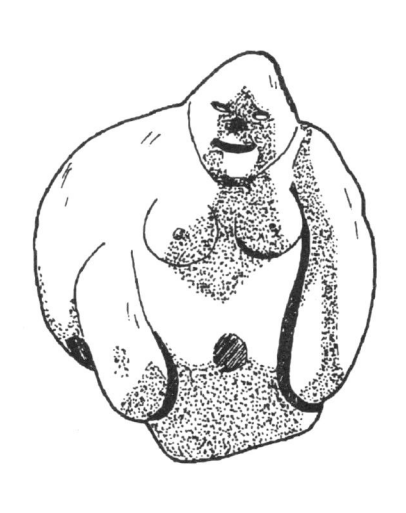

representing the Great Goddess is clearly correct, but there were certain features which seem to have been associated with Her throughout the eras of pre history.

Just a cursory glance at the figures noted above reveal one uniting feature to be the immense presence created by the exaggeration of their femaleness. The Catal Huyuk Goddess' power is further reinforced through an association with leopards and Her positioning on a throne while the Lausel figure holds a symbol for the crescent moon. The large proportions of these figures led to them being named steatopygous (a Greek medical term meaning the excessive development of fat on the buttocks), because archaeologists mistakenly believed that these were all models of women suffering from a disease which caused this. Ucko also discusses this as a serious possibility.

Marija Gimbutas and James Mellaart are two of the few archaeologists who have examined neolithic excavation evidence with gender issues in mind. Gimbutas sought identify the role women played in these early cultures. How did the social organisation of the Old European communities, which flourished from 7000–3500 BC, differ from that of the Kurgans who were to invade and subjugate them? The sheer volume of the evidence is astounding. Over thirty thousand miniature sculptures of clay, marble, bone, copper and gold were recovered from more than three thousand sites. Other archaeologists encountering evidence of the power assigned to the female in early cultures have ignored or devalued it. Female deities have been variously defined as fertility symbols or sex objects for men. Many scholars have even interpreted clearly female figures as male. Gimbutas, on the other hand, saw the figures as indicators of the high degree of importance that was attached to being female in the early societies of Old Europe [3]. She also found numerous pointers to these cultures being matrilineal with women playing key roles in all aspects of life.

Her findings were matched by those of Mellaart. His study of the arrangements of the buildings, burial practices and art work from his excavations at Catal Huyuk and Hacilar in Anatolia, revealed that these cultures were what he describes as unequivocally woman centred,

> That the civilization expressed at Catal Huyuk was woman-dominated, is . . . obvious.

The Meaning of Sacred Art

Catal Huyuk . . . was not only a matriarchal but a utopian society . . . Women were heads of households, they were reverently buried while men's bones were thrown into a charnel house. Above all, the supreme deity in all the temples was a goddess. [4]

Michael Dames, who came to the study of prehistory from an artist's background, has made detailed studies of the megalithic monuments and earthworks of Avebury in Wiltshire. His insights, which have led him to see the monuments as representing the life cycle of the Goddess, fit with the pattern of evidence in the rest of the neolithic world. Silbury Hill is plausibly described by Dames as representing the pregnant Goddess in profile. From the viewing platform close to the top of this sacred hill, if the 'ditch' area is flooded it is possible to observe the moon's reflection as it passes across the sky at the autumn equinox. It can be seen passing from the part of the hill described as representing the Goddess' vulva, to Her breast as She gives birth to and suckles the new infant. The construction of these great monuments would have taken the commitment and energies of the whole community.

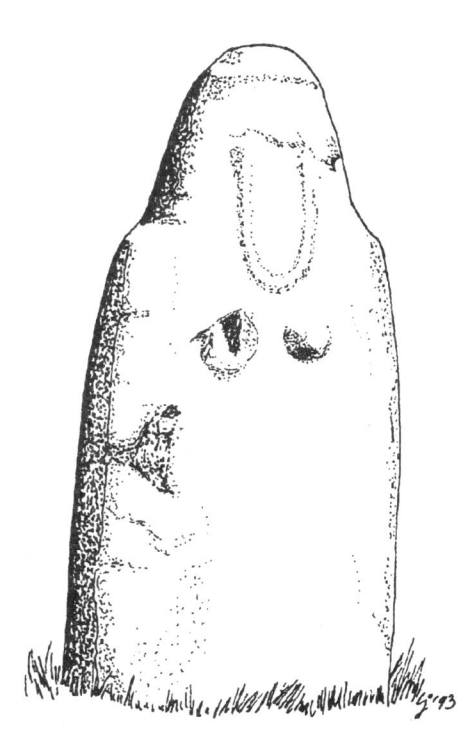

Fig. 16   One of the 'Grand Mother' standing stones with breasts. 2500–1800 BC. Found under the chancel of Câtel church, Guernsey.

The many and varied finds from Malta reveal a Goddess focussed culture where the power of the female is represented in numerous images of Her. Almost all of them exaggerate her female shape in the traditional style and they range from the small, though large proportioned, Sleeping Goddess (fig. 17) which has been compared with the massive hand-built mound at Silbury Hill in Wiltshire (fig. 18), to the towering figure from the temple at Tarxian (fig. 19). The outlines of the

49

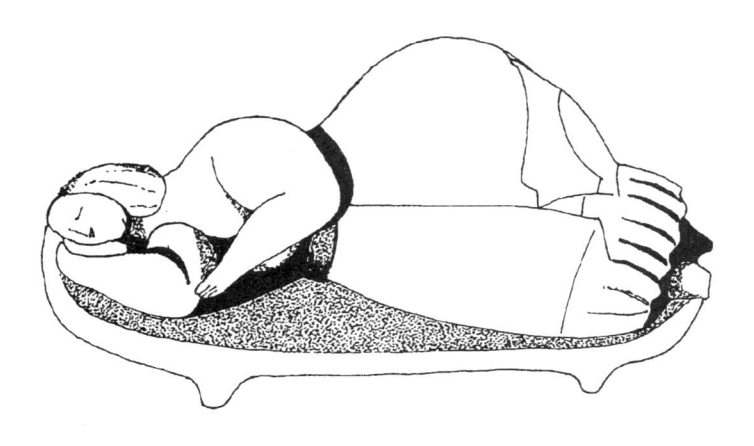

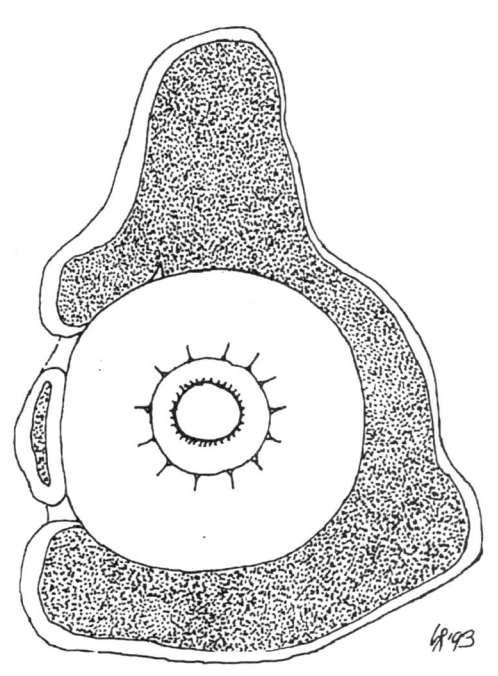

ABOVE Fig. 17
The Sleeping
Goddess, Malta
3800-3600 BC
122 mm long; clay
painted with red
ochre. Her form
resembles the outline
of Silbury Hill and
may be associated
with Mount Juktas as
representing the
Goddess.

LEFT Fig. 18
Bird's-eye view of
Silbury Hill, Avebury,
Wiltshire as pregnant
Mother Goddess
2500 BC.
(After Dames)

Fig. 19 Tarxian Temple, Globerina limestone, Malta 3300-2500 BC. The upper part of the massively-proportioned 8 feet-high figure was destroyed by farming. The inner temple threshold is decorated with spirals.

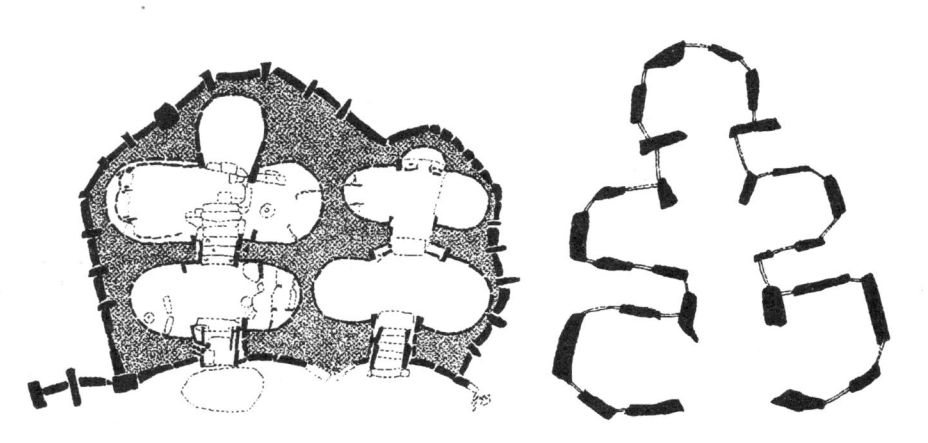

LEFT Fig. 20 Ggantija Mother and Daughter Temples, Gozo, Malta 3600–3000 BC
RIGHT Fig. 21 West Kennet Longbarrow, Avebury, Wiltshire 2000 BC. The outline takes the form of the squatting Goddess. The stones at its entrance form the shape of stylised ox horns.

great megalithic Mother and Daughter temples at Ggantija (fig. 20) on the neighbouring island of Gozo imitate the shape of the Goddess squatting to give birth. This same symbolism features in the West Kennet long barrow at Avebury (fig. 21). In the case of the long barrow the dead could be seen as returning to Her body for the cycle to begin again.

The megaliths of Jersey and Guernsey (fig. 16) have a special place in the overall spiritual picture of neolithic European artifacts. The single standing stones discovered here are formed with breasts which provide the key to understanding that the many thousands of standing stones that remain to the present day were set up to symbolise, the Great Goddess Herself. This symbolism no doubt contributed to ruthless destruction of so many individual menhirs and megalithic complexes under the direction of christian leaders in the 14th, 17th and 18th centuries [5].

Cretan Art

From the time when Arthur Evans uncovered the first treasures of Knossos in 1900, scholars from all disciplines have been unstinting in their praise of the uniqueness and perfection of bronze age Cretan art. C. Hopkins described its style as

[of an] entirely individual kind. Their exuberance and beauty, their grace and naturalism were astonishing. There were huge quantities of a vivid and beautiful pottery scarcely matched in later times; there was exquisite jewellery, enchanting miniature sculpture, extra ordinarily accomplished sealstone engraving, there was fresco-painting, faience work, work in bronze and gold. [6]

Archaeologist Nicholas Platon commented that:

It is the mass of excellence which is so impressive. The figures move with a lovely grace. [7]

Reynold Higgins of the British Museum felt that it showed:

Constant inventiveness, an understanding of form and movement and a sense of spontaneity and fun. [8]

The Meaning of Sacred Art

Just as in much earlier cultures, the inspiration for and focus of the art of the bronze age Cretans was their deity and religion which encompassed every aspect of nature.

The earliest examples of art works found on Crete are small Goddess figures from the neolithic tell at Knossos. These were made between 6000 and 3000 BC by the first settlers. It was towards the end of this period that the great neolithic structures of Malta (from 3500) and Avebury (3000) were being built.

Vincent Scully, a researcher who amassed evidence of sacred structures from many different areas claims that the siting of Crete's first settlement and the subsequent Temple Palaces had more to do with sacred than secular considerations. He points out that each site

> makes use . . . of the same landscape elements . . . first an enclosed valley of varying size in which the palace is set, . . . second a gently moulded or conical hill on axis with the palace . . . and lastly a higher, double peaked or cleft mountain some distance beyond the hill but on the same axis. [9]

Thus each Temple Palace is located at the symbolic vulva of the Goddess with Her pregnant abdomen represented by the conical hill. The double peaked mountains above are seen as Her breasts, the earth is the living Goddess. If we accept Scully's hypothesis then monumental representations of the Goddess were part of the bronze age Cretans' religious repertoire.

As time moved on, as well as being represented by the earth with its mountain peaks and sacred caves, the essence of the Cretan deity was also portrayed in small, detailed replicas of Cretan womanhood. There may also have been large-scale Goddess figures in wood or clay. Pairs of out-sized clay feet were found in religious contexts at Anemospilia and at Mallia and there is evidence of a large wooden statue from the East Hall of Knossos. Marinatos and Hagg have argued that such clay feet could not have taken the weight of a proportionally-sized wooden statue [10]. The design of later clay Goddesses from Karphi, with skirts thrown on the potters wheel and the separately modelled feet, suggests that large wooden figures could have had similarly hollowed-out skirts with the feet placed in a gap at the front.

All the surviving representations of the Cretan deity however were made, in contrast to those from neighbouring lands, on a distinctly modest scale. Jacquetta Hawkes comments that what is missing from bronze age Cretan art are the images, so common in the surrounding

Crete Reclaimed

patriarchal nations of Egypt, Messopotamia and elsewhere, of powerful and threatening deities. Such fearsome figures reflected the absolute power of their earthly representatives, the pharaohs and kings who commanded obedience and service. This monumental style was also used by the classical Greeks. The statue of Athena encrusted with ivory and gold that once stood as part of the facade of the Parthenon was forty feet tall.

In contrast, the women of Crete could see the great power that was at the centre of their belief system expressed in figures that looked and dressed as they did. The homely size of these figures would have made them easier to identify with and may say something about the priestess queens' relationships with their people. The daunting expression on the faces of these small statues sets them apart from representations of women in frescoes. The fresco figure known as La Parisienne (fig. 6), who was surely a Queen of Knossos, is dressed in a similar fashion to a small staue known as the Snake Goddess. The essence of the Cretan deity was expressed as both monumental and ordinary in the same image. Indeed it is difficult to say whether figures represent Goddesses or humans. This may be linked to a sacred tradition that involved the queen priestesses taking the role of the Goddess, as will be discussed later.

Cretan art is also significant for the total absence of the pomp and savagery so commonly found in other civilisations of the same era, like the Egyptians and Mycenaeans, and of subsequent periods, the Hittites and Assyrians. This absence, together with their choice of undefended coastal sites for their cities, has been described as the most telling indication of the whole tenor of Cretan society.

The Cretans' close neighbours and trading partners, the Mycenaeans and Egyptians, both glorified scenes of hunting and combat in their art. The supreme example of this is the Mycenaean dagger which depicts a lion hunt on one side and armed combat on the other. Hawkes notes that there is no trace of 'these manifestations of masculine pride and unthinking cruelty' on Crete, though many of these works with Mycenaean themes were undoubtedly executed by Cretan artists. There is no mistaking Cretan skill in the artistic field even when works are found in Mycenaean contexts dealing with subjects that were unquestionably Archaean. The volume of such artefacts suggests that Cretan artists either settled in the Peleponnese under the patronage of the palaces there or worked to export commissions.

In contrasting the content of paleolithic art with that of Crete, Hawkes notes that whereas the former depicted the animal in isolation as an object to be outwitted and dominated, the latter brought out the

The Meaning of Sacred Art

elegance and individuality of all aspects of nature with great reverence. The charm of the Cretan artists' work lies in the skill to capture the fleeting moment, the leap of the dolphin, the suckling of a calf, the caress of the mother goat for her kid.

Another contrast noted by Hawkes between Cretan art and that of its near neighbour Egypt was that no scenes of work or other practical activity are shown in isolation. There is rather a mingling of the secular with the sacred; play and sport are combined with ceremony. On the Harvesters Vase we see the procession to the harvest where music, dancing, frivolity and an air of companionable fun transforms toil into festivity. Baking or pottery-making, dancing and bull-leaping are clearly depicted as religious activities.

Peace, specialisation and dedication to the Goddess prompted the production of some of the most splendid artwork that has survived to us from the prehistoric world. The location of workshops inside Temple Palaces emphasises the religious importance of Cretan art. Just as present day currency is imprinted with the symbols which define the culture it is a product of, every aspect of the bronze age Cretans' artistic work is pervaded by the essence of the sacred.

The magnificent art works produced by the bronze age Cretans fall roughly into the following categories.

Stonework

The term stonework in this context can be misleading if we immediately think of granite, limestone or even marble. The Cretans sought their materials over a wide geographical area and chose them with care, to emphasise colour and veining. Their creations in this medium include vases, bowls and other carved vessels and sealstones cut from semi-precious gems. The stone vases from Ayia Triada are some of the best specimens in this medium. One of these, the Harvesters' Vase, has to be the supreme example of the stone carver's skill in any era up to the present day. The expression of feeling and movement portrayed through its low relief is quite magnificent but other, quite different, ritual vases are no less exquisitely carved. Some of the most popular subjects celebrated the natural world. The gold-painted Ox Head Rhyton, the Lioness Rhyton, the mountain shrine *rhyton* from Zakro and many other vessels carved from stone were used for pouring libations in rituals.

The carving of the sealstones that Cretans wore around their wrists is also unsurpassed. Their execution was made all the more difficult because they are cut in reverse, to give a positive image on the piece of clay that was to be stamped (figs 22–24). The scenes depicted on these semi-precious stones encompass such minute and intricate detail that

TOP Fig. 22
The Goddess holds out a staff, atop a mountain flanked by lionesses. Sealstone impression reconstructed from different fragments, 1500 BC, Knossos. To one side stands a sacred tripartite shrine facade, at the other an adorant in a typical stance of deference, shields himself from Her numinosity. It is this scene that the recently-discovered Master Impression seal from Hania most closely imitates.

MIDDLE Fig. 23
Goddess with stylised head seated on face-shaped stool flanked by lionesses. Cornelian lentoid seal from Mycenae.

BOTTOM Fig. 24
Goddess with stylised face. Sardonyx sealstone, 1400 BC, Knossos. This figure, which is described as having a bee face, is surrounded by Her symbols of power.

they could not have been executed without the use of magnification. Crystal lenses discovered in a Middle Minoan tomb at Knossos could certainly have been used for this purpose.

Pottery

Superb examples of pottery from all phases have been preserved and Cretan achievements both in design and decoration is beyond question. As we have already noted scholars like Robert Briffault and Erich Neumann have collected a catalogue of evidence which demonstrates that the art of baking clay was invented by women [11].

In the instance of Crete, Jacquetta Hawkes argues that Cretan pottery was especially feminine in taste with its pretty eggshell bowls and cups. Since the whole tenure of bronze age Crete was especially 'feminine', however, it seems inappropriate to use cultural definitions of masculinity and femininity as, according to all the evidence, such a dichotomy did not exist. Hawkes also points to the Pueblo Indian women of the south-west United States, who make exquisitely decorated pots, as an example of a culture where this craft is still in the hands of women.

Evans noted an example of a thrown cup where the marks of the potter's hands still remain in the throwing rings. He describes the marks left in the spiral fluting as having been made by fine slender finger tips [12]. He was in no doubt that the potters of bronze age Crete were women [13]. Maria Gimbutas was also convinced that Cretan potters were women. Yet, as Thompson observes, there were few known women potters in classical Greece. They were remembered only in the folk memory that gave rise to Athena being the patron of this art.

Pottery was central to Cretan culture. It was an important export and an essential element of ritual practice. Eisler believes that the actual process of making pots was considered a sacred activity. One of the shrine scenes from a tomb at Kamilari may support this view. It represents a ritual where figures appear to be either wedging clay or making bread inside a pillared temple. The delicate eggshell ware found at Phaistos and the Kamares ware from Knossos with its ceramic chains and appliqued flowers could not have survived daily use. It was clearly reserved exclusively for rituals. The strength of this religious association may have led to sacred wares being produced only by particular initiates.

The range in the style of the pottery is so great, has such clear developments and was of such central importance to Cretan culture, that Evans used it as the basis of his 'Minoan' dating system. There are however difficulties with assuming that all areas of the island and indeed other Cretan settlements in the Aegean followed the same ceramic fashions at the same time. An over-reliance on pottery styles may have led to the misdating of significant events like the abandonment of Thera.

Pottery dated as Early Minoan comes from a settlement at Fournou Korifi, which predated the construction of the Old Temple Palaces. Ceramics were already being used in complex shapes and being attractively decorated. The pots were characteristically dark surfaced and burnished. Vasiliki ware, named after the area in south-eastern Crete where it originated, also dates from this time. It is known as 'flame ware' because fire was used to produce the mottled effect which is one of its distinguishing features. It is so delicately made that its discoverers thought that the potter's wheel must have been invented and in use on Crete at that time.

Kamares ware is dated to the Middle Minoan phase, the time of the Old Temple Palace. The name derives from the sacred cave on mount Ida where it was discovered in large quantities. The context attests to its religious use. This ware is characterised by a sophisticated polychrome decoration on a dark background. By this stage the potters had developed a fine gloss paint with a metallic sheen in a wide range of colours for decorating the completed pots. As well as improving the looks of the vase this type of finish had the added effect of strengthening it. This same style of decoration reappeared centuries later on Greek vases.

The pivoted disc wheel, which was in use in Sumeria from around 3500 BC, was introduced from Egypt or Asia Minor to Crete around 1800 BC and, as a consequence, after Middle Minoan IA (100 years prior to the New Temple Palace period) only the largest *pithoi* were made by hand.

The later periods produced elaborate forms with naturalistic styles of decoration which included reeds, leafs and stylistic flowers. These themes were supplanted by the splendid marine designs in which octopus, nautili, dolphins, starfish, and conches were common themes.

The standard of pottery is said to have reached a zenith in the Old Temple Palace period and after what some scholars believe was a period of lesser quality, by 1500 (Late Minoan IB) ceramics had once again returned to the excellence of Middle Minoan II with potters attempting virtually every shape of vase and easily imitating those of metal or stone.

Although figures are seen carved on stoneware, it is a notable feature of Cretan pottery that the human figure was never painted onto ceramic pieces. The total absence of any figures on Cretan pottery indicates that this is more a matter of taboo than just a quirk of style. If it was a taboo

The Meaning of Sacred Art

then it was associated with the decoration of pots rather than with clay itself as there are many hundreds of figures in this medium. A clue to the reason for this absence may lie in later Goddess figures which are part-human and part-*pithos*. The deity is represented as part of the clay vessel itself. As clay is in essence earth it may have been, like a stalactite or exposed peak at a Peak Sanctuary, interchangeable with the Cretan deity. The *pithos* can be seen as representing the deity. Its dual role was to hold the products of nature and receive the dead for burial. If the clay of a vessel represented the Goddess Herself it would have been inappropriate to paint human figures onto Her.

If the essence of the Goddess was represented by the material of the pot this would add an extra sacred dimension to the ritual use of *rhytons*. These are vessels from which, in rituals, the water or oil or milk needed to sustain life could be seen as flowing from the deity Herself. This theory would also explain the many vases decorated with snakes (fig. 25) and topped by doves (as can be seen in a triple vessel in the Ayias Nikolias museum); both styles in which the Goddess is also represented in more figurative forms (figs 35 and 46).

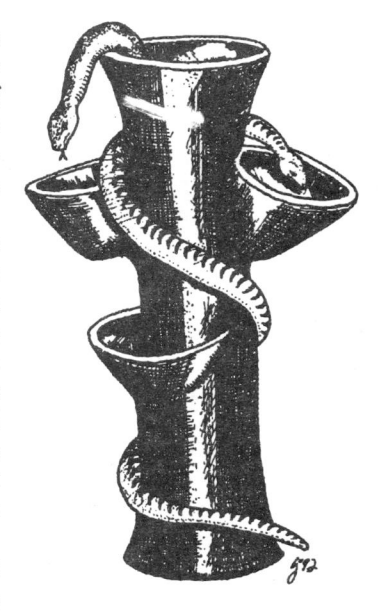

Fig. 25 Snake Vessel 1450-1400 BC.
This may have been how snakes were stored in tubes. It may also be an example of the Goddess as clay vessel. In this analysis the vessel is a symbolic representation of the Snake Goddess.

Faience and Ivory

Both these media were used by the Cretans to produce images of one of the best known symbols of Cretan religion, the Snake Goddess. This small 17th century BC representation (see front cover) is the one that most visitors to Crete will be familiar with. It was produced by a technique called faience which is achieved by preparing a core of quartz grains cemented together by the addition of an alkaline glaze during firing. This process was not rediscovered in Europe until AD 1570, around three thousand years later.

An astoundingly beautiful range of sacred goods produced in this medium was found in the 'Temple Repositories' at Knossos. As well as the famous Snake Goddess figures, there is a cow suckling her calf, a goat suckling her kid and, curiously, examples of women's clothing. These latter can be explained by a particular religious ceremony discussed in Chapter 4.

Ivory allows for the expression of fine detail, as in the bull-leaper from Knossos, where the tension of the action is captured in the muscles, sinews and blood vessels of the figure's arms. Other examples are a small sitting baby and the bull-leaper with an ornate apron who is poised, about to leap, her arms held in a gesture which resembles that of benediction (fig. 26). The ivory Snake Goddess now in the Boston Museum of Fine Arts in the USA, which is adorned by details in gold, is thought to have originated in a second Temple Repository at Knossos, adjacent to the one where the faience Snake Goddesses were found. This repository had been robbed and contained only fragments of gold leaf. Castleden, however, believes that this figure originated in the Great Goddess Sanctuary (Evans' East Hall) as part of an ivory group.

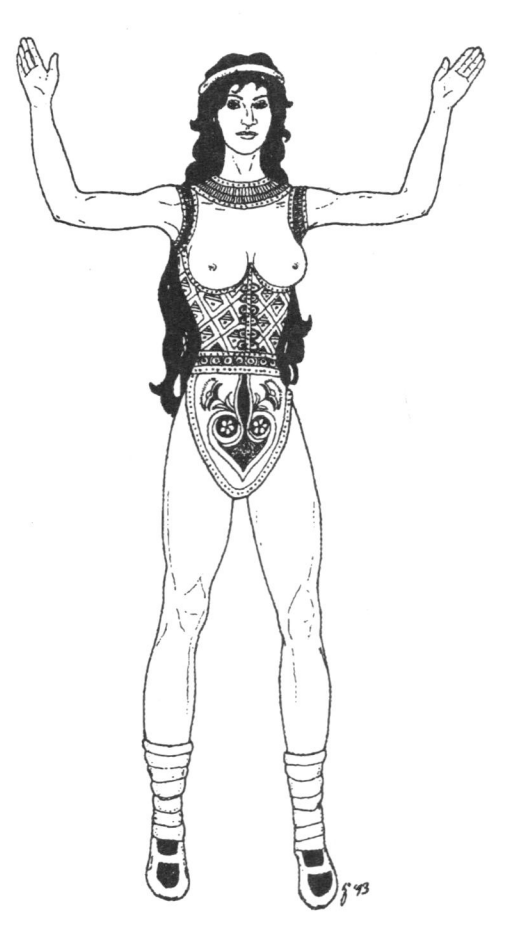

Fig. 26 Bull Leaper with decorative apron. Ivory, Knossos, 1600 BC. This figure's pose of benediction also replicates the ox horns.

Metalwork

The degree of accomplishment of Cretan artists was such that it is difficult to say which of the art forms they most excelled in. Superb examples are available in each medium. The Cretan metal workers used many different techniques in the execution of their art. Goldsmiths, for example, worked with sheet gold, gold wire, casting, embossing, filigree and inlay. Reynold Higgins, while Keeper of Greek and Roman Antiquities in the British Museum, argued that jewellery made from the most elaborate of these methods, filigree and granulation, indicated the royal status of the wearer or corpse it had once adorned. Such refinements are associated with finds at Knossos and Mallia. The bee pendant from the 'gold hole' burial site at Mallia combines several of these different techniques executed to perfection to produce a simple image in an elaborate style. Higgins also surmises that these objects would have been worn by women.

Fig. 27 Gold Signet Ring, Isopata 1500-1425 BC. Evans believed the central figure to be the Goddess descending to Her waiting adorants. Vegetation, a serpent and a crysalis also feature. A small hovering female figure is shown separated from the group by wavy lines (these also appear on fig. 3) which may signify a separation between this and an other world.

Some other delightful pieces are the finely-incised *labyris* from Archolochori and the gold and silver signet rings each incised with a sacred scene (fig. 27). Spyridon Marinatos was convinced that these rings, which he believed were never worn on the finger, belonged exclusively to women. In the royal burials at Phourni cemetery near Arkhanes, signet rings were found on the breast of one of the corpses. Two others were discovered in a position which indicated they had been suspended from one of the necklaces which had been placed in her tomb. Perhaps such rings signified membership of one of the sacred sisterhoods of priestesses mentioned in Linear B tablets, or were worn only by the priestess queens. Did the detailed scenes they depict originate from their dreams or trances, or did they represent rituals at which Goddess manifestation was enacted? We can only speculate.

The delicacy and refinement of their execution calls to mind James Mellaart's view that the neolithic people of Catal Huyuk were producing holes in their craft work so fine that no modern needle can penetrate them.

The exquisite design and intricate detail of two daggers (fig. 28) found in female burials at Mycenae, demonstrate the Cretan artist's skill at filling a small space. The first is a fine example of the marine style while the second takes a spiral form pattern. These artefacts, along with a large volume of fresco evidence, also attest to the high status of women amongst the Mycenaeans.

Fig. 28 Women's Bronze Daggers, 1600–1500 BC, Grave V, Mycenae. LEFT: Coral and nautali. These daggers, found with the remains of female corpses, show Cretan skills of filling a small space with intricate detail. RIGHT: Spiral decoration in gold.

Frescoes and Textiles

From about 2000 BC onwards frescoes, sometimes built up in relief, were painted directly onto wet plaster. These works have a grace and style which immediately identifies them as Cretan.

Marinatos notes with regret that all the Old Temple Palace frescoes were lost. He believes that they would certainly have been of a high standard judging, by the quality of Kamares ware pottery which dates from the same period.

The earliest preserved frescoes were simple linear designs like meanders and spirals, then animals and plants appeared followed by human figures. A complex adaptation of the linear design is the exquisite spiral and sun composition in stucco relief which covered the ceiling of the small sanctuary in which the Sacred Grove and Temple or Grandstand frescoes were discovered.

Frescoes were painted to different scales. There were life-size reliefs like the charging bull restored in the north portico of Knossos and the Lily figure which was partly in relief, and many other life-size figures that were painted flat. Perhaps the most spectacular full-size fresco is that which once decorated the Corridor of the Procession. This fresco comprised around 500 life-size figures depicted in two rows, one set above the other, filing into the Central Court. Another style records scenes as they would appear on a standard smaller scale, such as the paintings of monkeys stealing crocuses or raiding bird's eggs.

Perhaps the most interesting style is used for the miniature frescoes. For these the painters used a number of shorthand conventions to condense great scenes into a small space. There was no attempt at perspective and a number of scenes can appear in the same picture. One example comes from Akrotiri shows a pastoral scene, a meeting on a hill and a flotilla of ships leaving one harbour and arriving at another. We must infer that time is also condensed. Examples of miniature frescoes from Knossos are the Temple or Grandstand and the Sacred Grove Dance frescoes [14].

Frescoes tell us a great deal about Cretan culture and individual paintings will be examined in detail in the forthcoming companion volume to this book. A wonderful bonus is their record of the exquisite textiles produced by the Cretans. Whereas the frescoes just managed to survive the ravages of time, albeit in fragments in the many cases, fabrics, sadly, did not. Our limited evidence of their range, variety and accomplishment comes from frescoes, faience reproductions of gowns and another, rather more obscure source. Sinclair Hood has noted that the ceilings of Egyptian tombs were painted with patterns which imitated the Cretan textiles that were used to decorate the ceilings of Egyptian houses at the time [15]. It is an indication of the Cretan artists' and textile designers' skill and renown that their products were eagerly imported into a country with its own distinctive artistic style.

Evans noted a number of miniature fresco fragments which recorded the detail of embroidered robes. One, in which a woman is drawing up a fishing net, shows the swallow design on the fabric of her dress. In another, the fabric design incorporates the head of a figure with dark skin who is wearing large gold coloured earrings.

Archaeologists are in some doubt as to where the Cretans would have learned their artistic skills but are confident, because of its distinctive individuality, that it would certainly not have been Egypt. It is possible however that skills and techniques could have been learnt from other lands developed into quite separate styles on Crete. There is no reason why Crete would need to have borrowed from other cultures. Excavations at Catal Huyuk in Anatolia where the Cretans are thought to have originated have revealed that skills in sculpture and fresco painting were already well-advanced. Gimbutas argued that it was only the devastating attacks from the barbaric ancestors of the Indo-Europeans that halted the development of the neolithic peoples of Old Europe. Had they been left in peace their artefacts would undoubtedly have developed to a level comparable with Cretan art.

Nowhere on any of the Cretan pieces do we find the name of an artist. These magnificent works of art were not produced for personal gain, fame or greed or to express the power and importance of any individual. They were made for another purpose – to celebrate their deity, the Great Goddess.

3
Gender Roles

> The violence of the antagonism against the theory of
> matriarchy arouses the suspicion that it is . . . based on
> an emotional prejudice against an assumption so foreign
> to the thinking and feeling of our patriarchal culture.
>
> Erich Fromm, *The Forgotten Language* 1951

A Prehistorical Perspective

It is abundantly clear that there was an expression of reverence towards the female deity in prehistoric cultures but can we take this as reflecting the esteem in which women were once held? Part of the focus on women during paleolithic and neolithic times appears to have been around her sexuality, menstruation, pregnancy, parturition and lactation. Remnants of this have survived in the form of sheela-na-gigs which still adorn the walls of some British churches. This wild image of Celtic womanhood aggressively displays her genitals to anyone who dares to look. An illustration for *La Fontaine* by Charles Eisen called 'The Devil Deterred' is based on a tale about the devil pestering a young woman's village. She defeats him by lifting her skirt in his face, suggesting that the female genitals were once seen as a powerful protection against evil. One of the rites associated with Demeter in classical Greece was of women displaying their vulvas to the other assembled women. Later this practice was replaced by the use of sexually-explicit language [1]. The Cretans also made images of the Goddess proudly displaying Her vulva and clitoris (fig. 29).

The celebration of and respect for the positive powers of women's procreative functions (including menstruation) survived into historical times. Thompson notes that when crops of corn were attacked by grubs the traditional cure was for menstruating women to run naked through the fields at night. Among the Zulus of Africa the girls must be naked but need not be menstruating. Similar customs were described by Briffault as having survived among the European peasantry. Pliny recommended that women should walk through the fields barefoot, with loose hair and their skirts folded up to their hips as an antidote to crop infestations by noxious insects. Demokritis was of the same view. These Greek traditions are thought by Thompson to be the origin of the rites associated with Demeter. Among the Herero tribes of South Africa the herdsmen bring the morning milk to women in childbirth to consecrate it with their lips [2]. This is in sharp contrast to the judeo-christian notion of childbirth as something unclean.

Gould Davis refers us to the numerous historical reports of male genital mutilation which have the sole purpose of female imitation. European explorers of the 18th and 19th century reported the initiation rites and sex customs of peoples as far apart as Australia and Central America. These include penis mutilation, castration, mock childbirth and menstruation and the custom of carving the penis, with a sharp flint, to resemble the female vulva. In Australia the name for a man who has undergone this operation, which involves slitting the penis along the length of the urethra and keeping the wound open, is 'possessor of a vulva' [3]. Such men subsequently squat to urinate. The operation has no effect on sexual function, 'the erection of the member which has been so operated becomes very wide and flat . . . ' [4] The reason for this male genital mutilation was so that men might share in some of the power allotted to women by virtue of their sex. As Margaret Mead put it, 'Whole societies have built their ceremonial upon an envy on women's role and a desire to imitate it.' [5] It may be this desire to imitate women which is recorded in the Camp Stool fresco which depicts what appear to be men dressed in clothes usually associated with Cretan women.

Fig. 29 Decorated seated Goddess with emphasised vulva and clitoris. This figure is never featured in the literature.

Women as the Natural Leaders of Society

The decisive role played by women in the origin of civilisation is recorded in mythology and confirmed by archaeology. Thomson, expressing the view that he shares with Briffault and others, states that the invention of agriculture, one of the most momentous steps in human history, was initiated by women. This prepared the way for a sedentary life, allowed for the development of pottery, metallurgy, architecture, writing and the luni-solar calendar. Women are also the arbiters of a society's culture

> The groups, habits, norms of behaviour, inherited traditions, which constituted in their totality the nucleus of human culture, were formed and transmitted by the women. [6]

Matriliny, and its natural corollary matriarchy, is the logical basis for social organisation. Patriarchy can only be sustained by a battery of illogical and unnatural ideological, social and legal institutions. Zeus sought to circumvent and usurp one element of the power inherent in women. This sky god of the invading patriarchs who settled in Greece, gave birth (through his head) to Athena, the goddess after whom the locus of classical Greek civilisation was named. The patriarchal christians also attempt to reduce the role of woman as creator. In their religion it is a male god who created the heaven and the earth and the christian burial service emphasises that, 'Man born of woman hath but a short time to live'. Their male god, on the other hand, offers eternal life.

Physical Build

Elizabeth Gould Davis argues that all the evidence of myth, tradition and physiology, as well as that of anthropology, points to an original equality of the sexes in size and strength. Biologically speaking, as Michelmore puts it

> It is logical that the male should be the smaller partner
> .... The male in the view of nature, is only a 'glorified gonad,' in which size is irrelevant ... [7]

Women are certainly physically stronger than men in terms of biological survival, being better able to store fat, less aggressive, less prone to congenital diseases and heart disease, and having greater longevity. It is also possible that the weaker musculature of women has been achieved by many centuries of control rather than being inherent. Consider the different physiques of Princess Diana and the Olympic javelin thrower Fatima Whitbred. Which of these women would be considered to have the more appropriate build for a woman in a patriarchal society? Women are encouraged and rewarded for conforming to the feminine stereotype of weakness and dependency. As Gould Davis says:

> The probability that women were once the physical equals of men is indicated in such myths as that of the Lemnian women, who easily vanquished their menfolk in a civil war in which all males were slain, and in a similar legend of the women of Amathonte who steadfastly refused to have intercourse with the men, and in the legends, probably historical, of the Amazons who lived manless all but one night of the year. . . . The myths of such women as Atalanta who wrestled or raced all male challengers and the worldwide myths of maidens who chose as suitors only those rare males who could best them in physical combat also more than hint at an original physical equality.

Hawkes agrees that the athleticism of young women is expressed in the Atalanta myth and notes that Aegean women were loath to relinquish their involvement in sports [8]. Ionian women were famed for running and wrestling naked and, although women were barred from the main festival at Olympia, they held their own games which were sacred to Hera. Women and girls had competed in these all female races, the Heraea, every four years, long before the exclusively male Olympic games began.

Tacitus was a Roman, born 55 years after Jesus of Nazareth. Just after Saint Paul had been attempting to spread christianity and male dominance, Tacitus set out with a different mission in mind. He travelled throughout Europe recording what he saw. Among the people to the east of Germany he noted that, 'woman is the ruling sex' and in Fenni in what is now Lithuania he discovered women hunted alongside the men and 'insist on taking their share in bringing down the game'. He was also perplexed that 'Britons make no distinction of sex in the appointment of their commanders' [9]. These extracts from Tacitus' records indicate that these communities did not conform to those of the peaceful matriarchal mode. Their cultures were in transition but unlike the majority of Tacitus' fellow countrywomen, the women of these lands were not confined to domestic matters.

The Prevalence of Matriarchy

It would fit better with the matriarchal nature of society if we thought of the leaders of the great building campaigns not as astronomer-priests but as astronomer-priestesses, as wisewomen, the noble ancestress of the medieval and later witches who, devoted to the degenerated scraps of belief and love they had inherited, died at the stake for their inheritance.

William Anderson, *Holy Places of the British Isles*

In his book *The Prehistoric Aegean* George Thompson, considers the evidence for the pre-eminence of women in ancient society. Bachofen, in his exhaustive, scholarly study of ancient societies, *Myth, Religion and Mother Rite*, demonstrates that descent was once through the female line. His theories and evidence were later reaffirmed by Briffault. Thompson updates and corroborates these earlier works by quoting a wealth of information from a myriad of sources showing that the type of society I call matriarchal, one which was not only matrilineal, but also female focussed (matrifocal), the clans being headed by and organised around women, was once widespread. In order to support the evidence from the Aegean area Thomson uses examples from all over the world.

He also points out that the work of other scholars including Evans [10], Ridgeway [11], Harrison [12], Glotz [13] and Briffault [14] demonstrate the matriarchal character of prehistoric Greece. These writers were primarily archaeologists who catalogued the nature of matriarchal society without appreciating its significance. Rostovtzeff [15] for example, perceptively noted in his *History of the Ancient World* that it was 'democracy' which banished women from the street to the house. He makes no attempt to explain this statement but rather, along with other writers who cover a similar period, takes it for granted that democracy put women where we ought to have been all along.

Thompson cites numerous examples of matriarchies that have survived into living memory. Often these are isolated communities in remote areas where their customs and traditions are less affected by colonial intervention and missionaries. The study of such communities helps to shed light on the situation in bronze age Crete, adding substance to speculation. None of the examples he uses are undiluted matriarchies but rather cultures in transition from a matriarchal basis of organisation. The customs that each society developed show the strategies that were used in the transformation towards patriarchy. If, for example, the traditional custom is that a priest performs a ceremony but a priestess must always be present, this is an indication that it was the priestess who once officiated alone.

Linguistic Evidence

Thompson points out that Greek language gives unequivocal evidence of the matriarchal nature of the prehistoric Aegean. The typical Greek clan name has the termination based on *-id* which is feminine. In Attic the Greek word for clansperson was *homogalakles* which means 'fed on the same milk'. It follows then that the clan was structured around the women rather than men. Similarly the term *oer adelphe* means 'born of the same womb'. All Greek students know this, says Thompson, but they fail to ask 'why of the same womb rather than of the same father?' The Greek *adelphos* and *adelphe*, brother and sister, have no parallel in other Indo-European languages. They must therefore be derived from the indigenous language of one of the matrilineal cultures subjugated by the Indo-Europeans who eventually became the Greeks. From a complex analysis of the abundant evidence Thompson demonstrates how Greek-speaking invaders of the Aegean were so influenced by the indigenous cultures that they adopted their rules of matrilineal succession. The remnants of this persist in the concomitant new descriptive epithets, which eventually supplanted the title nouns of sister and brother.

There is also linguistic evidence to show how the focus was moved away from women as leaders of the clans to men as heads of the nuclear families. In Doric the Greek word traditionally used to describe the family group, *genos* ('tribe'), was replaced by *patra*, meaning 'fatherhood'.

There is evidence to show that these types of matrilineal institutions were once general. The Khasis of India, for example, have a similar linguistic heritage. The mother is recorded as head and source of the family by the name *shi kpoh* ('one womb') which is attached to clan members. A common saying amongst these matriarchal people was 'from the mother sprung the clan'. The implications of this went far beyond biology. As biological fatherhood was unknown, inheritance could only pass through the female line. If a son did come to own land, it reverted to the clan of his mother upon his death.

The Origins of Patriarchy

In the same book Thompson summarises different theories for the development of patriarchy. The casual reader may find these arguments difficult to follow, perhaps because not enough detail is given about the different stages of social development that he refers to. The current generally accepted view, which is shared by Thompson, is that during the Ice Age climactic changes caused the Middle East to become sub-tropical. The previously open grassland there becoming split into semi-desert with patches of green oases composed of riverbeds surrounded by jungle. It was this change, according to one theory, that caused the move from a hunter-gatherer economy to cultivation and stock breeding, each of which has implications for the attendant social structure.

The various stages of development Thompson discusses are: firstly, survival based on food gathering supplemented by small animals, a phase in which women predominate as providers. The second and third phases of hunting followed by stock breeding were, he believes, stages in which men took the main provider role. The forth stage is agriculture which women initiated and were the main practitioners of. In this latter stage women once again become the predominant providers. He therefore sees the optimal conditions for the survival of matriarchy being a rapid transition from the first stage to the forth. These also represent the best conditions for the development of civilisation.

Thompson's views are informed by Hobhouse who found, in his study of social organisation [16], matriliny in cultures based around hunting but that this declined rapidly in pastoral (herding) communities. This transition slowed down in agricultural societies. Some scholars argue that it was through the hunting economy that a contradiction developed between the male economic role and his social status. But more recent research questions whether there ever was a hunting economy, indicating instead a gradual progression towards agriculture and the domestication of animals with flesh from organised hunting only ever playing a minor role in human diet [17]. These early cultures are better described as gatherer-hunter because of the restricted role that meat is now known to have played in their staple diet.

The thesis that accords status to men because they hunt does not explain why the ultimate reverence that had always been given to women was superseded because men brought home occasional meat supplements to the largely vegetable and small animal or insect based diet which may have been provided by men or women. Hunting is usually claimed to be the economic base for the earliest societies yet the archaeological evidence from paleolithic and neolithic cultures, as we have seen, suggests a female-oriented ideology.

The devaluation of the female has yet to be explained by the hunter argument. There is evidence for the involvement of women in hunting from a wide range of sources over an extensive geographical area. Eleanor Leacock's research reveals less gender-specific roles among the Native American Innu, nomadic gatherer-hunters. All able-bodied members of the community participated in collective hunts, men expressed loving parenting skills and the society was organised on an egalitarian basis. However, decisions on major issues, plans for journeys and camp locations for wintering for example, were in every instance made by women [18]. We noted earlier the findings of Tacitus in Europe with regard to the women hunting in what is now Lithuania.

R.F. Willets also argued that the pure agricultural cultivators were matriarchal and matrilineal and that stock breeders are the cultures where men have the social and economic dominance. This theory, as propounded by, among others Friedrich Engels [19], is associated with the idea that, prior to stock breeding, the basic principles of reproduction were not understood and, once the male role was identified, patriarchy developed. It is difficult to believe that agricultural communities were not familiar with the reproductive physiology of domestic animals. Also, cultures like the Egyptians were fully aware of the male's role in fertilisation but still practised endogamy because it was the female who was considered to have the divine right to rule. It is only through patriarchal ideology that the male's contribution to procreation has become so misrepresented and over-inflated. His biological role in the fertilisation of the ovum could be done by one man for every hundred women, making the others superfluous, as is the case with present day agricultural stock. A knowledge of how irrelevant most men were to procreation could be a disincentive to patriarchal power rather than the opposite.

Matriarchal cultures which have continued into recent history are few due to the encroachment of patriarchy through colonisation, missionary work and the mass media, but they do exist. The key to their survival appears to be geographical isolation. Such cultures are often located on islands (the reason why the Cretans maintained their own integrity for so long) or in inaccessible mountainous areas. Two such societies whose matriarchal activities have been recorded during the past ten years are the disparately-located Chejun, who live on the island of Cheju off Korea, and the agricultural community of Galicia in western Spain.

Gender Roles

The Cheju women dive in the seas of Japan for shellfish and seaweed, leaving their men at home to look after the children. Their ancient religion tells not of a god but of the goddess who came from the sea bringing knowledge of rice cultivation and domesticated animals. The principal goddess Chil Seung, the female snake spirit, is the ruler of all their fortunes and the healer of women. This notion has interesting parallels throughout the rest of the matriarchal world, including Crete where Goddess religion is closely associated with serpents.

The notion of the divine female symbol is not alien to nearby Japanese culture of course. Japanese spiritual beliefs are pluralist but are dominated by the sun deity who is seen as female. Like the Hindus of India, however, their Goddess has been adapted from a once-matriarchal culture to suit the needs of one which is now fiercely patriarchal.

The Chejun islanders' diving kit includes heirlooms that are passed from mother to daughter. Unlike women in mainland villages, Cheju women are free to settle where they were born, as is the case in other matrifocal clan system, in order to work with their sisters and raise their families together. Men still go into the fields carrying small infants on their backs and grandfathers often watch the toddlers. Men also cook, store foods, dry grain and look after sick children [20].

There are no ready answers to the question of what precipitated the transition from matriarchy to patriarchy. It appears that hunting was never a very important role in human society but in some areas males chose to do it and may have made it exclusive as a way of increasing their status. We can see from Mycenaean artefacts that the men of that culture saw hunting as a way of emphasising their power in combat.

Barbara Lesko in her study of the ancient societies of Egypt and Sumer argues that a combination of factors stimulated the move from more egalitarian (matriarchal) to patriarchal societies. She postulates that a sense of security and optimism was important for the continuance of a more egalitarian system allied to whether the country needed a strong standing army. A third factor she identified was the dissemination of a culture of commercialism throughout the society. In Egypt, for example, where women continued to have a great deal of power well into the bronze age, there was need for a standing army, although most of the battles were fought far away and commercialism remained the province of the state [21].

All these theories describe a process of linear progression, in which one type of social organisation gradually transforms into another because of changes in the group's economic base, knowledge, or national security. These are theories of internal change but, as is the case of

Crete, Old Europe, Anatolia, Caanan, India, North and Central America, Africa, Australia, New Zealand and anywhere else that was invaded or colonised by an external force, change was not always a result of internal pressure. It is more frequently brought about by violent external assaults which then usually precipitate change on a gradual basis from inside.

Evidence relating to the early invasions of the Kurgans into Old Europe (fig. 30) suggests that diverse climactic and geographical forces created different types of social organisation that were contemporary with each other. It seems that not all cultures, at least from 7000 BC onwards, were matriarchal. Some pastoral cultures in peripheral areas did not benefit from a temperate climate, fertile soil and stable water supply. These were the prerequisites for agriculture and its corollaries - civilisation and the survival of a matrifocal basis of social organisation. These more hostile climates produced people with an individualist, fiercely competitive, patriarchal ideology and religion. As Old Europe specialist Marija Gimbutas put it, they 'worshipped the lethal power of the blade' [22].

This accords with Thompson's argument that where there was little agriculture women were not central to the society's means of production and as a result they did not hold the power that women in other neolithic societies did. Discontented with their own impoverished land to the north of the Black Sea and seeking an easier life they simply took over the areas previously occupied by the peoples of Old Europe. Gimbutas has outlined substantial evidence for several waves of attacks by these peripheral invaders that she called the Kurgans, on what were advanced and peaceable egalitarian (matriarchal) communities. The first one lasted from 4300–4200 BC. The results of these repeated incursions during this period are characterised by physical and cultural disruption and population shifts. In the face of these onslaughts 'the colourful pottery and sculptural art of Old Europe's incipient civilisations quickly vanished' [23]. Mellaart too found evidence of what he refered to as a pattern of disruption of the old neolithic cultures in the near east and in Old Europe [24].

Riane Eisler, drawing on Gimbutas' work, paints a comprehensive picture of the differences between the ideology and behaviour of these primitive patriarchal societies and the sophisticated matriarchal cultures they destroyed and replaced [25]. She describes the Kurgans pouring down from the arid lands of the north on horseback brandishing their sharp metal blades. As well as genocide they brought with them patriliny, slavery, the practice of suttee and above all the belief that right was determined by might. The effect was devastating, the first wave of assaults was followed by two other major incursions from 3400–3200 and

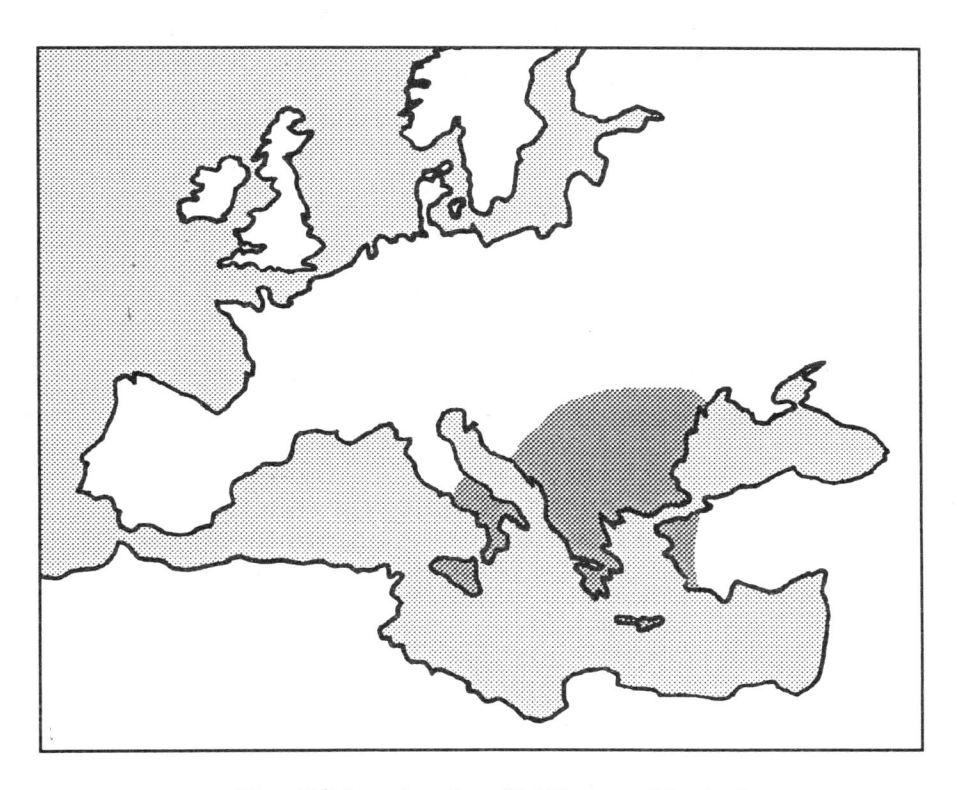

Fig. 30 Map showing Old Europe (shaded)

Crete Reclaimed

3000–2380 BC. The eventual result was the transformation of all matriarchal cultures in the area including, though at a much later date, that of Crete.

The association of patriarchal ideology and religion with harsher climates and poor natural resources can be seen in present day cross-cultural evidence. In Arab countries the bleak heritage of desert existence gave rise to a fiercely patriarchal culture. Oil wealth in these countries is still concentrated in the hands of a small minority and they are bordered by hostile neighbours and therefore have need of a standing army.

Another example which parallels the Kurgan invasions is when the geographically-impoverished Nordic countries sent hostile forces (the Vikings) into the European continent and Britain in search of wealth and a more hospitable environment during the first century AD. In the twentieth century, advanced capitalism has released Scandinavia from the mercy of the elements and these nations now benefit from some of the highest standards of living in the world. Sweden, in common with a similarly wealthy country, Switzerland, has also sought to remain neutral through two world wars, therefore avoiding military conflict for many generations. We can contrast the cultural mores of Islam in relation to women's rights, with the relative freedom of women in western Europe and in turn compare those countries with the advanced social and gender equality of the far wealthier Scandinavian nations, particularly Sweden and Iceland. A more egalitarian culture in Scandinavia has resulted in the decline of the male-dominated monogamous family. The incidence of children born to single-mothers is now greater than that of those born to married couples. The current president of Iceland is herself a single parent and women out-number men in the Swedish cabinet.

It is worth noting that the social roles within a culture are not necessarily determined by the rules of their religion. The teachings of Christ were radically egalitarian across gender and class boundaries and Islam, when it was created 800 years ago, was similarly liberal. It is the interpretation placed on religious teachings by a culture's oligarchies that determine social structure and gender roles.

Despite the calamities imposed by Kurgan invasions, ideological change was gradual and many of the peoples of the Aegean, including Crete, clung to some vestiges of matriarchy well into historical memory. In part this was due to the civilising effect that these advanced matriarchal societies had on the barbarian invaders who found it in their interests to preserve some of the population even if it was only so that they could benefit from their agricultural skills. Early invaders of the

Aegean, the Mycenaeans, who also originated from northern pastoralist (Kurgan) communities had settled for a compromise ideology which encompassed both a love of battle and the Goddess of peace and plenty. They were however superseded by the Dorians who destroyed their palaces around 1200 BC. A century later, in 1100, Crete herself was invaded and subjugated by the Dorians with their patriarchal ideology. Even then, as we see from the many positive elements of the Gortyns code written down around 500–450 BC (see Chapter 5) these invaders were also greatly influenced by Cretan civilisation. As a consequence the transition to patriarchy in the Aegean was a very gradual one.

The Devaluation of Women

When invaders, like the Kurgans in Old Europe; the British in America, India and Africa; the Spanish in South America; and so on, subjugate another culture, they impose their own cultural values onto the people of that area. In order for the new male (patriarchal) power to be imposed on matriarchal communities, the ancient high esteem in which women had been held has to be dismantled. We see evidence of this throughout history in the writings of christian missionaries and in the Bible where followers of Jehwah are incited to destroy everything connected with the old Goddess religion. The move to patriarchy was achieved through the use of myth, the institution of taboos or, more generally their adaptation, and the defilement of women and the Goddess. The sacred became profane.

From the earliest times cultures used taboos, a form of ritualised regulation, to indicate respect. Reproduction and group cooperation was essential to survival. As women are generally less interested in intercourse when pregnant, menstruating or lactating, men were discouraged from intercourse at this time by the establishment of formal taboos. As already noted menstruation had always been considered something to be celebrated, a symbol of a woman's divinity through her ability to create life. Men attempted to imitate female anatomy and menses and in cultures as far apart as the native peoples of north America, Australia and the Zulus of Africa, as already noted, saw menstruation as beneficial for good crops [26].

Once patriarchy came to be the dominant force in society this lack of interest and abstinence from men, an expression of self determination in women, had to be challenged and the sacredness once attached to women's procreative functions inverted. Women were proclaimed polluted, their sacred life giving blood unclean and lethal to men. As Briffault put it

Not only are her sexual functions treated as impure in themselves but the same condemnation attaches to her feminine nature as such. She becomes the root of all evil, Eve, a witch. [27]

There is no greater universal uniformity than the treatment of menstruating and puerperal women, comments Thompson. The deepest horror and aversion became attached to the once reified blood. Women were strictly segregated because a man might die if he touched her. These attitudes are not restricted to so called primitive societies. Only in 1993 did it become acceptable to advertise female sanitary products on television in Britain.

The immense power of ideology is demonstrated by the transformation that was achieved in making something which had once given women great power and esteem into a force for her oppression. The universality of these negative taboos serves to underline the ubiquitousness of the reverence which once attached to female sexuality, birth and lactation.

Patriarchy has taken control of all areas of women's lives particularly those from which we once derived most power, birthing (the creation of life) and breast feeding (which sustains it). In modern western society in complete contrast to that of ancient Crete, there is a taboo against women's breasts except when they are presented for the benefit of men. Breasts have become a symbol of women's sexual objectification, a statement of power turned against itself. A dire consequence of the success of this ideology is that less than ten per cent of babies in the west receive human milk after the first six weeks of life. In the west breastfeeding, like menstruation, has become a dirty secret, something to be hidden away. The mother centred French obstetrician Michel Odent has made a study of the inordinate lengths to which many cultures have gone in order to separate the new born infant from her mother's breast [28].

In a female-reverential society women have a great awareness of their own sexuality. This is clear from cross-cultural anthropological evidence and the archaeological evidence from matriarchal societies. Many Goddess figures display their vulvas or breasts or are depicted giving birth. Birth itself, potentially a profoundly spiritual experience has become something dangerous which must be controlled and managed by male obstetric technology [29].

In tandem with the process of devaluation of menstruation, birthing and breastfeeding, other symbols of women's power were either usurped (Zeus stole the *labyris* and gave birth) or discredited, as with

Gender Roles

the serpent and other sacred symbols in the Greek myths and the Bible.

Patriarchal mythology is a catalogue of the rape and defilement of the Goddess, women and the castration of female sexuality. Once the written word could record mythology we see a myriad of examples of the degradation of women. As the Freudian psychotherapist Lucy Goodison puts it in her book *Moving Heaven and Earth*, the mythic tradition was used to give a divine sanction to the subordination of women. Those in power used these mythical 'truths' to validate and reflect their own race, sex and class interests.

It adds to the weight of evidence for the former power of women that the new patriarchy was so concerned with establishing their downfall. Eisler and Merlin Stone, a sculptor, researcher and author of *The Paradise Papers*, draw attention to the practice of what Gould Davis calls hymenolatry [30] in the Bible. This misogynistic obsession with female virtue is in reality the defence of the man's property rights which extended to his daughters and wife.

Classical literature and drama, like the Bible, is obsessed with the rape and murder of women. In the play *Oresteia*, the author even feels the need to establish that a mother has no blood relationship with her child but is merely the vessel in which it grows, the caretaker for its father. This play, by Aeschylus, which was performed at great state occasions to huge audiences, includes the lines 'The mother is no parent of that which is called her child', she is 'only nurse of the new planted seed that grows'. Eisler finds it interesting that the Greeks needed to continue making such forcefully misogynistic statements a thousand years after the Achaeans had taken control of Athens in 500 BC [31]. Perhaps this is not really so surprising since similar statements still abound and both women and men left the Church of England in hordes because the could not tolerate the 1994 'blasphemy' of women being ordained to perform sacred duties in their patriarchal church.

Another example of the new patriarchy's need to destroy the respect women once commanded is a prototype for the Eve myth in the Bible. Hesiod, the Greek landowner and poet, writing in the 700s BC describes how woman was created as a punishment for a man's (Prometheus') misdeeds

> [Pandora] with the mind of a bitch and a deceitful character . . . [was the] founder of a race of women who lived among mortal man as a source of misery to them . . . a confederacy of troublemakers. [32]

Crete Reclaimed

The great founding fathers of the classical age used the debasement of women as a way of validating themselves. In the fourth century BC Aristotle's *Metaphysics* defined women as inferior to men. This is a curious notion given that these barbarian patriarchs had taken over the culture, script, mathematical systems, architectural methods, poetry styles and sports of a matrifocal culture. Those scholars, philosophers and social thinkers who insisted on differing from this view were silenced and their work obliterated. Aristotle ordered the burning of texts which did not conform to his version of history.

Greek myths are rife with violent expressions of male domination. Zeus raped Hera in the form of a cuckoo and as a bull he abducted and raped Europa. In a further embellishment the Cretan Queen Pasiphae (clearly a symbol for a powerful female ruler given the Greeks' need to show dominance over her) is forced by the sea god Posidon to fall 'in love' with a bull. The result is that she gives birth to a creature half-bull half-man. This was the genesis of the myth of the minotaur which the Greeks used to discredit the graceful matriarchal culture of Crete and to retrospectively justify their invasion and colonisation of this island paradise. The ideologies that form the basis of Greek and christian mythology have been used to sanctify the rape and enslavement of people throughout patriarchal history.

Matrilineal Endogamy

The ideological transition to patriarchy played out in myth and religion was mirrored by social behaviour. Endogamy is a good example. This is the rule, prevalent in many transitional matriarchal cultures, which allowed for the principle of matrilineal succession to be reconciled with patriarchal power. It was a fundamental element of the transitional process. In accordance with this rule a daughter, the natural heir to the throne, married her brother in order to ensure that his children, which were also the children of the heir (his sister), would be entitled to inherit the throne. The best-known practitioners of this were the Egyptian Pharaohs but other examples were widespread. Similar codes of inheritance can be found in the Iraquoi in America and the Roman monarchy. The succession was from male to male, but in the female line. Why would this convention have existed at all, had it not been that women had held ruling power in matrifocal societies?

Evidence Recorded by the Classical Greeks

Because of the subject area of the present book I have not included evidence of matriarchal social organisation in India, China, Africa, Sumer, Spain, Ethiopia and the Hittite, Semitic, Etruscan and North

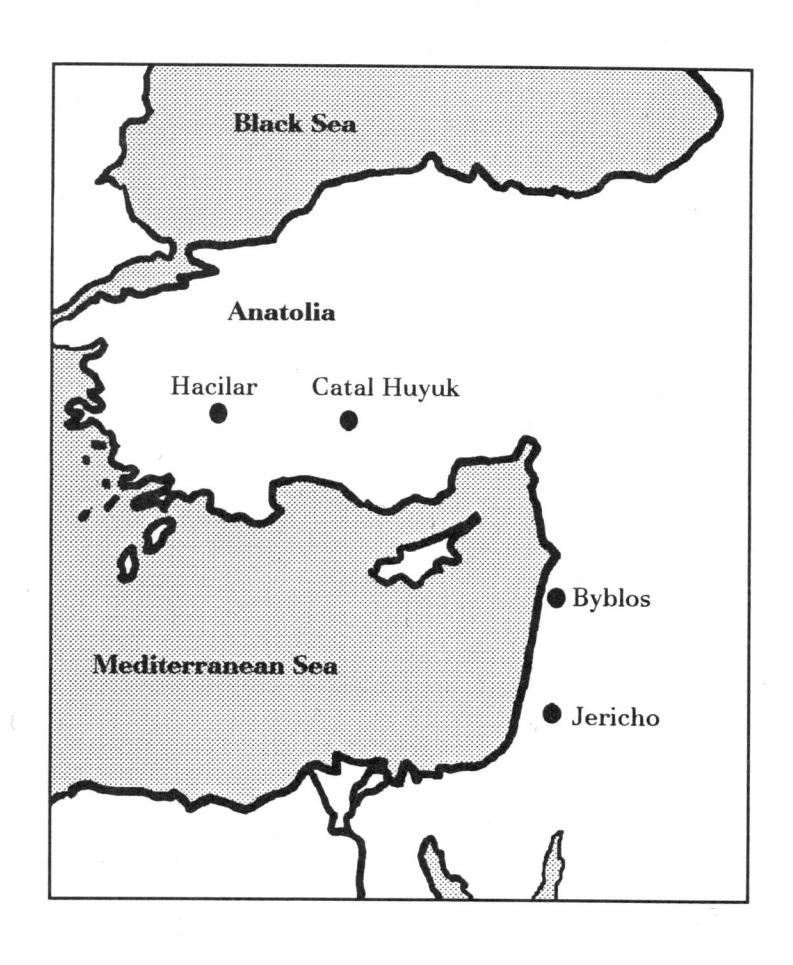

Fig 31. Anatolia map.

American cultures. I have concentrated instead on evidence recorded by the Greeks.

Even while patriarchal ideology was working to establish a new social order in the Aegean, Greek men, as part of their empire building activities, were recording their impressions of cultures similar to those they had supplanted. They were fascinated (if not appalled, as later christian missionaries were to be) by the difference in status between the women of other cultures and their own. Chroniclers often accompanied the expeditions and duly recorded these remarkable differences.

Herodotus (484–424 BC) travelled widely in the eastern Mediterranean in order to study people and places. He is the first historian whose works have survived and they claim to cover the period up to his own time. He is an important source of information about social organisation in the countries he visited. He recorded that in Lycia, a land to the south-east of Caria on the west coast of Anatolia (fig. 31), children were still named after their mothers. If a man is asked who he is, he wrote, he replies by naming his mother and his mother's mother. It was also the rule there that a child born of a slave by a free man was servile but a child born of a free woman by a slave was free [33]. He believed that this Lycian custom was partly of Cretan origin though all indications show that this was a practice common throughout the Aegean and therefore shared by the Cretans. He also observed that, among the Maclynes of Lybia 'sexual intercourse is promiscuous, they do not live together but copulate like cattle' and consequently have no concept of individual paternity. Reporting on what Thompson calls the Egyptian matriarchate, Herodotus noted that sons were not obliged to support their parents but daughters were, thereby reflecting the laws of inheritance.

Another important source was Eusebuis, the bishop of Caesarea in Palestine. He lived from AD 265–340 and was the author of *Chronicle*, the Greek universal history and chronological tables which are the foundation of much of our knowledge of dates and events in Greek and Roman history to AD 325. He recorded that the women of the Geloi of Scythia (a central Asian people who moved into southern Russia about 700 BC) 'till the soil, build houses, do all the work and lie with any man they like' [34].

Areas with cultural norms alien to those of the classical Greeks often feature in their legends. In the *Golden Fleece*, the Arganauts put in at Lemnos, a land ruled by women under Queen Hypsipyle. According to the story, the women of this land had caused offence to Aphrodite who, as a punishment, had afflicted them with such a terrible smell that their men had left them. In revenge for this insult the women slaughtered all the men except for Hypsipyle's father. Bachofen interpreted this myth as the survival of matriarchy in a degraded form. The Greeks used this tale as a reminder that matriarchy was unacceptable to the new order 'for none respects what the gods abominate' [35]. Elizabeth Gould Davis points out that the Lemnian women were easily equal to the physical task of vanquishing the whole of their menfolk.

A number of scholars have noted the obvious indications of matriarchy in passages from the *Odyssey* where Nausikaa, the Phaeacian princess, gives instructions to Odysseus as to how he should approach her royal parents

> When you enter the palace, walk straight across to my mother. . . . My father will be sitting there . . . but pass him by and clasp my mother's knees - then, however far away, you may be sure of a safer journey home.

Odyssey Book 6, 303-15

This message is reinforced by a girl whom Odysseus meets.

> Not only he [Alcinous the king] but her children and the whole people honour her. They look on her as a goddess when they salute her as she passes through the streets.

Odyssey Book 7, 66

The Greek Mainland and the Aegean

According to evidence from sepulchral inscriptions, the Lycians from Anatolia and other Aegean peoples were known for raiding the Nile Delta in the 13th century BC. In the 12th century some of them and the Carians had migrated to Palastine where they were known as the Philistines. The clash between the Israelites and the Philistines is symbolised in the Bible as the fight between David and Goliath. The Philistines had matriarchal institutions including matrilineal decent and succession and their basic social unit was the matrifocal household.

The Carians, a matriarchal people from south-west Anatolia, are known to us from historical times because of the activities of Alexander the Great. We know that the Carian King Mausolos derived his title through his marriage to his sister Artemesia, the Queen of Halikarnassos. Artemesia was the active ruler of her country. Heradotus

Crete Reclaimed

records that during the Persian war she supplied Xerxes with five warships for the invasion of Greece, to be commanded by herself. In time the throne passed from Artemisia to Ada and it was to Ada that Alexander deferred during his occupation of her lands and for her (rather than any husband or male counterpart of hers) that he expelled the Persians. Matrilineal endogamy was practised there up to the fourth century AD.

The Persians seem to have had similar cultural mores. In his *Life of Themistocles*, Plutarch describes the identity of three young captives as the sons of the Persian king's sister Sandake.

The strenuous part played by Macedonian women in the struggles of their monarchy, notes Thomson, is indicative of there being a matriarchal culture there too.

Attic law stated that sons inherited on condition that the daughter's share was given at marriage (dowry). If there were no sons the daughter received all the inheritance but she should then marry her own uncle. The same law applied at Gortyns, in

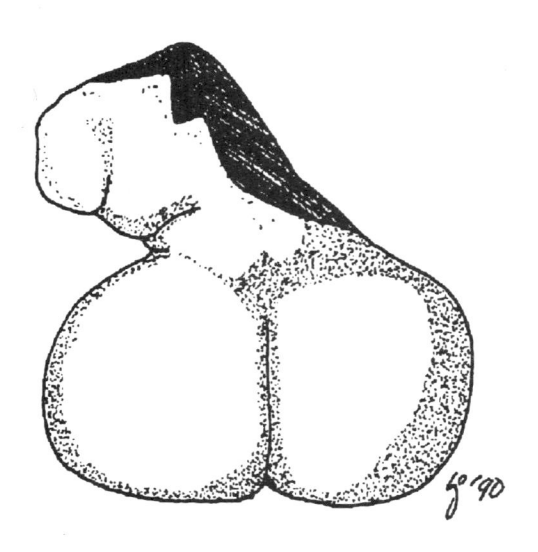

Fig. 32 Neolithic Goddess 4000 BC, Saliagolis, Cycladic Islands. This example has typically large proportions and may be intended to symbolise the Goddess as the earth in the form a rock or mountain (see also fig. 8).

Dorian Crete, but here the daughter had a share in her own right and could refuse to marry her uncle by buying herself out.

In a number of Aegean islands, including Lesbos, Lemnos, Naxos and Kos, matrilineal succession to real property was the rule as late as the end of the 18th century AD. The surfeit of Goddess figures found on the Cycladic islands, including the 4000 BC Goddess as Rock statue (fig. 32) from Saliagos indicate that their culture was focussed around the Goddess.

Thomson cites evidence that other parts of Asia Minor (the area now roughly covered by Turkey) were ruled by women [36] and Jacquetta Hawkes comments that

> It seems, however, to show a perverse prejudice in scholars when they are unwilling to allow significance to the fact that, in western Asia Minor, with its close and persistent contacts with Crete, matrilineal inheritance persisted until the fourth century. [37]

After the decline of matriarchy there, women's publicly-acknowledged privileges became confined to religion but this did not prevent them exercising unobtrusive influence on secular affairs.

The Attitude of Classical Greeks to Matriarchy

As already noted, the classical Greeks looked back to bronze age Crete, the source and foundation of their civilisation, with a sense of longing and regret. This attitude is summed up by Hesiod in one of his celebrated texts, *Works and Days*, he describes the history of the world as falling into five phases of peoples. The first was the 'golden age', which seems to approximate to the neolithic and bronze age cultures of the region with Asia Minor and Crete being supreme examples. 'The fruitful earth poured forth her fruits unbidden in boundless plenty . . . In peaceful ease they kept their lands in good abundance . . .' [38] This was surely what the Old Testament describes as the Garden of Eden, the neolithic era, whose philosophy survived throughout the bronze age on Crete. This was a time when, in many fertile regions of the world, people lived together in peace, harmony and plenty. To Hesiod they were 'pure spirits' and 'defenders from evil'.

Then there came a 'race of silver', who were in their turn replaced by a 'race of bronze', a people in no way like the silver, they were 'dreadful and mighty', they 'ate no grain but hearts of flint were theirs, unyielding and unconquered' [39]. Historian John Mansley Robinson writes that these men are known to us. They came from the north about 2000 BC

Crete Reclaimed

with their weapons of bronze and settled on the mainland in the Peleponnese to become the Mycenaeans. But Hesiod describes the Mycenaeans as a fourth category. He separates the barbarians who arrived in the Aegean and the people they became after adapting and softening through their contact with the refined cultures of the region, into two distinct races. We know from the archaeological evidence of the sophistication and refinement of their palaces, their frescoes of important women and the art works they commissioned, that the Mycenaeans were greatly influenced by the matriarchal communities they came into contact with, not least in Crete.

In her 1995 critique of Marija Gimbutas, Cambridge University archaeologist Lynn Meskell suggests that Gimbutas' theories of the Kurgan invasions of Old Europe are a result of her experiences as an Eastern European refugee from the Russian occupation of her own country [40]. But here, more than two millennia earlier Hesiod describes the process that Gimbutas was to glean from the excavation evidence.

After the Mycenaeans came the fifth race of men, that from which Hesiod himself was descended. 'Would that I had no share in this filthy race of men. Would that I had died or afterwards been born', he rails, because now, 'one man will sack another's city . . . Right shall depend on might and piety shall cease to be.' [41] This fifth race was of course the iron age Dorians, worshippers of Ares, their god of war.

The role of this new race of Greeks was pivotal in the final dissolution of matriarchal culture in the region but there was no immediate and simultaneous takeover. The struggles, conflicts and eventual victories of the patriarchate, their ruses and ideological justifications are recorded in the literature, plays, legends and mythology of the time. Sadly there are two rich veins of history which are absent from these records; the one which was never written because women, on the whole, were excluded from scholarly works (though we will be looking at some notable exceptions) and the other, written by women and men who did not align themselves with the aspirations of patriarchy, which was destroyed.

Historical records show that in classical Sparta monogamy was not binding. Kekrops, the legendary first king of Athens is accredited with the invention of matrimony. Before then in Athens and Sparta at least, but by implication throughout the Aegean, 'there had been no marriage; intercourse was promiscuous, with the result that sons did not know their fathers, nor fathers their sons. The children were named after their mothers' [42]. This evidence of life in ancient Athens, corroborated from so many different sources, confirms that matrilineal 'group marriage' had once prevailed in Athens. As Thompson points out there is, 'no reason to doubt this as they would not have invented a story that

Gender Roles

represented their ancestors as "savages"'. Yet Aristotle claims in *Polotis* that, 'male dominated marriage with slaves is the original nucleus of society'. This latter argument claimed that the Greek economic tradition of private property, slavery and the subjugation of women rested on natural justice. The result of this conflict of opinion was the destruction of the writings of the later materialists, Demokritos (Aristotle had his works burnt) and Epicurus. What remains to us is a one-sided view of Aegean history, recorded by one particular faction of Greek patriarchalists with the occasional suggestion or hint of a less-subjective reality.

Some records do survive of Greek men who were aware of an alternative view. Pythagarus insisted on the equal treatment of women and men in his school; Plato, one of his scholars, advocated education and political equality for women in his *Republic*. This seems only appropriate since Pythagarus was taught ethics by Themistoclea, a priestess of Delphi whose power and learning give an indication of the roles which women had previously played in the region before the arrival of the patriarchal invaders. Similarly, Socrates who, as an old man was executed for his heresies, had been taught by Diotema, a priestess of Mantinea [43]. This information is somehow censored out or ignored in the Greek history and philosophy taught today.

A series of three plays and Lysistrata by Aristophanes also managed to survive despite the strong feminist sympathies they expressed. Although we know little of the women of classical Greece, it seems clear that the old traditions were still popular and that there were many great scholars among them. The vestiges of a strong female literary tradition are represented by Sappho and her women's university.

Eisler cites a number of other notable Greek women whose works have survived to us, usually because of the writer's association with a man. Aspasia, a companion of Pericles, was a scholar and stateswoman who sought to educate ordinary Athenian women. The philosopher Arignote was the author of a number of serious sacred works [44] and there is some speculation that the *Odyssey* was written by a woman. It seems that women also headed philosophical schools (universities) of their own. One of these, Arete of Cyrene, was primarily interested in natural sciences and ethics and believed in a 'world in which there would be neither masters nor slaves' [45]. Telesila of Argos was known for her political songs and hymns and Corinna of Boeotia, a renowned poet and Pindar's teacher, is recorded as having won five times in poetic competitions against Pindar [46]. Proximal is remembered as a myth teller in simple language, though sadly her works have been lost.

Crete Reclaimed

From the scraps of evidence that did survive it is clear that the ideas and learning of the Greeks did not materialise out of thin air. The Greeks were, as Hesiod put it, a barbarous people who conquered and subjugated far more advanced and highly sophisticated cultures who each had a rich tradition of scholarly knowledge. Although we know that some of the greatest names of classical Greece, Pythagarus and Socrates, received their education from priestesses of the old matriarchal tradition, we know very little of these and the other women from whose knowledge the foundations of classical Greek culture were built. Their works were collected for many centuries in the great libraries that were destroyed by muslim and christian fanatics with Hypatia, the keeper of the library at Raquote (now Alexandria in Egypt) being hacked to death with shells for the blasphemy of being an educated woman.

It is easy to see how we lost this rich written heritage that is the basis of western civilisation. Even now, over 2000 years later, the only modern texts in which information about our early female scholarly heritage appears are, with rare exceptions, those written (and on the whole read by) women. Elizabeth Gould Davis, Merlin Stone, Riane Eisler, Jacquetta Hawkes and Elise Boulding being some of the best known. The male mainstream of archaeological and historical texts (those used in schools and, though women students and scholars are ensuring that this is changing, in universities) silence women just as efficiently as their book burning ancestors of ancient Greece.

The Aryans that were to become the Dorian Greeks took control of the thriving matriarchal cultures of the Aegean. The different clans of the region were gradually subsumed into the Greek tradition. One of the social mores in the cultures these northern invaders encountered was the rule that religion was the sole reserve of women. Because this tradition was too strong to break immediately the Greeks allowed it to continue in a form which was adapted to their own ideology of male dominance. In one instance, quoted by Thompson, women were allowed to perform religious ceremonies but were barred, on pain of death, from the sacred inner sanctum. In this way, firstly the control and gradually the whole of religious practice was taken over by men.

A similar approach was used at the Olympic Games which were started in 776 BC and served to draw the various nations of Greece together. These games were based on the sports that had long taken place in a religious context on Crete. Even the same style of boxing gloves were used. The only event lacking was bull-leaping. The timing, every forth year, was taken from the exclusively women's sports festival, the Heraea.

Gender Roles

Because the games had such important political overtones, underpinned by religious ideology, the Greek ruling elite used that forum to enforce the marginal role that women were to take in their new 'democratic' society. Women were barred from competing in the games but their skills (as weavers, artists and designers) were greatly prized and awarded to those (men) who triumphed in athletic feats. The exclusion of women as competitors was again achieved by the penalty of capital punishment.

Fig. 33 Mounted Amazon Attic Vase 600-400 BC.

Perhaps this is why athletes at the games competed naked so that women could not enter in disguise. Why were men so afraid of female competition? The feats of the Cretan women bull-leapers, the legends which surround the Amazons and Atalanta (who out-raced all male challengers) suggest that they had good cause. This policy is reminiscent of Hitler and how his Aryan supremacy claims were in tatters after the victories of black athletes at the 1936 Berlin Olympics. The Nazis' book burning activities also find parallels in the activities of these early patriarchs.

The Amazons

A rich source of information about the Greeks' attitude to the matriarchal peoples of the Aegean, and the other lands with which they traded or sought to invade, are the legends and historical reports of the Amazons. These bands of warring women (fig. 33) arose as part of the backlash or resistance to invasion and subjugation. There are strong indications that at the time of the Dorian influx into the Aegean there was dispersal and resettlement of the indigenous population. It may have been some of these peoples that the Greeks called the Amazons, though the term seemingly grew to encompass any matrifocal nation they encountered where women took up arms against their would-be oppressors.

Crete Reclaimed

Amazonian phenomena are interwoven with the origins of all peoples. They may be found from Central Asia to the Occident, from the Scythian north to West Africa, and beyond the ocean. Everywhere Amazonianism is accompanied by violent acts of bloody vengeance against the male sex. [47]

It is clear that the Greeks encountered warring women and as a consequence many legends have grown up around this enigmatic group. Subjugation was not to be imposed easily and would certainly not be passively accepted by the great queens of the old order. Women as heads of the clans were responsible, according to clan law, for avenging the death of a clan member. This is why, in Aeschylus' play *Oresteia*, it is Clytemnestra who avenges her daughter Iphigenia by executing her husband, Agamemnon. Under the old matrilineal law her husband was not of their clan so his killing did not infringe the clan taboo. Acting from similar convictions and motive Queen Boudica of Britain wrought terrible revenge against the Romans in the name of her daughters and in defence of her country. We might also say that she made a stand for women's rights. She made sacrifices to the warrior Goddess Andraste in Her sacred groves and was the only British monarch to have any success against the Roman invaders, wiping out many highly-trained and well-armed legions before she was finally suppressed.

Thompson argues that the legend of the Amazons began with the true story of tribes of women in the Aegean and was expanded, by the Greeks, to encompass the many matriarchal tribes that they came into contact with in their colonisation of and search for slaves among richer, better-developed and more refined cultures than their own. The epithet came to represent the struggle of the women of other continents who were reduced to servitude by the patriarchal traditions of barbarous invaders. They included the Cretans, the Pelasgoi, the Leleges, the Lycians and the Carians, the Lydian Omphale, the Lemnian Hypsipyle, the Assyrian Semiramis, the Queens and Queen Mothers of Egypt and Ethiopia, the Tomyris of the Massagetai and the many other matriarchal women of Arabia, Lybia, Italy, Gaul and Spain.

He believes that the original Amazons may have come from the north coast of Anatolia or further east in the Caucases. They have been identified with some Caucasian tribes where the women did all the ploughing, planting, pasturing and horse breeding [48]. In Herodotus' version the Amazons were defeated and taken prisoner by the Greeks but they overpowered their captors and escaped by sea to the Crimea where they became friendly with the Scythians [49]. Diodoros Siculus writing in the first century BC describes them thus

> The Amazons were a people ruled by women . . . The women were trained for war; being obliged to serve under arms for a prescribed period, during which they remained virgins [meaning to be without men]. After being discharged from military services they resorted to men for the sake of having children, but retained in their own hands the control of all public affairs, while the men led a domesticated life just like the married women in our own society. [50]

They were also, of course, matrilineal [51]. These classical records are corroborated by archaeological excavations. Throughout the Aegean and along the north coast of Anatolia there are local monuments called Amagoneia and legends commemorating the adventures of these warrior women. Statuary groups of women, votaries of the Goddess, who are either hunters or warriors, have been excavated in these areas by Lethaby, who believes that they show clear signs of Hittite influence [52].

The actual name Amazon derives from the women of Ephesos who, as well as taking to warfare, were, as was the custom for women throughout the Aegean, responsible for agriculture and were in the habit of reaping (amao) with girdles (zonai) round their waists [53]. The idea that the name is associated with being breastless, that Amazons had one or both breasts cauterised in infancy, still persists despite the lack of

Fig. 34 Amazon (Sosikles/Capitoline type 440-30 BC). Greek artists made such figures for sculpture competitions.

91

documentary evidence. In all of the representations of Amazons in Greek art they are shown to have the full mammary complement (fig. 34).

Patricia Monaghan, researcher and author of *Women in Myth and Legend*, describes the Greek's belief that a land populated entirely by women lay just outside their borders. Plutarch, among others, writes of its existence stating that this nation invaded Athens. Once or twice, a year, so the legend goes, the women of this matriarchal borderland had intercourse with men from neighbouring tribes and any resultant male children would be returned to these tribes. Interestingly the tradition was for two Amazon queens to share the throne (see page 107). One of them took care of domestic affairs whilst the other presided over battle. They produced artistic treasures that were 'coveted far outside their borders'. One of the greatest of these was the queenly belt of office. 'For some 400 years (1000–600 BC) the Amazons held sway over the part of Asia Minor along the shores of the Black Sea.' [54]

Gould Davis also discusses the Amazons, suggesting a connection with Crete. She too refers us to Diodorus who, in his mammoth *Library of History*, names Queen Basilea as having

> 'brought order, law and justice to the world, after a
> bloody war against the forces of evil and chaos. She was
> a warrior Queen after the Celtic fashion, a prototype of
> Cartismandua, Veleda, Budicca and Tomyris.' [55]

She became the Great Goddess 'of a hundred names and yet only one personality' who was subsequently revered throughout the ancient world as Basilea the first ruler of Atlantis.

The Women of Ancient Crete

> It seems likely enough that the custom of the kind
> described as matriarchy (mother rule) persisted in Crete.

Sinclair Hood [56]

As we have already noted, the evidence from so many disparate parts of the world confirms that the Cretan matriarchate did not exist in a void. From every corner of the surrounding area and beyond, as far as China, southern Africa and Spain, there is unequivocal evidence that the structure of society was matrilineal (inheritance passed through the female line). A natural corollary of this was matrifocality (women having central roles with society organised around them) and therefore matriarchy (women being responsible for leading the clan or nation). In societies organised in this way these aspects of earthly culture were mirrored by a religious tradition which saw the deity as female. It was when social organisation moved away from this female-centredness that equivalent changes took place in the religious sphere. Society creates the deity in its own image.

The image associated with ancient matriarchal cultures of an omnipotent yet benevolent creator of the universe should not be confused with the meagre vestiges of female deities which form part of the male-oriented pantheons of religions like shintism, hinduism and christianity. The Virgin Mary, for example, for all the reverence bestowed on her in the Catholic tradition, is a bit-part player in patriarchal religion. Her role is defined in relation to an all male trinity. She is the ideal of femininity, the identity invented for women by patriarchy, a castrated role-model, divest of the female sexuality that patriarchy finds so threatening. She has nothing in common with her predecessor, the omnipotent creator of the universe, she is the passive and pure earthly vessel of the all-powerful male god. Similarly the hindu's Kali is a product of Indo-European colonisers. The indigenous matriarchal Indians had celebrated the Great Goddess under the name of Danu or Diti. Just as Athena represented the old Aegean Goddess transformed into a war deity, this once-beneficent provider was transmuted by the Indo-Aryans into a deity of war, death and violence.

Against a backdrop of a world mostly in transition towards the new patriarchy, Crete survived as a matriarchal culture. The island was protected by geographical remoteness against incursions from the horse-riding barbarians of the northerly Steppes that had halted and reversed the cultural progression in most of the rest of Old Europe. As a result Crete survived and grew to be a great civilisation, the blueprint for the legends of the lost island paradise of Atlantis and the Garden of Eden.

It is difficult to know whether the priestess queens would have been the culture's leaders right up to 1100 BC when, with the arrival of the Dorians, there was a move to a more patriarchal way of life. Arguably there were some earlier transitional changes due to Mycenaean dominance of the island from 1450 BC, but as we will see in Chapter 5, the evidence for this is now questioned.

The Problem of Ethnocentricity

The only concrete evidence we have for what any aspect of life was like on bronze age Crete comes from archaeology. Such findings depend on interpretations which are inevitably influenced by the accumulation of millennia of patriarchal ideology. But the evidence is too persistent to be ignored and scholars have acknowledged that

> There are certain indications including the evidence for late survivals in the historical period that the Minoan social organisation was matrilineal . . . There is no denying the high social position of women in Minoan times.

and

> A matrilineal social organisation could account for the dominating role of the Mother Goddess. In such a social system the woman would have played the leading part in maintaining the clan and household cults. [57]

Referring to the social norms of the ancient world in general Seltman points out that

> Among the Mediterraneans as a general rule society was built around the woman even in the highest levels where descent was in the female line . . . religion and custom were dominated by the female principle. [58]

Matrilineal rights are, of course, unassailable, whereas patriliny needs all sorts of complex institutions to support it. There is no evidence, from matriarchal times on Crete, of marriage or the nuclear family which are the corner stones of male dominance. Nor is there a patriarchal religion which is imperative for the enforcement of the rules governing the patrifocal monogamous family. The family unit on Crete, as in the rest of the ancient world until it was overthrown by patriarchy, was based upon the matrilineal clan system. As Butterworth put it

> The attack upon the matriarchal clans destroyed the power of the clan world itself . . . the matrilineal world was brought to an end by a number of murderous assaults upon the heart of that world, the *Potnia Mater* (Great Goddess) Herself. [59]

Gender Roles

On Crete as in the rest of the matriarchal world, matrilineal decent dictated that women were the leaders of the clans. As the civilisation developed it is reasonable to assume that the clan leaders took responsibility for the religious activities and social welfare of the wider community. Nicholas Platon, a greatly-respected scholar of bronze age Crete puts this another way. He describes Crete as a theocracy, its rulers deriving power from their association with the deity but he completely misses the implications of this. He argues that the Cretan system of the offering of first fruits, the voluntary but regular giving of part of the harvest to the deity for administration and the organisation of public works, leads to

> . . . the indispensible conclusion . . . that the social and political system in Minoan Crete was theocratic and that the importance of the priesthood found expression in the members of the royal family, who as a divine genos were blood relations to the deity. [60]

No one who has seen the archaeological remains could reasonably dispute Crete's theocratic organisation, the essence of the deity is everywhere. From this convincing statement, which is grounded in the archaeological evidence, Platon then makes the ethnocentric and completely unsupportable assumption that this theocratic power was vested in male priests and kings

> 'The kings of Crete, having acknowledged the king of Knossos . . . lived in harmony among themselves.' [61]

He somehow manages to circumvent the royal burials at Phourni, the numerous frescoes, signet rings and sealstones depicting priestesses and other important court women that proffer themselves as candidates for the role of 'ruler' and claims as his 'evidence' for this assertion the so called 'Priest King' or 'Lily Prince' fresco, which a number of respected scholars, including Mark Cameron, believe to depict a female. In the whole of bronze age Cretan archaeology there is not a single representation of a figure who could be considered to be a king or a male priest. But Platon ignores this, together with the fact that the deity was female and that Her representatives on earth were unlikely to be male, as well as all the artefacts that would lead an unbiased viewer to different conclusion.

The archaeological remains give unequivocal evidence for there being not kings but queens of Knossos, Arkhanes, Ayia Triada and

Akrotiri (on Thera). We know what the great Cretan queens looked like. The models of the Snake Goddesses resemble the fresco portrait known as La Parisienne; the royal burial at Phourni near Arkhanes revealed a woman dressed in a similar way, and there are clear images from Akrotiri. Figure 35 is an artist's conjecture of the Queen of Knossos performing a snake ritual, perhaps in this role she represented the Goddess.

Because this was a matriarchal culture the deity had such a distinctly female identity. Though a tautology, the pre-eminence of the Goddess in Cretan religion meant that women were central to the rights and ceremonies performed for Her. Sacred associations of priestesses are recorded

Fig. 35 Artist's impression of a Priestess-Queen taking on thee persona of the Snake Goddess. Clebrantss express their deference. All figues and architecture based on original artefacts.

in Linear B scripts which date from Knossos' final year. As Sinclair Hood points out, 'The queen as representative of the Goddess may have sat upon the throne [in the Knossos Throne Room].' [62]

The undeniably female emphasis of the Throne Room has led some scholars argue that it was probably not the true seat of power but merely a ritual throne. Matters of state, they claim, would be conducted in the 'Hall of the Double Axes' (the rooms designated by Evans as the King's residence). Even if this were true, the excess of *labyris* symbols associated with the latter (from which its title is derived) also clearly associate it with the Goddess and therefore it is just as much the rightful place for the queen-priestesses as the Throne Room. The *labyris* was never associated with a male until, in classical

Gender Roles

mythology, it was stolen by the new patriarchal order as part of the process of legitimating itself (see fig. 52).

Perhaps a more significant change in the attitude of male academics is indicated by professor of archaeology Gerald Cadogan who cautiously admits, in the preface to the 1990 edition of *Palaces of Minoan Crete,* that

> . . . I am much less certain that the rulers of Minoan Crete until 1450 were men . . . rather than women.

Yet the evidence from after 1450, the time commonly assigned to the arrival of the Mycenaeans at Knossos, is overwhelmingly in favour of female rule. This is the time when Cadogan, Evans and other scholars believe the Throne Room was redesigned and redecorated in a way which, as Arthur Evans put it, heralded the establishment of a new order at Knossos. If this is so then, by these scholars' own logic and definitions, this 'new' order was a powerfully female one.

Movable artefacts are also the subject of ethnocentric postulations. Glotz, for example cites numerous instances of female figures depicted with wild animals or carrying the equipment necessary for the hunt. One of his examples, from Tiryns, is of two women in a chariot, decorously dressed in high necked tunics. It is generally accepted that they are on their way to hunt [63]. He then states that 'hunting was not *of course* a common sport of women in Minoan times.' It may well not have been, but if so, perhaps it was not common for men either. It is among the Mycenaeans not the Cretans that men's dominance over the hunted animal and the gore of the kill is glorified in art. On Crete we see both sexes depicted in the hunting and capture of live wild bulls.

Martin Nilsson wrote his study of Minoan and Mycenaean religion in 1948 and continues to be accepted by many scholars as the best authority on the subject [64]. Overall, he agrees that the mass of evidence points to the pre-eminence of women on Crete. Occasionally however he slips back into androcentric mode. He makes much of the absence of a 'God or Lord of the Animals' and is concerned that no example is recorded of a male grasping wild animals in a dominant fashion after the manner of the Goddess when She is depicted as the Lady of the Animals. He has a similar approach to the scenes on the Ayia Triada sarcophagus. Nilsson acknowledges that it is women who officiate at the altars but insists that the men are carrying *heavy* objects (two model boats and a model dog!).

Evans himself is the supreme example of the androcentric scholar confused by the plethora of matriarchal images that it was his privilege

Crete Reclaimed

to uncover. His comments, on the group of Goddess figures recovered from a temple at Asine (on the Peleponnese coast near Tiryns), encompass his ambivalence

[there was] no indication of a beard, nor have we any call to recognise, in the midst of this motley harem, Dodarna's Lord [Zeus]. [65]

To his credit, he is immediately aware that the long pointed chin of the Mycenaean style head is not a beard (the whole face is white indicating that it represents a female) and that the group is clearly associated with the Goddess rather than with Zeus. Yet he feels it appropriate to refer to this sacred group in his academic texts as a 'motley harem'.

Present day archaeologists who are decidedly more aware of the dangers of ethnocentric interferences are not immune from such lapses of clarity. James Mellaart, who excavated Catal Huyuk, believes the enthroned Goddess found in a grain bin at the neolithic settlement there to be 'giving birth to a *probably male* child' [66]. Only the head and neck of the newborn is showing but because Mellaart's concept of neolithic Goddess religion includes a male consort-son, he has superimposed this idea in an entirely inappropriate fashion. A similar bias that leads him to offer no comment on the fact that, in what he described as a 'hunting shrine' in Catal Huyuk's level III, only Goddess statues and female burials were found [67].

Fortunately, in the light of the development of a rigorous reappraisal in other social sciences, a new generation of archaeologists is becoming more aware of the ethnocentric prejudices that scholars bring to their discipline. Michael Shanks and Christopher Tilley are staunch advocates of this new consciousness [68]. They appeal to colleagues to be aware that their subject involves bringing the past into the present with all the associated contamination that this entails; that archaeologists can never produce a purely objective account; and that politics are present in archaeology but in a covert rather than an explicit way. Julian Thomas has similar concerns though these are somewhat obscured by his rather terse verbiage [69]. He points out that, by describing the unfamiliar object from the past, we are making it familiar and less 'other' in our own present, thereby necessarily losing some of its essentially distant essence.

Gender Roles

Despite this desire for an increased sensitivity to the present's influences on the past, the effects of sexism are so strong that an acknowledgement of the gender bias in archaeology is the last stone to be unturned. As Shanks and Tilley note

> A feminist archaeology . . . is likely to be substantially different in orientation from current archaeological practice . . . *Homo Artifex* is not *Femina Artifex* ; such concepts are male and refer to *man*kind. To obscure this may be to perform an ideological service for mankind. Archaeology, significantly, although eminently well placed to do so, has not paid much attention to the origins, nature and development of sexual repression and exploitation. [70]

But this glancing professional awareness of their discipline's male bias is the only attention these authors pay to the issue. Shanks and Tilley's main empirical interest in the book from which these quotes are taken, is beer packaging. They acknowledge in the preface to their new edition that, 'We might have made more of gender issues in the present work.' Given this inertia, which is probably a combination of lack of interest and an inability to identify with the marginalisation experienced by women, I am not inclined to hold my breath in anticipation of the discipline of archaeology becoming less gender biased. Fortunately, there are notable exceptions who do address the *Homo Artifex* issues but, predictably, these are women. Joan Gero and Margaret Conkey's *Engendering Archaeology* is a pioneering example.

The Archaeological Evidence

Frescoes

Women are, without exception, the central subjects of these cameo recordings of ancient Cretan society. Time after time we see them, always elegant, often regal; La Parisienne (see fig. 6), the woman in the garden scene from Ayia Triada [71], the central figure in the Processional fresco, the three Ladies in Blue and so on. These women are clearly either queens, priestesses or leaders of some kind.

While the importance of particular women is emphasised in these frescoes, others (like the Temple [Grandstand] fresco, the Theran miniature fresco and the Sacred Grove Dance fresco) inescapably stress the importance and centrality of women generally. This is done by:
1. Depicting women as of disproportionately larger size.
2. Recording their privileged positions in areas reserved exclusively

for them. These are either central, in raised areas, or in sacred enclosures.
3. Adding extra detail to their faces when they appear in the crowd scenes with men.
4. Restricting men to crowd scenes.

The Palanquin fresco, found close to the Processional Corridor, is fragmentary but we can see that it represents a major public ceremony attended by large crowds. At the centre of the activity is a figure in an unflounced dress. Her importance is emphasised by depicting her carried in a litter (palanquin). A similar litter with the remains of a female figure seated in it was found, together with miniature sanctuary equipment, having fallen from the sacred East Hall at Knossos. The other objects in this collection included the Bird and Pillar Epiphany (fig. 36).

The many restored frescoes of court life could leave us with the impression that almost all the important women featured as priestesses, princesses and queens appear to be younger women. But we should not be misled by what may be a preoccupation of the restorers. Also, it would be quite difficult to give sufficient facial details to indicate age, particularly in a miniature fresco where the artists needed to incorporate a mass of information into the picture before the plaster dried. Most probably the emphasis would be given to creating a clear message rather than nuances of facial features.

The women in Cretan, Mycenaean and Theran frescoes were invariably depicted bare breasted and with varying, though distinct, categories of mammary development, sometimes enormous and sometimes pendulous. Breasts may have been used as a measure of seniority and, to some extent, age. The female bull-leaping athletes depicted in frescoes have large chests rather than breasts. The Lily

Fig.36 Bird and Pillar Epiphany, Knossos. May symbolise the Goddess as pillar with a bird as her crown.

Gender Roles

Figure, which was described by Mark Cameron as the 'princess of the bull ring', leading in a bull, shares this lack of mammary emphasis. Yet this convention appears to be reserved for the medium of frescoes. The breasts are clearly depicted on an ivory carving of a bull leaper (see fig. 26).

There is no evidence that the sexuality of bronze age Cretan women was male-defined or male-focussed. Women appear to have displayed their breasts as an expression of their power, perhaps through their identification with the deity. All the names that derive from the Great Goddess on Crete, whom the priestesses represented, clearly identify Her as virgin, that is, spending Her time apart from men (see Chapter 6).

Frescoes indicating the pre-eminence of women in bronze age Aegean society are not limited to those found on Crete. Many depictions of important women were found at Akrotiri (the contemporary Cretan port of Thera). Lyvia Morgan, in her studies of the miniature Theran frescoes, noted that women were shown as disproportionately larger than men, even in scenes of daily life. Commenting on the fresco of the arrival town from the walls of Room 5 of the West House at Akrotiri, she points out that the higher status of women is established by the privileged position of their seats for viewing the arrival of the ships and their close proximity to the Horns of Consecration. Women appear at the top of some buildings, all of which are painted blue or gold. On either side of them some, much smaller, men are depicted but in separate, red buildings.

There is, however, something strange about the way these women are represented. Curiously, only half of their torsos are shown and these are presented in an unusually stylised way. In addition, it is unprecedented for women and men to be represented together in this way in Theran frescoes. Morgan therefore believes that the artist may have used this mode of representation as a way of stressing the importance of the occasion by indicating that a number of royal women were present. The actual women that these stylised images may represent (queens? officials?) could well have been involved in other, more weighty matters at the time, engaged in ritual or preparing to receive the new arrivals as their guests perhaps.

The representations of women from Thera and from Mycenaean sites indicate that the high status of women was current wherever Cretan culture was established. Many of the frescoes from Tiryns (fig. 82) and Mycenae (fig. 83) feature elegantly dressed women. Evans noted the disproportionately large women looking down from a balcony or window in fresco fragments from Mycenae [72]. Women are frequently portrayed as looking down in this way, perhaps observing some sacred performance from a privileged vantage point (figs. 37 and 58). Alternatively, as will be discussed in Chapter 4, they may have been involved in the religious practice of appearing in the role of the deity.

Even though bronze age Cretan women and men wore similar clothes for sports and had similar hairstyles we can be sure, at least in frescoes, which are which by the colours that were consistently used to distinguish them. Women were white and men were brown. The fresco painters' unfailing adherence to this code does not however prevent some inveterately ethnocentric archaeologists from ignoring it. Swedish archaeologist Gösta Setlund argues that the boxing children of one Theran fresco are girls, because they are wearing earrings and girdles whereas boys (e.g. the fishers) in Theran frescoes are usually shown naked [73]. The sash or girdle may however be associated with the sport whereas it would be more sensible for the young fishers to be naked. Decorative jewellery was worn by both sexes.

There is no indication that these colours were, as Hans Wunderlich suggested, a reflection of reality. Women were not preoccupied with keeping their skins white. Fresco evidence tells us that women took part in every aspect of society, dancing in olive groves, performing death-defying leaps over bulls, drinking with each other, overseeing religious performances and ceremonies or walking in gardens.

Other fresco fragments, which have not yet been reconstructed into full figures or scenes, depict women athletes. These include fragments in high stucco relief from the East Hall at Knossos [74]. It appears from one of these, which shows a bare female leg under stress, that either pugilism or acrobatics was represented [75].

In order to see better the effects of the tunnel vision that patriarchal attitudes have imposed upon us, it is helpful to imagine that the sexes of the figures depicted

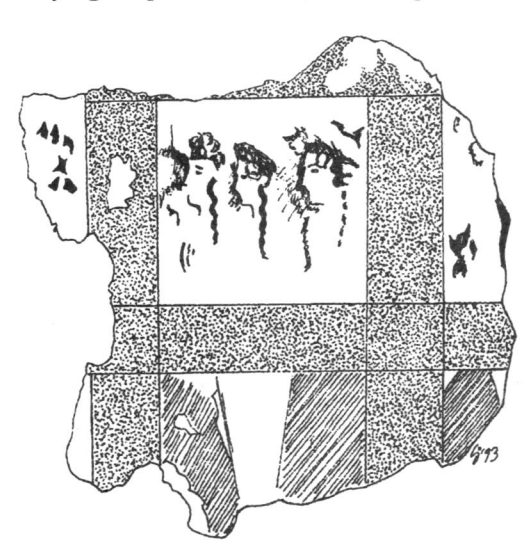

Fig.37 Minature fresco fragment of women at windows. From the western fresco heap, Knossos.

Gender Roles

in the frescoes are reversed and that La Parisienne, the Blue Ladies group, the figure in the garden from Ayia Triada, the women at windows and balconies and the central figure of the Processional fresco, restored holding the *labyris* and being revered, were all men. Could we believe for one minute that there would be any doubt that these figures represented kings or highly placed officials, members of a ruling group? Is it possible that La Parisienne and the figure restored holding the labyris, if they were male, would not be proclaimed the Kings of Knossos or the central figures in the Temple fresco cited as the high officials of the Labyrinth? The answer is clear from the way the fresco of the so called 'Lily Prince' has been treated.

Goddess Figures

The vast majority of the frescoes, excluding the one from Akrotiri where the figure is extraordinarily large, attended by a griffon and having crocuses heaped at her feet, are considered to represent mortals. This picture is reversed with Cretan figures. It is generally agreed that those which represent the deity (see front cover) are distinguishable from representations of mortal women by their crowns, abstracted forms, exaggerated proportions or the animals which accompany them. The two best-known snake Goddesses both wear distinctive crowns. The issue is complicated by the ritual practice, of which there is a growing scholarly acceptance, in which the priestess took on the identity of the deity. Thus the figures may show the mortal priestess at the moment that she has been transformed into the Goddess.

These considerations aside it is clear, as Jacquetta Hawkes notes, that the Cretans saw the supreme divine power in terms of a female principle incarnate in a woman whom they portrayed exactly as themselves. She believes that Cretan women would have shared in the power of the Goddess both psychologically and socially. A figure so supremely powerful, completely independent of men and yet so vividly aware of Her own sexuality would have presented a wonderful and natural sense of self-validation for Cretan women. We can see this in the aura of confidence and self-assurance that emanates from fresco images. Hawkes suggests a direct link between the accepted sexual freedom and high social status of women and their dress. She points in contrast to the complete veiling and seclusion of women in cultures where their religion imposes total control over their lives and denies them even a soul [77].

Commenting on these representations of an omnipotent Goddess, Hawkes notes that if a king had existed he would be confronted on all sides by images of his part as a 'subservient instrument or worshipper of the Goddess' (figs. 22 and 88). This, she argues, would be intolerable for a sovereign prince of a worldly power, which is one of the reasons why she believes that men did not rule on Crete.

Lucy Goodison describes the Goddess figures as expressing an essence of power. Each seems charged with an awareness of her own intrinsic importance, at the centre of what is necessary and sacred. She sees them as an embodiment of the awesomeness and centrality which is woman's by nature.

Vases and Models

Once we move away from the clear (to some) distinction of the sexes made by the fresco painters there is more room for (mis)interpretation. This is partly because many bronze age Cretan activities may have been common to both sexes and for athletic activities, including bull-leaping and hunting (for live animals), both wore the same style of dress – the simple short apron and cod-piece. According to the fresco evidence the only clear exceptions were the higher echelons of society and religious ritual, where women alone presided.

Three famous carved stone vases were found at Ayia Triada. Of these, the Boxer's Vase shows some figures which are obviously women while others are of indeterminate gender. The Chieftain Cup shows figures that have been described as boys, but as children there is nothing to distinguish their sex, so they could be either girls or boys. Some of the figures on the Harvesters Vase appear to be men but the nature of the carving makes distinguishing gender difficult.

Other figures add even more confusion. A ceramic group from Kamilari shows women performing a sacred circle dance surrounded by Horns of Consecration. The figures' breasts and the sacred activity they are engaged in clearly identify them as women but their 'cod-pieces' seem wholly inappropriate to the modern western eye. As already noted the codpiece was worn by both sexes as part of athletic garb. If the cod-piece was there as a symbol of sexuality for men then we must assume that it had the same meaning for the women who wore it. As such it would have been representative of the clitoris for women and the penis for men. The cod-piece as worn by men bears no relation to the actual, much smaller, size of the penis. It is symbolic. Perhaps the dance itself was to celebrate sexuality and sensuality.

Sealstones and Signet Rings

Many of the scenes, particularly on the rings, show religious ceremonies where there are a group of women with one of them placed

Gender Roles

centrally or being revered (figs. 27 and 77), though in some it is not clear whether the spirit of the Goddess is represented by one, more than one or none of the figures. While many of these cameos clearly stress the spectacular power of the Goddess some may depict mortal rituals perhaps with a priestess queen taking the role of the Goddess.

Mycenaean rings were also used to express the omnipotence of the Goddess. While the archaeological, early historical and legendary evidence suggests that the Cretan deity resulted from the matrifocal nature of that culture, it is not clear that Mycenaean social organisation reflected such a model of human female rule, though it may have done. Perhaps the key to this anomaly is in the source of these rings. They were undoubtedly executed and probably therefore designed by Cretan artists but they would have expressed the religious beliefs of the wearer. They may even have been worn by Cretan priestesses living in Mycenae and neighbouring cities in the Peleponnese. Perhaps the surfeit of Mycenaean frescoes and rings, which incontrovertibly express the pre-eminence of women, was the result of Cretan settlers in Mycenaean palaces who ordered the decor of their rooms and the design of their jewellery accordingly.

Until recently all the sealstones and seal impressions discovered which featured human figures clearly expressed the centrality and omnipotence of a female deity. In 1983 however, a single exception was recovered from the Kastelli region of Hania where a joint Greek–Swedish team is currently excavating a site destroyed by a great fire around 1450. This seal's find context was a Late Minoan II dump though its discoverers, Yannis Tzedaskis of the Greek Ministry of Culture and Erik Hallager of the Swedish Institute in Athens, believe that it was originally part of a Late Minoan IB destruction deposit. One of their reasons for this conclusion is that there is no evidence of a fire in Late Minoan II which may have preserved the seal [78].

The seal describes what appears to be a large muscular male figure who is unlike any other male figure seen elsewhere in Cretan art. The impression is by no means clear but the head could be that of a lion or a bird. The figure leans back with left arm bent and right arm extended holding a staff in imitation of the much earlier Goddess of the Mountain Peak sealing (fig. 22). Long flowing locks fall down his back. He stands on top of a tall structure and towers high above what seems to be a city. There are a number of familiar symbols in the scene; the splitting cell border from the Throne Room at Knossos and what may be intended for Horns of Consecration atop the buildings. If this figure was intended to portray a male deity it stands in complete contradiction to the vast array of other bronze age Cretan artefacts. There is no evidence from Knossos of any similar change of focus towards a male deity and that particular edifice may have survived until as late as 1150 BC. This find may be explained by reference to another from Anemospilia. Here the single incidence of human sacrifice on the island was discovered. It is associated with the skeletal remains of a man too large to be Cretan and wearing a ring unlike anything else found on Crete. The Hania seal may also have been associated with a particular break away cult of Mycenaeans or others familiar with Cretan religious symbolism.

The seal has been named the Master Impression and no doubt it will receive a disproportionately large share of scholarly attention and the mass of evidence for female centrality on Crete will pale into insignificance in the face of this single burly usurper.

The Celebration of Intimacy between Women

An important theme of bronze age Aegean art and later classical Greek legend which dealt with matriarchal peoples, is the royal and sacred female couple. Women were often depicted in situations of intimacy with other women. In some instances this is indicated by their physical closeness or by sharing part of the same physical body (fig. 38). It is difficult to know what this might indicate but the evidence is there and cannot be ignored.

Mark Cameron was a much respected scholar from the British School of Archaeology at Athens who was a specialist in Cretan frescoes, until his untimely death. He established that the large woman, La Parisienne (undoubtedly a queen) from the Camp Stool fresco (fig. 6), had a companion, a similarly-dressed woman whose importance was also emphasised by her large size [79]. The female figures in the chariots on either end of the Ayia Triada sarcophagus are also depicted in pairs.

In the Processional fresco Evans had only one central adored queen restored but Christos Boulotis believes that there

Fig.38
Double Goddess, marble. Shrine VIA10, Catal Huyuk, 5800 BC.

Gender Roles

may have been other women who were singled out for special attention in this extensive fresco, each of whose importance is marked by the way in which the procession is interrupted to focus around them [80].

The miniature Temple Fresco shows important women sitting in pairs most of whom are touching each other. The women in the Blue Ladies fresco are also shown touching. Schliemann points to a seal carving where the Goddess and Her female companion are shown as happy and sad with butterflies flying around them. On the 'Ring of Minos' found near the Temple Tomb, the Goddess, naked, breaks a sacred bough while in the foreground her female companion or one of her priestesses wearing a flounced dress, steers a boat fitted with a double altar through the waves (fig. 39).

The regularity with which women are depicted in pairs may be indicative of shared queenship. We find other evidence of this in Linear B texts found at the palace of Pylos. They mention 'Two Queens and Poseidon' and the 'King and Two Queens'. The position and role of these queens is somewhat enigmatic but they are in this context associated with the new godling Poseidon who, for the Mycenaeans, was more important than Zeus. The theme of joint female rule is also recorded in the legends of the Amazons where one queen would be responsible for domestic rule while her partner or sister took care of military matters (see page 92).

The Etruscan religion features a sacred female pair: two Goddesses, thought to be Thanner (Goddess of Childbirth) and Alpnu (Goddess of Harmony), who are depicted embracing [81]. Intimacy between women is also the theme of a small ivory figure group found in a shrine in the citadel at Mycenae (fig. 40). It features two women wearing the typical Cretan split skirt costumes and wrapped in a single shawl. One woman has an arm around her companion's shoulders. The second caresses the other's hand with one hand whilst her other hand steadies the child at their knee. The group has been described as two nurses and an infant but why would it be necessary for one infant to have two nurses at the same time? The elegant

Fig.39 Detail from 'Ring of Minos', Knossos. A priestess in an animal/bird-prowed sacred boat is a Cretan artistic theme.

Fig.40 Goddesses or queens with child. Ivory. Mycenae, 1395–1350 BC.

Gender Roles

clothes of the women and their tender embrace of each other suggests that their status was quite different. They were certainly important women, perhaps goddesses or queens. Were they sisters or perhaps lovers? Although the group is from Mycenae, the exquisite crafting and style of dress show the work to be the product of a Cretan hand.

The sacred female couple is associated with a child in other mythical traditions. For example, in Egypt Osiris, the year bull, was said to have been born as the result of the union of two Goddesses, Nepthys (a cow goddess) and Isis (sometimes depicted as Hathor). Thus the sacred bull is created from the coupling of Egypt's two most sacred cows.

The importance of this theme of two Goddess as joint mothers is reinforced through its imitation by the classical Greeks. As part of their efforts to earn legitimacy for their new godling with ambitions, Zeus, the Greeks claimed his surrogate parents as the goddesses Amelthae (the goat) and Melissa (the bee), by whom he was raised on milk and honey.

Another Greek example of the suggestion of a sacred female pair is the large votive relief from Eleusis 440–430 BC in the National Museum of Athens. It shows two women both dressed in elegant classical robes each holding a staff; between them is a young male.

In this context the myth of Demeter and Persephone takes on another dimension. It relates the story of the Goddess and the vegetation. The role of vegetation is in other cultures taken by a male who is variously described as a lover or a son. Here, in a tradition which is thought to have been brought to the mainland by settlers from Crete, we have both parts played by women and there is no blood sacrifice but merely a disappearance for the duration of the winter. A more careful exploration of the genesis of Demeter and Persephone reveals that they were originally part of an all-female trilogy. Thompson describes their association with Hecate, the Moon Goddess. In the earliest version of the story she and Demeter were the mothers of Persephone.

In the later, transitional, phase of religious development, the Great Goddess was allocated a son who gradually usurped Her role but it appears that this may have been in imitation of earlier and contemporary traditions in which the duo or trilogy would have been all female. There are many examples of images along the theme of the Goddess with what appears to be Her daughter (see figs. 77, 78, 79, 80). A complete inversion of this ancient tradition is accomplished by christian mythology in which the son has two fathers, the god and the Holy Ghost. The patriarchal practice of transposing their ideology, sacred sites and holy days onto earlier matriarchal traditions suggests that the male trilogy, by stages, replaced an all female one. I am not of course referring here to the Triple Goddess concept of maiden-mother-crone, which was a result of the transition to patriarchy.

The importance of the sacred female trilogy in matriarchal religious tradition suggests that it may have been based on reality with priestess-queens ruling in pairs and raising the next generation of leaders. The deity is created from the ideology of the ruling group, in their own image.

These pieces of evidence may seem of little consequence when viewed individually, but together they are too important to ignore and the questions they raise need to be addressed. Why were scenes of intimacy between women such an integral part of Cretan art? What is the significance of the frequently-depicted shared lower female body with two upper parts shown embracing? (see fig. 39). The fresco evidence and the separate areas for the sexes in Mycenaean palaces indicate that women spent most of their time with each other. It could have been this preference of earthly women for female companions that was reflected in the conceptualisation and depiction of the Goddess pair.

Sappho's community on Lesbos may have been a survival of something which was a common feature in the past. Sects of priestesses would have studied and practised their rites together. Thomson points to a number of mainland Associations of Women, which survived into classical times, who spent their time together drinking and performing readings of their poetry. Hawkes informs us that it was the fashion amongst certain groups of women of that time, old and young alike, to spend whole nights 'on bare hills' in dances simulating ecstasy, their intoxication being partly-alcoholic and partly-mystical. Although, she continues, the male members of their families may not have been pleased, they would not have interfered in matters of religion. At Samos and elsewhere at the Feast of Adonis young women customarily held drinking parties at which they would spend their time devising and solving riddles. Was it in emulation of this that Greek men developed a tradition of homosexual relationships? Or was that too a left-over from the era before the imposition of compulsive heterosexuality?

The Men of Ancient Crete

There is no evidence that Cretan men were oppressed and subjugated as women and girls are under patriarchal rule. Many feminist scholars shy away from the term 'matriarchy' because they see it as implying a mirror image of patriarchy. There is however every indication that this was not the case. There is nothing to suggest any of the equivalents of the gender oppression that are the worst demands of patriarchy; suttee, foot binding, cliteroidectomy and infibulation, for example.

The ideology of a culture sets the boundaries of that group's behaviour. The vengeance and cruelty of Zeus, the almighty power of the Old Testament god and the gods of judaism and islam do not find a parallel in the philosophy associated with the Cretan Goddess. Her relationship to Her people was one of beneficence and provision. Having seen that the demands of this almighty power amounted to the heaping of crocuses at Her feet, it is easy to believe that Her people were not taught to fear Her.

Matriarchy was not the equivalent of patriarchy with women in charge. If we accept the evidence of Gimbutas, Mellaart, Gould Davis, Thompson and many other scholars, the social organisation of matriarchal peoples was much more liberal, peaceful and egalitarian than in patriarchal cultures. It does appear however, from Mellaart's evidence and from the Cretan frescoes and sealstones discussed in the present book, that in some areas of society women were allotted a different status to men.

According to Mellaart's findings at Catal Huyuk, and even more so at related Hacilar, these neolithic Anatolian cultures were matrifocal. Women, for example, were accorded more status in burial than men. This could have been because the dwellings uncovered were all shrines and, as the intermediaries between the people and the deity, women (as priestesses) were buried in them rather than men. Because Mellaart was forced to abandon his excavations we do not know whether all the buildings at this settlement would have had a combined use as shrine and dwelling or whether this was something peculiar to the limited area that was excavated. What is beyond doubt is that 'buried skeletons were far more apt to be women's than men's' [82].

Further evidence for the comparative status of women and men in neolithic cultures comes from the grave cemetery of Vinca in Old Europe. Here, Eisler reports that Gimbutas found that hardly any difference in wealth could be identified in the equipment and grave gifts that had been buried with women and men in this clearly non-patriarchal society. In Gimbutas' words, 'the same can be adduced of the Varna society; I can see no ranking along a patriarchal masculine feminine value scale.' [83]

It is clear from the archaeological evidence that men were involved in most professions on Crete. They would have been athletes and farmers, metalworkers and ship builders along with women; they even participated in the sacred activity of bull-leaping. The most popular team sports are still, in the west, reserved for only one sex. The unisex nature of the athletic garb of Cretans and the many depictions of the bull games, shows that there, around 4000 years ago, such activities were common to both sexes.

There is every indication that the whole tenor of neolithic and early bronze age culture was devoid of the rigid role and status divisions apparent in later patriarchally organised societies. The practice of painting women and men in frescoes in different colours may itself imply that many roles were not gender specific. The sexes might otherwise have been indistinguishable given that they shared so many similarities such as hair style, degree of muscular development and clothing.

The areas indicated by fresco and other evidence as those from which men were excluded were, in pockets around the Aegean even in later classical times, still exclusively associated with women. These included religion which would also have encompassed healing and childbirth and, as the evidence from Cretan artefacts powerfully suggests, matters of state administration.

What must have affected Cretan men as much as it did the women was the ubiquitous image of what Jaquetta Hawkes calls 'a splendid Goddess queening it over a small and suppliant male.' Whether the figure to which she refers represents a godling has to remain a matter of opinion. Male figures on sealstones and signet rings usually appear as adorants. The addition of a figure which may be considered to be a minor deity, is the result of the adoption of the Great Goddess by the Mycenaeans who sometimes represent Her with a diminutive and clearly subservient male (fig. 88). Is this how they saw the great Zeus or mighty Poseidon refered to in Linear B texts?

Although this male addition is part of Mycenaean rather than Cretan symbolism, Hawkes' point is none the less valid. A similar impression is given by the many frescoes of important women portrayed at the expense of male figures. She believes that this religious concept must surely have expressed some attitude present in the human society that celebrated it. Moreover the powerful position of women, which mirrored that of the Goddess, was strong enough to sustain itself despite the contrary examples that were to be found, in differing degrees, in Egypt and the Levant – countries with which the Cretans were in regular contact.

Almost all the artistic depictions of men show them as young, lithe, beautiful and clean-shaven. They wore either long or short skirts depending on the activity they were engaged in and were naked from the waist up. The male figurines from the Diktian Cave, now in the

Gender Roles

British Museum, show the long decorative aprons they wore. This style of apron appears to have been derived from women's dresses, as can be seen in the two best preserved faience Snake Goddesses. The unisex broad, tight metal belt emphasised the waspish waists of the men and women though its small circumference may well have been over emphasised in artistic representations. In common with women, men went barefoot indoors or in sacred places and wore sandals and boots outdoors.

The hair fashion and adornments of the men demonstrates that there was little differentiation between the sexes with regard to pride in personal appearance. The Cup Bearer fresco shows that, when taking this role in processions men's naked torsos and limbs were decorated with anklets, armlets, necklaces and bracelets and they wore seals at the neck or wrist. Other men in the Processional Fresco are carrying vases and cups. Although some have been restored playing musical instruments there was no direct evidence from the original fresco to suggest this. Evans used the male musician on the Ayia Triada sarcophagus to guide the restorations of these figures. All that was found of them were their feet and in some cases, the lower hems of their robes.

In frescoes, as on sealstones and rings, men are usually depicted as carrying something or in an attitude of reverence, roles which serves to emphasise the importance of the women in the scene. In the case of the Ayia Triada sarcophagus dated around 1450 it is still the women who take the

Fig.41 Artist's impression of a bronze age Cretan man. Figure and artefacts based on Cretan originals.

central and more sacred roles in the proceedings. As in the Processional fresco the men on the sarcophagus form part of the background in which the ceremony takes place. It is interesting to note however that they wear exact replicas of women's clothing. Were it not for the tradition of indicating the sex of the person by colour it would be difficult to distinguish them. Thomson presents a wide range of evidence to support the view that it was through imitating women, first as their assistants and then as deputies that men came to supplant women as the main participants in religious and secular spheres. Even to the present day in Britain and elsewhere in the christian church the male priest wears what is to all intents and purposes a *long dress*. If he is discharged from holy office he is 'de-frocked'.

The elegance and beauty of Cretan men, the time and attention lavished upon their hairstyles and general appearance and the pride in their sexuality expressed by the cod-piece shows that they were not lacking in self-esteem (fig. 41).

Bronze age Cretan men have been described as calm, dignified, tender, peaceful, gentle and meditative. Evidence from many sources including the jollity expressed in the Harvesters vase present an image of people far from unhappy with their roles. There is nothing to suggest that they were oppressed or subjugated in any way.

There is little indication that Cretan men changed much in the period up to the Dorian invasion. Images of elegant and gentle young man with long flowing tresses were still being produced up to around 1200 BC.

4
Religion,
The Goddess and
Her Symbols

> The priestesses long presided over religious practices.
> Woman was the natural intermediary with the divinities,
> the greatest of whom was woman defined . . . the
> participation of men in the cult was, like the association of a
> god with a goddess, a late development . . . . it is the high
> priestess who takes her place on the seat of the Goddess,
> sits at the foot of the sacred tree or stands on the mountain
> peak to receive worship and offerings.
>
> Gustave Goltz, *Aegean Civilisation*

The Goddess Tradition

As we have already seen the conceptualisation of a female deity existed at least 24,000 years prior to the development of classical Greek civilisation and continues, it could be said, in a much metamorphosed form, in the guise of devotion to the Virgin Mary [1].

The Cretan Goddess was a local form of a once-universal deity. She was celebrated in ways similar to how the Great Goddess had once been revered in Asia Minor, India, Malta, Syria, Egypt and throughout Old Europe. On Crete She continued to be celebrated in a monotheistic form far later than in most surrounding countries including the mainland of Greece and nearby Egypt, where polytheism had long since sounded Her death nell.

Fig. 42 Bell skirted Goddess from the shrine at Gazi. The modelling has become more stylised, perhaps this indicates a cessation of the practice of priestesses imitating the Goddess. The pose of benediction and the symbols incorporated in the crown remain traditional.

Her symbols (serpents, *labyris*, spirals, diamond shapes and Horns of Consecration) were common to many areas. The Snake Goddesses found at Gournia, for example, are similar to those from Romania and a female deity carrying a *labyris* was characteristic of neolithic cultures of the Tarn and Garonne. The prehistoric people of the northern Delta region of Egypt worshipped their supreme Goddess as a Cobra using the name Ua Zit (Great Serpent) [2] and the benefactor of the Chejun women of Japan was personified as a serpent goddess. In the transitional matriarchal cultures of India, Mesopotamia and Sumer the Goddess was associated with serpents as was the Canaanite Goddess. This same symbol was appropriated by the new classical religion through its associations with Zeus and Athena. It later became the object over which the new patriarchate had to assert their dominance and hence incurs derision in the Bible.

The earliest Goddess figures found on Crete date from neolithic times. Nilsson describes them as 'exclusively and exaggeratedly female, of the type called steatopygous, similar to examples from all over the world.' These images appear from the remote times of the paleolithic age and are spread over a vast area of south-east Europe and the Near East including Crete. They illustrate, continues Nilsson, a belief in a monotheism for the primary (female) deity which creates and nourishes all life. Manifestations of this belief in the neolithic era can be found in the thousands of surviving figures from all over the area known as Old Europe.

A series of about 20 of this style of figure was found in the neolithic strata of Knossos, together with clay birds and animals. In contemporary deposits at Phaistos a clay representation of the squatting Goddess was

The Goddess and Her Symbols

found along with the remains of shallow clay bowls, pectunculus shells and a large lump of magnetic iron.

Contrary to Wunderlich's opinion, that the Cretan Goddess figures were lamenting women or erotic reminders of the living world for the (male) dead, they are rarely found in Cretan tombs. The Late Minoan period was outstanding for rich tomb deposits, but Goddess statues were noticeably absent. The exception is the tomb of a woman discovered at Ayia Triada. Its contents were found greatly disturbed but among them were several bell-shaped Goddess figures.

The standard position of the arms of Cretan Goddess statues mirrors that shown on the ritual scenes of gem stones and precious rings and is interpreted as a greeting to votaries or a gesture of benediction. The consistency of this gesture, which is also reflected in the contours of the *labyris* and the Horns of Consecration, establishes its significance. The hands and arms are held in a position that can be seen as imitating the female reproductive organs. In this analogy the body of the Goddess becomes the uterus, the focal point of the creation of life. In some of the bell-shaped Goddesses (figs 10 and 42 are examples) this notion may be further reinforced by the lower half of Her body representing a *pithos* (used for both the storage of food and for burial).

Fig. 43 The many surviving Taula on Menorca can be seen as a symbolic shorthand for the Goddess with upraised arms.

The positioning of the arms in this way was not limited to the Cretan deity, the same shape is evident in the pre-dynastic Nile River Goddess or Nathor. She is usually portrayed with a bird-like head and her arms stretched up and back. In Menorca, a Spanish island replete with neolithic monuments to its then Goddess religion, this symbolism has been abstracted into the *taulas* which is formed by a long vertical slab with a short horizontal placed on top of it (fig. 43) [3].

Hawkes points to the contrast between the high civilisations of both south-west Asia and north Africa and Crete in how they responded to their deities. In the former the cultural ideology was that human society should be an earthly reflection of the cosmic hierarchy. Consequently, unbounded power was given to the holy kings, queens and priests. Conversely, she believes, the Cretan's approach to life demonstrated a sense of liberation of the human spirit from enslavement to its gods. The bronze age Cretan's response to this female metaphor for all things wonderful was not the service and unquestioning obedience demanded by patriarchal religion. Their conceptualisation of the divine form was one of benevolence and nurturance, their response one of joyous celebration. For this reason I have, throughout this book, used the term 'celebrated' rather than 'worshipped' to describe the Cretans' relationship to their deity.

The cultures which celebrated the Great Goddess preserved a close link between nature and humanity and this is reflected by the symbols that were associated with Her. As a scholar of prehistory, Horace H. Wilson pointed out in 1948

> The Goddess is recognised already in the steatopygous Neolithic idols. Later She appears accompanied by snakes which chiefly testify to Her underworld connections. Cows and goats suckling their young, flowers, fruits, shells and flying fish . . . . suggestive of the different gifts of the Earth Goddess, Mother of all and her functions in connection with the production of life and the nourishment of all young things. [4]

This close association between the Great Goddess and the natural world has led to Her being named the Earth Mother by many scholars. Such a narrow definition may have influenced Peter Ucko who believes that neolithic Cretan figurines, in common with those from a number of other neighbouring contemporary cultures, do not exhibit divine features. Although he never says what these features would be, his comment that none of the Cretan figures is holding a child, seems to indicate that he is looking for a fertility goddess or earth mother [5].

Pioneering feminist researchers like Elizabeth Gould Davis and Merlin Stone have, however, transcended this restrictive image for us.

The Goddess and Her Symbols

Stone points out that referring to the Great Goddess as the earth mother is a refusal to admit the truth of Her real power.

And despite the fact that the title of the Goddess in most historical documents of the Near East was the Queen of Heaven, some writers were willing to know Her only as the eternal Earth Mother. [6]

She was revered throughout the world as the Creator of the Universe and was known variously as:
Isis . . . the Goddess from whom all beginning arose . . . Mistress of Heaven . . . more excellent than any other god. (Thebes, Egypt 14th century BC)
Arinna Sun Goddess . . . [who] controllest kingship in heaven and on earth. (Boghazkoy, Turkey 15th century BC)
Ishtar . . . Goddess of all things . . . Lady of Heaven and Earth . . . the Queen of Heaven, the Goddess of the Universe, the One who walked in terrible Chaos and brought forth life by the Law of Love; and out of Chaos brought us harmony . . . (Babylon 18th–17th century BC)
Nana . . . the Creatress . . . the dignified . . . the Glorious One . . . the Mighty Lady (Sumer 19th century BC) [7]

These testaments to the omnipotence of the Great Goddess are given even more weight in that they all date from a time when the transition to patriarchal rule and religion was well under way in these parts of the world. If that was Her power then, what must it have been earlier before there were any other gods?

Professor Spyridon Marinatos saw the various Cretan Goddess figures as representing the same deity in Her different roles, the Snake Goddess as Goddess of the House and Underworld; the Dove Goddess as the Goddess of the Heavens and Love, and the Poppy Goddess as associated with health and fertility. Another of Her manifestations is as the Lady of the Beasts who governs domestic animals and all wild nature. She is depicted as companion to and revered by wild beasts and is associated with cows, goats and lions suckling their young. All these aspects were elements of Her total power. She had no particular name and represented no one particular aspect of creation. She was simply the manifestation of the spirit or energy that created and nourished all things. In Marinatos' view, 'She was Queen of the mountains, animals, the sea and the powers beneath the ground.' [8] She was every single one of these elements and all of them at the same time.

The many symbols associated with Her can be seen as expressing these different aspects. The serpent, Her connection with the underworld the spiral, Her agelessness, and the diamond shape representing Her squatting to create new life. Her provision of sustainance as the governor of germination is indicated by the *kernos*. The Cretan version of this vessel consisted of a large circular stone with a cup-shaped indentation at the centre and smaller ones around the rim, one of which forms a lip, onto which seeds or first crops would have been placed for blessing.

She was the giver and sustainer of life and the embodiment of the reproductive and regenerative powers of nature. Ancient peoples everywhere were totally dependent on Her cycles. In fertile areas this dependence was welcomed and rejoiced in, for She was a proficient provider in those early settlements around the temperate Mediterranean. She was the product of peaceful, agrarian, sedentary matriarchal communities, the descendant of the Golan Goddess, the Goddess of Willendorf and the enthroned birthing Goddess of Catal Huyuk; and the ancestor of the myriad of classical, Roman, and judeo-christian goddesses and gods that were to follow. She was also celebrated in written mythology for donating many gifts to humanity - the seed corn, the olive tree, the tools of agriculture, the fishing net, and so on.

Symbolism

The belief system of the ancient Cretans was as intricate as that of any other religion. The complexities of its religious symbolism can be better understood if we look for a moment at what happens when we attempt to approach christianity with a similar naivety. At the centre of christianity is its most important symbol the cross, an instrument of torture and death. The most sacred ritual associated with this patriarchal religion is the symbolic eating of the flesh and the drinking of the blood of the revered leader Christ, whose mother is a virgin and whose father is a ghost. Such an interpretation is problematic if we approach christian symbolism literally and in abstraction. We need to appreciate symbols for what they are, a shorthand for the network of beliefs that are the basis of the religion.

The symbols of the Goddess on Crete were primarily associated with Her powers of creation and regeneration. Archaeological evidence has established that these were the *labyris*, snakes, spirals, birds, bees and wild and mythical animals. Her cult, which was exclusively practised by priestesses, was also associated with the sacred caves and peaks, *adyton*, Goddess manifestations, Horns of Consecration, bull leaping, altars, dancing, pillars, boughs and trees, *kernos*, poppies, lilies and the Sacred Knot.

The Goddess and Her Symbols

The Labyris

The *labyris* was the primary symbol of the Great Goddess on Crete and was described by Nilsson as being as 'omnipresent as the cross is to christianity or the crescent to Islam' [9]. The symbol itself is very ancient. Representations of it dated to the paleolithic have been found in a cave at Niaux in south-west France and the neolithic tell of the Halaf culture in Iraq [10]. The name *labyris* derives from *labrys*, the Lydian word for 'double axe'. *Labyris* have been found in every possible form on Crete. They were carved onto stone, shaped from stone, painted on ceramics and frescoes, and many thousands of them were cast in bronze, silver and gold. No large *labyris* were found at Phaistos or Mallia but this may be because of later ransacking for metals. Large bronze *labyris* blades were found at Nirou Hani together with offering tables and other ritual objects. *Labyris* set into Horns of Consecration were the typical ritual objects used in Cretan shrines and were found in the Shrine of the Double Axes at Knossos and the hilltop shrine at Gournia, both of which were in use after the 1450 destructions.

Stone pyramids and Horns of Consecration, socketed to take the *labyris*, were found throughout the great Temple Palaces and in other important buildings on Crete. They were used to signify the sacredness of an object or an area or the essence of the Goddess in a room that had been sanctified or consecrated to Her. Their use for this purpose is recorded on the Ayia Triada and other sarcophagi, on gem stones, on *pithoi*, and carvings on altars, sacred and structural pillars and blocks. In the lightwell of the Hall of the Double Axes at Knossos, for example, the *labyris* appears 17 times. This ubiquitous symbol, the holy of holies, can be seen held by women but it is never depicted in association with a man.

Nilsson believed that ritual use of the *labyris* came from its practical application for hewing timber which was done by women [11]. Marija Gimbutas sees it as a symbol for the epiphany of the Goddess as a butterfly. The various stages of the life cycle of this insect can be seen as representing the cycle of life (caterpillar), death (chrysalis), and rebirth as the butterfly goes on to create more life with a new clutch of eggs before her own death. There are a number of representations of chrysalis and butterflies in Cretan art including the Ring of Nestor and the Vaphio Ring.

It is claimed that the Goddess as butterfly is represented on the gold signet ring (1500 BC) from the Isopata tomb near Knossos, which shows Her dancing with Her attendants. They all appear to have insect heads and hands (fig. 27). A seal from Zakro depicts a butterfly with eye markings but a clearer association comes from a seal dated 1600 BC from the island of Mochlos. It shows the deity with large breasts, a human head, butterfly wings and animal legs (fig. 44). Many of the butterfly images from this period are associated with the Mycenaeans (fig. 45) and butterflies also feature on the Theran miniature marine fresco.

The lily is closely associated with the *labyris*. As represented stylistically by the Cretan artist its form closely resembles that of the labyris, and is consequently a popular feature in sacred landscapes. The *labyris* shaped lilies of the restored fresco of the Throne Room at Knossos were created under Evans' instructions but there are many authentic blooms which trace this form (figs 46 and 47). We also see *labyris*-shaped lilies in the setting in which the Lily Figure from the Processional fresco is walking and in the intricate bodice worn by one of the priestesses in a fresco from Thera (fig. 5).

The *labyris* shape is also reflected in the *waz* or papyrus wand, a symbol associated with the Egyptian Delta Goddess. Stylised representations of papyrus are a common feature of Cretan art (fig. 48).

The shape of the ox horns and the crescent moon can also be seen in the *labyris* shape. Marija Gimbutas believed that the *labyris* set between the Horns of Consecration was a compound expression of the Goddess' power of regeneration. She explains this association by referring to the ancients' belief that swarms of bees were regenerated from the carcasses of dead oxen. Bees swarming from the carcass of a lion are mentioned in the Bible (Judges 14:8).

ABOVE Fig. 44 Goddess as butterfly. From Mochlos, 1600 BC.

BELOW Fig. 45 Butterfly Dress Ornament, gold plate. From grave III, Mycenae citadel; one of 701 such discs.

The Goddess and Her Symbols

Fig. 46 Goddess with headdress, Mycenaean gold brooch, 1600 BC. Two waz lily motifs and three papyrus stalks curving round on either side with hanging blossoms. The shapes of the flowers and skirt recall the labyris form.

Figs. 47 and 48 Jars decorated with forms representing the labyris and stylised papyrus.

The shape of the *labyris* can also be seen as resembling the arms of the Goddess in benediction. This is illustrated by a stylised Late Minoan I *labyris*/Goddess painting from Mochlos (fig. 49) and Mycenaean Goddess figures (fig. 50). Other stylistic representations of the Goddess shows Her in the pose of benediction but the symbolic derivation here is the trident, another sacred symbol found carved in Cretan shrines. The Middle Minoan I faience Goddess from a votive pit at the ancient harbour of Knossos (fig. 51) illustrates the development of this concept although the face painted on Her body is incongruous.

As noted in the preceding chapter, this pose of the Goddess traces the stylised form of the uterus and fallopian tubes, the source of life itself. As Cretan burial customs included excarnation they would have been conversant with anatomy and could soon have noted the part of a woman's body that held a foetus. In this analysis the *labyris* actually represented the Goddess as the source of life.

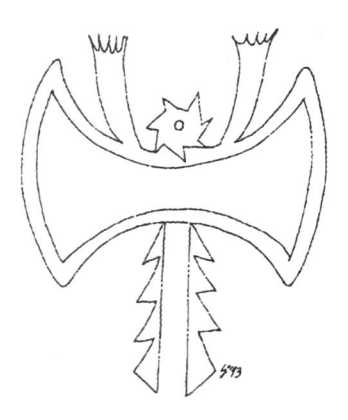

Fig. 49 Goddess as labyris. 1500 BC painting from the island of Mochlos.

Fig. 50 Mycenaean bird-like Goddess. Painted terracotta 1300 BC.

The Goddess and Her Symbols

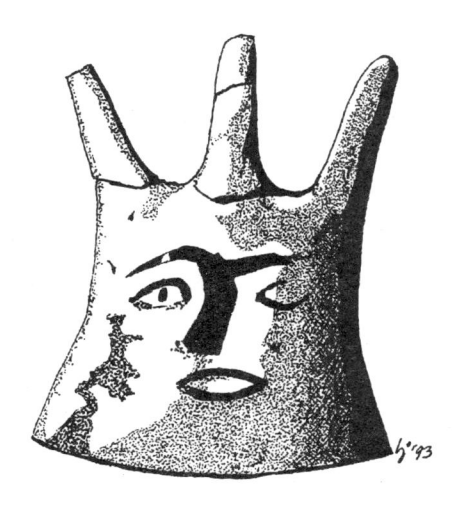

Fig. 51 Bell-shaped Goddess, with face painted on Her body. Faience, 2000-1800 BC. From a votive pit at the ancient harbour of Knossos.

Fig. 52 The New Holy Trinity. Attic vase, 600-400 BC. A symbolic representation of the establishment of patriarchy. Zeus gives birth to Athene seated on the sacred throne, Poseidon holds the trident and Hephaistos hold the sacred labyris. This new patriarchal trinity each have something which was once exclusively female and had sacred associations with the Goddess, something they have stolen.

Jungian analysts and researchers, Ann Baring and Jules Cashford, in their book *The Myth of the Goddess* claim that 'The sacred axe (labyris) was the ritual instrument that sacrificed the bull . . .' [12]. They also however, acknowledge that this sacred symbol 'never appears in the hands of a man or a male priest' [13], and later claim that, 'It is most probable that the ritual slaying of the bull by a priest took place. . .' [14]. Unless, in the second comment, the authors are referring to the post-matriarchal period on Crete, these statements clearly contradict each other. The bead seal cited by Baring and Cashford as evidence of bull sacrifice [15] shows a man stabbing a galloping horned animal which bears little resemblance to a bull. It is dated vaguely but late at 1400–1100 BC, a time by which large numbers of Mycenaeans are thought to have been present on the island. Besides its late date, this image is unique and cannot therefore be taken as representative of Cretan religious practice. There is no evidence that bulls were sacrificed as part of bronze age Cretan ritual.

In later times the Greeks took advantage of the power invested in the symbolism of the *labyris*. In classical art works it is shown as associated with the Amazons and features in their myths. But the Goddess had to be destroyed and denigrated in order for patriarchy to prevail and this is exactly what we see played out in Greek myth. When Heracles killed the Queen of the Amazons he stole the *labyris* from her. It was then passed, through a woman, to Zeus, in whose hands it became a symbol for lightning. A classical painting from an Attic vase depicts a trilogy of gods exhibiting their new found powers which have been stolen from the preceding Goddess tradition. Zeus sits on the throne of the Goddess giving birth, Hephaistos holds the *labyris* and Poseidon the sacred trident, three of the most powerful symbols of Aegean religion (fig. 53).

The Snake

Where the supreme deity took human form an accompanying snake was very frequently portrayed, as in the Snake Goddess from Knossos. The symbolism of the serpent She holds is the survival of the Neolithic Mother Goddess iconography.

Arthur Evans

The Goddess on Crete is an expression of the neolithic Mother Goddess which survived almost unchanged as an ideology although the deity on Crete derived Her physical expression from the contemporary

The Goddess and Her Symbols

Cretan priestess. The Great Mother no longer needed the huge proportions of Her predecessor but Her power was, nevertheless, as absolute and universal, at least for the Cretans. Cretan art is replete with images of the serpent in religious contexts. The tall-hatted Snake Goddesses has three snakes coiling over and around Her body while Her smaller, more famous, contemporary holds a small snake in each raised hand. Other figures which date from both earlier and later periods show the Goddess holding snakes (fig. 53) and even as part-woman part-snake.

One of the earliest surviving representations of the serpent in a sacred context dates from 16,000 BC when they were carved on a plaque from Siberia. The series of spirals on the reverse of the plaque confirms the early association of these two symbols [16].

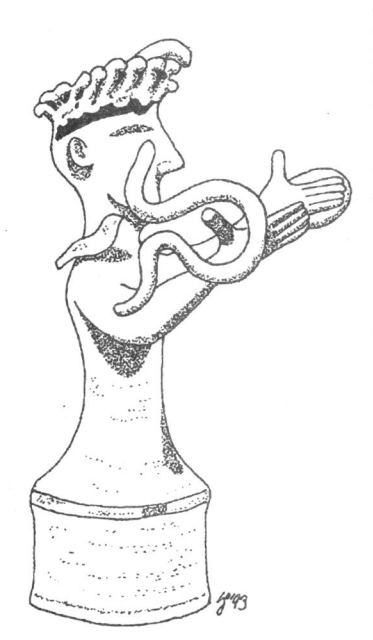

Fig. 53 Snake Goddess, post-1450 BC, Gortys sanctuary. The serpent encircled arms are held up in benediction but the hands face towards the figure. She has a rayed crown topped by a serpent and a dove perches on Her neck.

The snake probably derived its symbolic importance from its ability to slough off its skin (or mortal coil) and its practice of moving between the worlds in tombs and caves. It forms spirals with its body and resembles the first source of life, the *umbilicus*, the life-giving cord which connects the new life with its source, every mammal with its mother. Further magical associations offered by the snake may have derived from its venom which could have been used for medicinal and trance inducing properties. Snakes are also able to confound nature by paralysing their victims into a state of living death.

References to the snake in mythology throughout the world are legion. The Melanesian phrase for 'everlasting life' means literally 'to cast off the slough' and in Greek the word for slough, *geros*, is the same as the word for old age, the snake's sloughed skin epitomizing rebirth. At the temple of Asklepios healing powers attached to the snake's facility for changing its skin. In Africa, among the Zulus, the dead are thought to appear as snakes at burial grounds and the soul of a notable Masai person is said to enter a snake.

Evans cites the representations of snakes found on Malta and points out the association of the snake with chthonic (manifesting the regenerative power of the earth) and fertility deities in many religions. In Egypt, where life was so dependent on the annual flooding of the Nile, the snake symbolised the winding, life-giving river on which everything depended. It was also seen, along with the cat, as the protector of the dead as it would eat small animals who came to steal food left as nourishment for the after life in Egyptian tombs. In the *Egyptian Book of the Dead*, the deceased prays to become like the serpent, 'I am the serpent Sata . . . I die and am born again.' [17]

Above all, the serpent was a symbol for the Goddess Herself. Mythology specialist Joseph Campbell cited the snake as signifying, 'the naked Goddess in Her serpent form.' [18] In the sacred wood of Apollo in Epeiros, on the Greek mainland, the snakes were tended by a priestess (in memory of the early religion) who fed them with honeycakes, only she being allowed to enter. The same ritual and rules also applied to the shrine of Eileithyia at Olympia in Greece. In Athens a serpent lived in the Erechtheum, the sacred temple adjacent to the Acropolis of Athena.

The Sumarian Snake Goddess is both serpent and human and in the Rica villages of Albania each household had a snake known as the 'house mother'. In Scotland the tradition of the snake was associated with Bride (the goddess of plenty, learning, culture and skills) who, in the form of a serpent, would visit Hebridean mothers in labour. In Ireland too the people had celebrated the Great Goddess under the name of Bride or Bridgit. St Patrick, the bringer of christianity to this pagan island, could not rest until all the snakes (vestiges of matriarchy) had been ousted. In this instance the snakes may have been a metaphor for the Druids, the transitional pagan religion which temporarily blocked the acceptance of the new style patriarchy.

The serpent, as a symbol for the Goddess Herself, appears in the Bible where She is the temptress of Eve. She is used, by patriarchal Hebrew priests to represent all that is evil and is portrayed, in tandem with woman kind, as being responsible for the downfall of the whole human race. At the root of Old Testament ideology, the justification for the dominance of man over woman is presented as the Goddess Herself. Thus one of the most potent symbols of the sacredness of women is desecrated and its power, having been harnessed by a conflicting ideology, is reversed. As Eisler puts it, 'the part the serpent plays in humanity's dramatic exit from the Garden of Eden only begins to make

The Goddess and Her Symbols

sense in the context . . . in which the serpent was one of the main symbols of the Goddess.' [19] She compares the Mesopotamian Goddess of 2400 BC who has a serpent coiled around her throat with an almost identical figure from 100 BC India and continues:

> The fact that the serpent, an ancient prophetic or oracular symbol of the Goddess [*], advises Eve, the prototypical woman, to disobey a male god's commands is surely not just an accident . . . she eats from the tree of Knowledge. [20]

* This was the role of the Oracle of Delphi where the resident goddess was a serpent who was slain by Heracles and later the Sibyl of Rome where a priestess was the vehicle for divine revelation and wisdom.

The message, to the original audience of the Bible, the matriarchal Canaanites, was that women brought their own suffering on themselves by continuing in the ways of the Goddess [21]. The new patriarchs insisted that humanity must follow the laws of their god Jehovah with blind obedience and no longer seek knowledge and wisdom for themselves. This indicates a clear differences in the social philosophy of the two cultures. The matriarchal Canaanites emerge as participative, in contrast to the authoritarian patriarchal Hebrews.

This biblical obsession with the debasement of the serpent is paralleled by the behaviour of the heroes of patriarchal Greek mythology. Zeus, Apollo and Heracles all slayed serpents (destroyed the Goddess tradition). Medusa herself is a prime example of the degraded symbolism of the Goddess. Serpent and woman are combined in her persona to produce unparalleled power. She inspired fear and awe and was slaughtered as a proof of the hero's cunning and prowess. Another route to undermining the power of the old traditions was to appropriate them. It was in the guise of a snake that Zeus Kresios seduced (a euphemism for abducted and raped) Persephone, the new goddess of vegetation.

Folklore and mythology are rife with references to the serpent in either her standard or more elaborate, winged, dragon guise. She is always the object over which domination must be established by the new patriarchate. She is often described as protecting a treasure belonging to the earth, a jewel of some sort which is a symbol for the

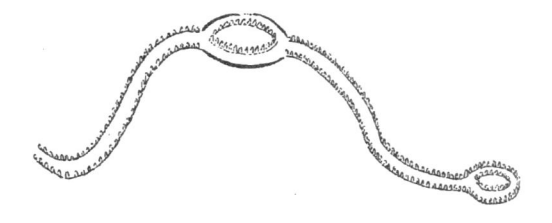

Fig. 54 Stukley's 18th century reconstruction of the 2600 BC Snake Avenues of Avebury.

earth itself. Eisler refers to the pertinent legend of the serpent who guarded the sacred fruit tree of the Goddess Hera. She was slain by Heracles (Hercules). The gravity of this event is compounded by the knowledge that this tree was given to Hera by the primaeval Goddess Gaia.

Conscientious attempts were also made by the new patriarchal religious leaders to eradicate the physical evidence of massive monuments to the Dragon-Serpent-Goddess tradition. At Avebury in Wiltshire little remains of the original massive stone avenues described by the 18th century antiquarian William Stuckley as representing a great serpent (fig. 54) [22]. The medieval church found the power of the old beliefs so threatening that they had many of the massive stones smashed and buried or reused.

Fig. 55 Earthwork Serpent. 1350 feet long bank, Ohio. A relic of the 2000 year old Hopewellian culture.

Fig. 56 Traditional Aboriginal Snake Sand Drawing.

Despite these concerted attempts at eradication many examples of serpent earthworks have survived such as the neolithic Dorset Courses, Dragon hill in Dorset, St Michael's Mound in Cornwall [23], an underground temple at Margate in Kent (discussed in Chapter 5) and a 2000 year old Serpent mound and squatting Goddess in a 1350 foot long bank in Ross County, Ohio (fig. 55). The Rainbow Serpent is the traditional sand drawing of the Aborigines of Australia (fig. 56).

Centres of Celebration

Because of the identification of the Goddess with the natural world, even at the height of their material achievements, the Cretan centres of celebration tended to be natural sites - caves, mountain peaks and sacred groves. Jacquetta Hawkes refers to Her as the 'Goddess of the wild places and the unconscious mind'.

Caves

The limestone of the Cretan landscape is honeycombed with caves many of which are very large and elaborate. Of the approximately 2000 caves on Crete, only 35 are known to have been used for religious activities. Those which were especially favoured for ritual use are situated near to mountain peaks; they also have dramatic rock formations and a pool of water which could be used for sacred purposes. The caves were the original labyrinths, a term which had two meanings. The latter part of the word means 'home of' as with Corinth, Zominthos, Hyakinthos and other Greek place names. Thus *labyrinth* is 'the home of the *labyris* '. A labyrinth is also a meandering walkway associated with the sacred paths and corridors of the Temple Palaces. With their complex passageways and tunnels, and the hundreds of sacred *labyris* found in them, the caves were labyrinths in both senses of the word.

The sacred cave represented access to the underworld. It provided a sense of being between the worlds and, to some extent, imitated the foetal experience. By entering these great caverns celebrants entered the symbolic sacred womb of the Goddess and could express their adoration of Her as the giver of life and receiver of the dead. In the sacred semi-darkness of lamp light, rituals would be performed and offerings left.

The importance of the cave in bronze age Cretan religion is attested to by the quality and sheer volume of the sacred objects discovered in them. A hoard of votive *labyris*, many of them gold, were found in the sacred cave at Archolochori. Three terracotta birds came from the Patso cave and the Kamares cave revealed a cache of exquisite ceramic bowls and other sacred vessels. The many hundreds of votive offerings from the Psychro cave include a wide range of objects. They can be seen displayed together in the Ashmolean Museum in Oxford, England.

The lower levels of the Temple Palaces, Wunderlich's 'many dark, windowless rooms set aside for ritual use', may have been intended to recreate the atmosphere of the sacred caves. Examples at Knossos are the warren of rooms surrounding the Throne Room and the complex of chambers behind the Tripartite Shrine. There are also numerous dark passages from which one would have emerged into the brilliant daylight of a lightwell or courtyard. Many of the passages are not straight or direct but of a dog-leg character clearly reminiscent of the meandering passageways of the great caves. Sacred pillars, symbolic of great stalactites, were also recreated in these religious complexes.

The Vernofereto cave at Kato Pervolakia in the Sitia district is the site of a unique cave painting which dates from around 1400 BC. The painting features the crouching figure of a woman with her arms upraised holding a bow and arrow, her faithful dog stands close by. This figure may be a priestess or represent the Goddess. Beneath her three people in boats are casting nets into the sea in which we see octopus, dolphin and starfish.

The power of the caves as foci of the Goddess tradition made them important targets for the arbiters of the new patriarchal religion. Thus a cave was chosen as the birthplace of Zeus, the principle god of the Greeks.

Peak Sanctuaries

The Peak Sanctuary was another natural location where the bounties of the Goddess were celebrated. The largest and most impressive of these was Psili Korfi on Mount Juktas' highest point. Juktas lies 7 km south of Knossos, from where its peak is visible. The shrine here could be said to represent a Temple Palace in miniature. The date of the remains of its massive walls (originally 740 metres long, 3 metres thick and probably 4 metres high with a 130 metre circumference) on Juktas' northern summit, has been estimated to date from 2100 BC. Thus ceremonies were practised here 200 years before the Old Temple Palaces were built. Even here on this great hill the emphasis is still on the earth as the womb of the Goddess. In the most sacred part of the sanctuary, indicated by the remnants of a row of five small rooms which once stood at the edge of the steep, west-facing cliff, there is a cleft in the rock which leads to a small cave. Here the remains of a pyre and altar were recovered. Large numbers of clay votive figures were found in this area along with fragments of offering tables and bronze figurines. Thirty sacred *labyris* were also recovered from the site.

As well as simulating the atmosphere of the sacred cave in an urban setting there is evidence that the Cretans also sought to recreate the mountain peak. There are indications that the actual summit peak itself was celebrated as sacred. A spur of exposed natural rock was discovered in a number of religious contexts. These sites include Anemospilia and Phaistos on Crete itself and Mycenae and Eleusis on the mainland.

The list of mountain sites grows as more are discovered. The 35 located throughout the island so far are listed in Castleden's *The Minoans* (1990). Clay figures and limbs dating from Middle Minoan I were excavated at the site of a hill sanctuary at Petsofa and a head showing an elaborate beehive hairstyle was recovered from Piskokephalo mountain sanctuary which is thought to have been in use from Middle Minoan I to Middle Minoan II or III.

Following the mass destructions the focus moved away from mountain peaks though cave sanctuaries remained in use. Nowadays, as elsewhere in the world, christian churches have appeared on many of the sites formerly sacred to the Goddess. These small white buildings can be seen marking the ancient peak shrines and at the mouths of the once-sacred caverns.

Groves

The most appropriate places for dances and ceremonies to celebrate the fruitfulness of the Goddess were Her sacred olive, fig and pomegranate groves. Celebrants would have left offerings at the low walls that formed the enclosures of the sacred groves just as present day christians do at the altar rails of their churches. Artefacts suggest that altars and *labyris* stood just outside these enclosures. Libations would have been poured over the sacred boughs placed there and we may deduct from the practices recorded in the exploits of the Greek mythical figure, Jason, that sacred liquids may also have been sprinkled onto the trees themselves.

A 16th century BC miniature fresco from Knossos records a sacred performance held in the open air. The event, which may be a dance or a ritual enactment of some other nature, takes place beside an olive grove surrounded by a low walled enclosure. As Cameron has pointed out, the state of growth on the trees suggests this festival took place in spring rather than autumn.

Public and Private Rituals

Dance

According to Greek legend dancing originated on Crete. The Goddess Rhea taught the Kouretes to dance and clash their shields in order to disguise the cries of the infant Zeus to protect him from his father Kronos. The centrality of dance to the religious life of Knossos is recorded in the *Iliad* where Homer describes the dancing area that Daedalus built for Ariadne, the princess who represents the remnants of matriarchy on Crete. This myth may have recalled the original dance floor in the Theatral area.

The style of dance performed in the bronze age may have been the Crane dance (*geranos*) which, in the myth, Theseus saw being performed by Cretan maidens.

During Evans' time on Crete both women and men took part in a 'mazey' dance around Knossos. It was always performed left to right 'widishins' or anti-clockwise. Examples of early earthworks in the form of mazes have been found throughout the world. The cut turf mazes of Saffron Walden and elsewhere in England and others in Scandinavia and Northern Russia are reminders of the widespread nature of the sacred maze dance.

Several ceramic representations of women performing a sacred round dance have survived. One, from the tholos tomb at Kamilari near Phaistos, shows four women holding their arms around each other inside a circle defined as sacred by the surrounding of Horns of Consecration. In another composition found at Palaikastro four women dance as a fifth plays a lute or lyre (fig. 57).

As well as the statuary groups depicting small circle (*hyporchema*) dances, which are still performed in parts of Crete, and the fresco of a larger group of women dancing, there are representations of individual dancers. In these the fresco painter

Fig. 57 Circle dance with lyre, Palaikastro 1400 BC.

has captured the movement and life of the moment in which the dancer's hair flies out as she swirls around.

Some people have suggested that opium or even a derivative of snake venom may have been used in these ecstatic dances in order that the participants should gain an altered level of consciousness. As anyone who have witnessed the rhythmic gyrations of the whirling Dervish, African tribal dances or even attended a dance workshop will know however, nothing but the power of dance is needed to induce a special state of consciousness.

All the archaeological evidence shows the sacred dancers to be women. Just as men are never depicted holding the *labyris*, they are never shown involved in sacred dance rites. In this context it is notable that the legends associated with the great neolithic stone circles of Britain concern young women who were said to have turned to stone for dancing on the (patriarchal) sabbath.

Harvest Rituals

From the evidence of frescoes and other scenes like that on the Harvesters Vase, the *kernos* discovered at several sites and the festivals associated with the harvest which have survived to modern times, it is clear that this was a time of great celebration. We know that in later classical rituals *kernos* were associated with the first fruits of the harvest. As Nanno Marinatos put it, within the harvested ear of corn both death (of the plant) and the germ of new life (the seed) are present. She has suggested that rituals associated with the harvest took place in the west courts of the Temple Palaces where raised walkways meet to form a triangle next to the corn silos or Koulouras. At Knossos a passage leads from this walkway into the labyrinth along the Processional Corridor.

A clue as to the type of rituals the Cretan priestesses performed may be found in the Eleusian mysteries, which are said to have been brought by settlers from Crete. Ears of wheat, torches, the chalice, the Cretan rosette, a poppy and pomegranate were carved on the external temple walls at Elephsus. We know little about the rites because initiates were sworn to secrecy, but we do know that a great fire burned in the temple which was shared by the initiates who each carried a flaming torch. There was also a sacred cave where a priestess representing Persephone reappeared from the underworld and an ear of wheat was reaped and displayed to the assembled crowd in silence. The dancing which would have formed part of the proceedings, continued to be performed by torchlight in the name of the Goddess right up until the 1930s, when the police put a stop to it.

Goddess Epiphany

Frescoes, sealstones, Temple Palace architecture and cross-cultural parallels all suggest that Cretan priestesses made appearances in imitation of the Goddess at windows (fig. 58) and doorways. In historical times this ceremony was associated with Artemis of Ephesus who was expected to appear in specially designated windows high in her temple's pediments. This custom was already an ancient one at the time the temple was built in 600 BC and had been common practice in Anatolia, Syria, Mesopotamia and Egypt [24].

Fig. 58 Woman at Window. From west fresco heap, Knossos.

Robin Hagg has suggested the facade of Knossos overlooking the West Court as an appropriate location for crowds to have gathered to see the priestesses make appearances at windows. At Arkhanes the Temple Palace ruins include a tower-like structure which had windows overlooking the courtyard which may have been used for this purpose.

The Throne Room at Knossos and the specially designed rooms (known as Chancel Screens) that are to be found in many of the fine houses (shrines) around Knossos and in Country House Shrines like Tylissos would have been ideal locations for a more private version of this ritual for particular initiates.

In the Throne Room for example, we can imagine that, having prepared herself in the adjacent ante chapel, the priestess, dressed in sacred robes, would make her first dramatic appearance at the doorway between the griffons of the west wall of the Throne Room. These fantastic creatures are associated with the Goddess on sealstones, rings and frescoes. Perhaps the best example of the latter is the fresco from Room 3a of a sacred building on Thera. She would then move over to take her seat on the sacred throne.

The Goddess and Her Symbol

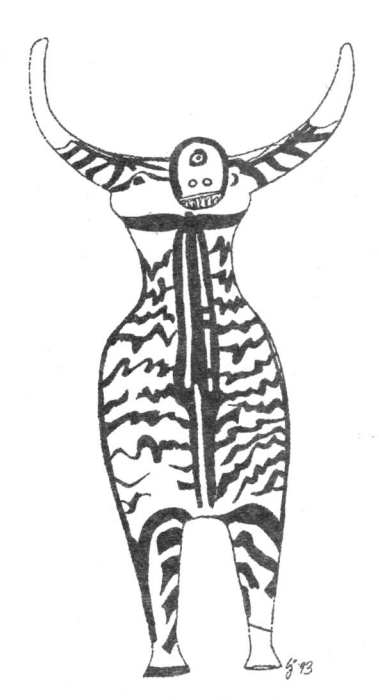

Fig. 59 The Goddess as Ox. Front view of a bovine figure, Crete.

The robes, which we see suggested in frescoes from Thera and Knossos and modelled in faience amongst the treasures stored away in the Temple Repositories and on sealstones, appear to be connected with this ceremony. Rituals involving sacred robes also survived into the classical period as part of the mysteries of Athena and Artemis. Book 6 of the *Iliad* describes the embroidered robes that were carried by a procession of female elders to the Trojan Athena. In Athens, it was the custom to take down the statue of Athena Polis at the summer solstice so that it could be washed and reclothed in a new, specially woven, robe. A similar rite was associated with the temple of Artemis at Ephesus.

Bull Leaping

We know that bull leaping was a sacred activity by the many representations of this act at Knossos and by the sacred symbols, pillar shrines and sacral knots, which accompany its depiction on sealstones.

Artefacts indicate that bull-leaping was a common activity, taking place even as part of the bull hunt. An ivory box found in a Late Minoan III tomb at Katamba close to Knossos shows a woman leaping over bull's horns in the midst of a rocky landscape. An even more vivid depiction is on one of the Vaphio cups where a dramatic encounter between a bull and two of its would-be captors is recorded. A male figure has failed in his attempt to secure the bull and has been thrown under it, his arms flailing up behind him. Evans notes that he has the appearance of the stricken lion hunter who features on the shaft of the Mycenaean Lion Hunt sword, for whom it looks as if death cannot be far away. In the same moment a young woman has thrown herself onto the huge, agitated beast and is shown enveloping its horns with both her arms and legs [25]. Evans points out that, 'This sudden onslaught with the full weight thrown on the bull's head, has twisted it half round and threatens to bring him down in full career if not to break his neck.'

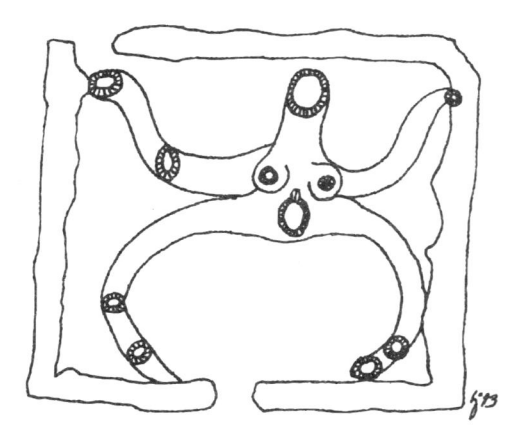

Fig. 60 Hilltop feature known as the Square Enclosure, 3700 BC. (After Dames) Viewed from this direction this figure is the squatting Goddess with breasts, a prominent womb or vulva and upraised arms. When turned upside-down, however, She transmutes into an ox head.

This, he adds, is precisely what the later Thessalian youths are recorded as doing as they sprang from ponies [26].

Evans noted that the 'special elegance of ornaments and headdress' singled out the young women bull leapers as of gentle birth and high rank. Although, he comments, their dress was the same as the male leapers 'even to the imitation of the male "sheath"' [27], he was quite clear who the women were because of the luxuriance of their locks. A curling fringe above the forehead with tresses partly bound in a chignon was a common feature. In frescoes women are more clearly identified by their white body colour.

All the evidence shows that a great deal of effort was made to capture bulls in a humane manner. The only pictorial image of a probable bull sacrifice in this long period of Cretan archaeology is from the Ayia Triada sarcophagus which dates from around 1450 BC and, as is indicated from the building in which it was found and many aspects of the scenes depicted on it, more representative of an alien tradition than indigenous Cretan ritual.

The shape of the bulls horns imitate the position of the arms of the Goddess raised in benediction and therefore take on symbolic importance as an expression of the Goddess herself (fig. 59). This association can also be seen in the configuration which Dames has suggested from the neolithic hilltop feature known as the Square Enclosure at Windmill Hill near Avebury. Pot sherds found in the earthworks that form the figure date it to around 3700 BC (fig. 60).

The Lustral Basin

The Lustral Basin, also known as an *adyton*, is a ritual cleansing area set into the earth and approached by (usually spiral) steps and was central to bronze age Cretan religious practice. They were often faced with gypsum, a porous material, so it is clear that they were not used for conventional bathing and they did not have the plugs usually found in ordinary baths. Their religious identity is confirmed at Zakro where an *adyton* was discovered decorated with altars and Horns of Consecration in white on a red background.

The location of Lustral Basins, close to the northern entrances of Knossos and Zakro, suggests that they formed an important part of the preparation for those wishing to enter the sacred confines of the Temple Palaces. Other *adyton*, their inaccesiblity to the casual visitor emphasised by the series of sanctuaries that surrounded them, indicates that they also featured in more sophisticated rituals which may have been reserved for initiates.

Pillar Libation Rituals

Other private rituals which we could imagine were reserved for certain initiated priestesses, involved the use of pillar crypts. These were located in the dark inner sanctuaries of the most sacred areas of the Temple Palaces and other large religious houses. We can only guess at the secret rituals that took place here but we know from their structure that they involved pouring fluids - oils, milk and perhaps mead or another form of liquid honey. Many hundreds of *rhyta*, which have a small hole at one end, have been recovered that were specifically designed for this purpose.

In the Royal Villa, one of the sacred buildings close to Knossos the central pillar in the crypt has a channel cut around its base with deeper squares set along it to catch the sacred libations. The nearby Little Palace has three pillar rooms, two of which stand side by side in the basement. Between the pillars in these two crypts there are cists with a central hole which could have held a sacred bough or a *labyris* on a pole. The third contained sacred goods which had fallen down from the shrine above. A pillar crypt was also discovered in the Temple Tomb, another of the important buildings close to Knossos and two labyris marked pillars were found in crypts at Mallia. The pillars in the crypts of the Temple Palaces and large houses may have been seen as a convenient way of representing the stalactite pillars of the sacred caves.

Altar Rituals

It is clear from the late shrines, found almost as they had been left at Knossos, Gournia, Gazi and Ayia Triada, that an important part of Cretan religious practice involved the placing of Goddess figures on a plaster bench. Ritual equipment like tripod stands for tall cone-shaped *rhytha*, smaller altars and Horns of Consecration were also involved. These small shrines were intended for the use of either one, two, or at the most a small group of people at any one time. The one at Knossos, the Shrine of the Double Axes, had its own *adyton*. Other bench altars can be found throughout the Temple Palaces and are sometimes confused with seating.

Some of the scenes depicted on the Ayia Triada sarcophagus may record indigenous Cretan religious practice. Three spiral-decorated altars are represented, two on one side and one on the other. At one of them a priestess holds her hands just above a bowl. A jug and a dish which may indicate wine and fruit are depicted above her. Behind this altar is a pillar-mounted *labyris* set into a pyramidal stand and topped by a bird. The adjacent altar or sacred enclosure is decorated with spirals and topped by four sets of Horns of Consecration. The sacred branch or bough shown at the top of the enclosure recalls those seen in religious scenes on sealstones and signet rings. At another altar a priestess pours libations between pillar-mounted *labyris* which are also topped by birds.

Trees, Boughs and Sacral Ivy

Temple groves play a central role in ancient texts like the Tablets of Sumer and the Bible where the destruction of the sacred groves of the Queen of Heaven are recorded [28]. Even when ceremonies were performed in the more formalised settings of the Temple Palaces, trees and boughs continued to have great significance. We see them depicted in ritual scenes on Cretan and Mycenaean gemstones and rings. In these exquisite cameos of ritual celebration a common theme is of attendants, priestesses and other votaries almost caressing a sacred bough or tree in the presence of the Goddess. Occasionally, as on the Ring of Mochlos we see a sacred bough being transported by a priestess in a boat. The branch usually appears to be perched on an altar. Two branches can be seen on one of the altars of the peak shrine depicted on the Zakro rhyton. It seems more probable, however, that many 'altars' are, in effect, sacred enclosures into which the bough has been placed or is growing thereby maintaining the effect of it being partly in the earth (the under/other world) in the way a free standing bough could not.

The ubiquitousness of this symbol can be seen in the following examples. On a signet ring from the royal burial in Tholos tomb A we see it being uprooted in combination with an expression of mourning. One sealstone depicts a priestess blowing a triton shell, presumably to evoke the Goddess. She stands beside a bough set between Horns of Consecration. On other gemstones there are depictions of what Nilsson described as 'ecstatic or orgiastic scenes of the tree cult'. He seems to be

The Goddess and Her Symbols

referring to the dancing. The only participants in these so-called 'orgiastic' scenes are women. The exquisite gold ring from Mycenae features three votaries approaching the Goddess seated under a tree while a forth is touching it. The superb detail of the carving identifies the piece as the work of Cretans.

A lavishly decorated Late Minoan I (1550 BC) *pithos* from the Gulf of Mirabello in eastern Crete is replete with Goddess symbolism. We see ox heads, *labyris* and branches of foliage which have been described as sacral ivy or lilies (fig. 61).

The tree may have symbolised the connection between air and earth, life and death. Its sustenance is drawn both from the earth through the roots and the atmosphere from light. Just like the cave or mountain it may have been thought of as symbolising the Goddess, the initiator of all life. As Nilsson put it, the tree could be seen as holy in itself or as an embodiment of the Goddess. The tree also expresses the cycle of life and death through the seasons. It produces new life in the form of buds and seed, provides fruits for sustenance and in the autumn the leaves die and drop off so that the whole cycle can begin again.

During the bronze age, Crete would have been covered in oak, cypress and fir trees but it seems that only certain types of tree were considered sacred, as with the fig tree in parts of India to the present day. On Crete the most likely candidates were the olive, the pomegranate and the fig. The pomegranate and fig trees would have derived particular importance because of their fruit which are filled with a mass of lush red seeds, symbolic of fecundity and sacred female blood. The fig's significance is aknown from the Bible as the tree from which Eve and Adam took leaves once they discovered their nakedness in the Garden of Eden. The olive was an important crop, providing oil and fruit both of which lend themselves to preservation and storage. It also lives to a great age and has the

Fig. 61
Pithos decorated with labyris, ox heads and foliage. 1550 BC. Island of Pseira, Gulf of Mirabello, East Crete

Crete Reclaimed

ability to send out shoots from a seemingly lifeless trunk thereby reviving each year.

Reverence of sacred boughs continues to the present day, if in a somewhat disguised form. Fir trees are the central symbol of one of the most important days in the modern western calender and May poles are the focus for one of the greatest national celebrations in Scandinavia. In the festivities surrounding the welcoming of summer, the May pole is raised not as a phallic symbol but as one of general fertility. The Scandinavian May pole is not a single pole, it has a cross-piece from which circles of foliage hang on either side of the central upright, perhaps in imitation of the fillopian tubes and ovaries. At Easter, a time the Scandinavians associate with witches, branches of birch are brought into the house and decorated with painted eggs and feathers. The sprouting of new leaves on the bough heralds the spring.

Ivy is a common decorative feature on Cretan stone lamps, swords and metal cups [29]. Evans was able to isolate a symbol which represented ivy in both Linear A and Linear B scripts and it features on the Mycenaean Ring of Nestor whose subject is the Tree of Life. It too has survived into present-day celebrations. In one christian carol which has pre-christian associations, the evergreen holly with its menstrual blood red berries is paired with the parasitic ivy which grows in living spirals in the wake of death. Ivy can also be seen carved on 19th century grave stones in English churchyards.

The Pillar and Stalactite

The stalactite, created as a result of the forces of nature is an obvious representation of chthonic energy, another embodiment of the Goddess. The concretions of limestone that make up stalactites are an expression of the earth in a 'living', growing form.

That the pillar is intended to represent the Goddess can be seen from images carved on sealstones and other artefacts. The human female figure as a symbol for the Cretan deity is interchangeable with the pillar. Lionesses, griffons and other noble animals seen flanking the Goddess in Her human form (fig. 22) are portrayed, in other instances, standing in the same relation to a pillar. On a gold ring in the Iraklion museum the Goddess is depicted both as a pillar flanked by lionesses and in Her epiphany as a butterfly. This same symbolism is expressed on the massive lintel at the entrance to the great city of Mycenae with lionesses on either side of the Goddess as pillar (fig. 62).

The stalactite in the Eileithyian cave at Amnissos has a long history of reverence, with supplicants taking gifts there right up to classical and even into christian times. Heaps of pottery fragments from many

The Goddess and Her Symbols

different eras were found in the farthest chamber of the cave. Any more valuable offerings would have long since been rifled from Amnissos and other similarly accessible caves.

Both the natural pillars in the sacred caves and spurs of rock were seen as embodying Goddess energy and as such were reproduced symbolically in the Temple Palaces and the sacred rooms of other buildings. The *labyris* engraved on pillars at Knossos (as many as 29 on a single pillar) may have played a similar role to the gold and silver labyris that were placed between the stalactites of the sacred caves. The downward tapering columns of the Temple Palaces that would once have been encountered at every turn, also representing the sacred pillar. They were often painted red, another direct association with the deity's role as creator.

Fig. 62
Lion gate at Mycenae, 1500 BC. An illustration of the symbolism of the Goddess as pillar. This style of downward-tapering pillar is ubiquitous in Cretan art and architechure. Compare with fig. 22.

The bees...

The famous Mallia pendant, exquisitely worked in gold, attests to the high esteem in which bees were held. There are several other surviving images of bees and the Goddess is sometimes depicted in this form. One example is the onyx gem sealstone (1500 BC) from Knossos where the Goddess as a bee is flanked by winged dogs. The sacred horns and *labyris* are above Her head.

The special status allotted to this industrious insect in Cretan religion was perhaps because its social organisation mirrored that of the bronze age Cretans. In both instances the success of the whole

ABOVE: Fig. 63
The Tate and Lyle emblem depicts bees swarming from the carcass of a lion, accompanied by the words 'Out of the Strong Came Forth Sweetness'.
RIGHT: Fig. 64
Octopus chalice encompassing bee and serpent symbolism.

population was dependent on the cooperation of all its elements. Each individual worked for the good of the whole group and takes particular care of the queen.

Bees were also associated with reincarnation. The cycle by which death is succeeded by new life can be observed everywhere in the natural world. Leaves are renewed every year and maggots thrive in the wake of death. In the case of bees they would have been observed swarming (deriving life) from carcasses, an image that was capitalised on by Tate and Lyle (fig. 63). In Greek mythology the first swarm of bees appears from the wound of a mountain lion killed by Aristaeus (the Pelasgian Hercules) [30]. The veteran collector of ancient myth, Robert Graves, claims that

> The Goddess is herself a queen bee about whom male
> drones swarm in midsummer, and as Cybele is often
> pictured; the ecstatic self-castration of her priests was a
> type of the emasculation of the drone by the queen bee in
> the nuptial act. [31]

Some artefacts suggest an association between the bee and the serpent, as in the representation of an octopus on a palace style vase from Knossos (fig. 64).

The ancient Cretans cultivated bees, and honey was an important part of their diet. It would also have been used in medicines and unctions

The Goddess and Her Symbols

and mead (an intoxicating drink made from honey) would have been an appropriate libation for religious ceremonies.

Bees are also of course responsible for pollination and in this role they express the essence of the Goddess as provider of food. The Mycenaeans, probably following in the ways of the Cretans, sent great jars of honey to the sacred cave of Eileithyia. During the Venetian occupation of Crete (1206–1669) the island and its capital (now Iraklion) were known as Candia, a name which continued to be used for Iraklion right up to Evans' time there, due to its fame for fruits candied in honey. Honey remains an important part of Cretan diet and exports.

The high standing of this 'nectar of the gods' is emphasised in the mythology surrounding Zeus who was raised by the goat goddess Amelthae and the bee goddess Melissa on milk and honey.

The sacred associations of this insect continued into classical times. Baring and Cashford note that the omphalos at Delphi is shaped like a beehive and that Pythia, the chief oracular priestess there, was called the Delphic bee. They also point out, that through the common root of the Greek word *ker*, there is a link between the ideas of honeycomb, Goddess, death, fate and the human heart.

The bee hive was a popular architectural form on bronze age Crete. *Tholos* tombs which took this shape were used on Crete and at Mycenae and the remnants of beehive shaped storage silos at the Temple Palace of Mallia were probably of a similar style to those used throughout the island. This beehive form is still the standard shape for storage huts in modern day Crete.

... and the Birds

Birds were frequently used as symbols to indicate the presence or identity of the Goddess or to sanctify a location as sacred. The Bird and Pillar Epiphany from Knossos (fig. 36) comprises three pillars, each topped by a bird. As we have already noted the pillars represent the Goddess while the birds confirm Her identity. Representations of the Goddess in human form are sometimes accompanied by birds. Birds can also be seen perching on the pillared *labyris* on one of the altar scenes on the Ayia Triada sarcophagus and the Mycenaen model of a temple (fig. 81).

The birds sitting atop an elegant triple vase complex in the museum of Ayios Nikolias may represent the Goddess, come to partake of the libations [32]. The association of bird and female to express the deity was used in other parts of the Aegean and neighbouring lands. Breasted jugs from Melos found in the Temple Repositories take the form of exotic birds and the Goddess as a bird is the subject of a 1500 BC

Crete Reclaimed

Figs 65 and 66.
Kamares-style bird-like jars with reflected images.
2000–1700 BC. Old Temple Palace, Phaistos.

sacred jug from (see fig. 75) Thera and many Cretan jugs (figs 68 & 69). The most popular Goddess of the Mycenaean culture was fashioned as part woman part bird and the much earlier pre-dynastic Goddess of Egypt, Nathor, had distinctive bird-like features.

The source of the bird as a symbol for the Goddess may have been its relationship with the air, its sense of freedom through flight putting it above human life. Bronze age peoples would also have been aware of the migratory habits of birds who seemingly disappeared (or died) on a cyclical basis only to return the following year.

Spirals, Diamonds and Mazes

The spiral image was commonly used in neolithic times and is associated with the labyrinth or maze form which was widespread in ancient Europe (fig. 67). Diamond forms (a symbolic shorthand for the squatting, life-giving Goddess) are also often associated with the spiral. This juxtaposition of the diamond and spiral can be seen in the Hebredes (off the mainland of Scotland), Ireland (on the kerbstone of New Grange, a neolithic chamber tomb), Malta and Crete over a timespan covering the neolithic (New Grange is dated at 3200 BC) to the stirrup jar from Zakro made around 1450 BC.

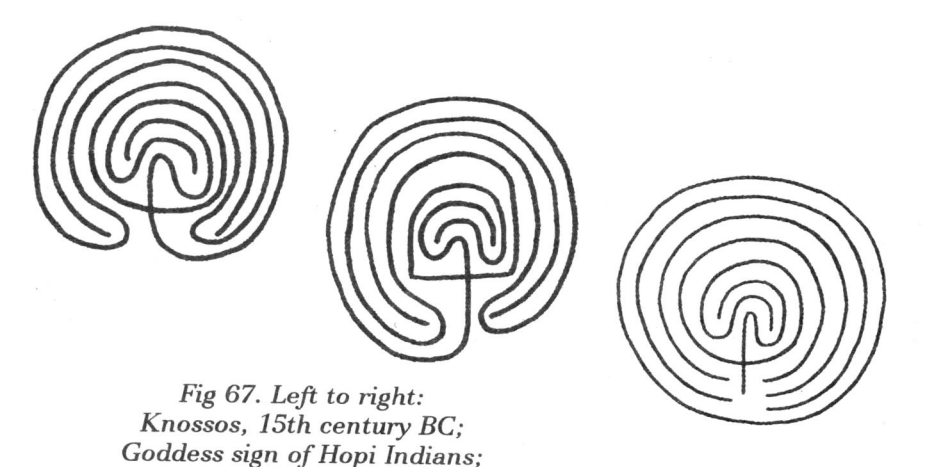

The Goddess and Her Symbols

*Fig 67. Left to right:
Knossos, 15th century BC;
Goddess sign of Hopi Indians;
rock engraving, Tintagel, Cornwall
(probably 18th century AD).*

The spiral form abounds in bronze age Cretan decorative art, appearing on ceramics, frescoes, sarcophagi, sealstones and pithoi. It is thought to express the repeating pattern of death and rebirth that reverberates throughout the mysteries and symbols of Cretan religion.

The Splitting Cell and the Opposing Pair

The portrayal of twins, crescents, doves, lions or griffons facing each other was another important symbol. Examples include include the bee pendent and the lions flanking the Goddess as pillar on a mountain top. The Kamares style bird jugs (2000–1700 BC) from Phaistos (figs 68, 69) are examples of the use of the opposing or mirror-image symbolism.

The layered and split cell is an important associated image which dates from at least 4000 BC. It was incorporated into symbolic frescoes in the main ceremonial rooms of the Temple Palaces, like the lower border of the Throne Room at Knossos.

In the Hall of the Double Axes, frescoes of decorative animal hide shields were set onto a border of spirals. These may represent a splitting ovum/egg or other dividing cell. Indications of a splitting cell form can be seen in what would otherwise seem unnecessary elements of design: the central rib (which could represent the stretching of the cell's nucleus into an elongated shape before it divides), and the dotted circular outline which is depicted as just on the verge of splitting into two separate circular forms.

Fig. 68
Fresco showing shield set in spiral background. Mycenae.

The symbolism of the shield is compounded by its overall shape which represents the Goddess in human form. In the Mycenaean Adoration of the Shield painting the shield is actually depicted as a living being by the addition of limbs.

Because so few Cretan texts have survived it is difficult to know how much or how little they knew about cell biology. Obviously they would have come across open eggs with single, double and not-yet fully-separated yolks. We can also assume a good knowledge of chemistry and metallurgy which would have been necessary to sustain their ceramic, textile, metalwork and aromatic oil production. They also had close contact with the Egyptians who were skilled at mummification and the preservation of different parts of the body, and we know that they were familiar with the concept of magnification which would have been essential for the minute detail which is a feature of their art.

Could the ancient Cretans have used their crystal magnifying lenses to observe cell division in some reptile or primitive life form? If so this splitting cell shield form is the ultimate illustration of what the Goddess represented, the source and origin of life itself (fig. 68).

The Colour Ochre

The 30,000 year old Venus of Willendorf was found to have been stained with red ochre, the sacred colour signifying the life-giving abilities of the Goddess and symbol of this power in all womankind. Human bones dating from the paleolithic and neolithic eras were similarly stained. In these earlier phases of prehistory it is thought that people believed that life was created from menstrual blood. When a child is born she comes accompanied by a quantity of 'unformed' blood

The Goddess and Her Symbols

reinforcing the idea that it was out of this that the child was created. As a result of this belief women's blood was seen as having magical properties and was revered as sacred in its own right.

This idea was extended to include fertility in all things and the power attached to this life-creating blood was used to enhance crop production (see page 65). The sheer power of women's blood can be sensed in the extremes of the taboos which still surround it. As recently as 20 years ago, in parts of Britain a woman was considered unclean unless she had been purged of the contamination of childbirth by 'churching'. In north London where the Hesidic Jews from eastern Europe settled, special pools were built by the community so that women could ritually cleanse themselves after menstruation and childbirth.

Bones uncovered at Phourni cemetery, near Arkhanes, had retained their red colouring by being sealed in a *larnax*. The excavators said they looked as if they had been dipped in wine. The Cretans also appear to have used the colour red to signify the sacredness of an object or a place. Many of the unglazed clay Goddess figures were painted with ochre and it was incorporated into the fabric of the Temple Palaces in the form of red plaster which was used on the walls of sacred rooms and between stone floor slabs at both Knossos and Phaistos. In the Peristyle Hall and a nearby niche at Phaistos, these flagstones were lozenge (squatting Goddess) shaped.

The importance of the use of this red colouring by the Cretans is suggested by Plato who lists it as one of the features of Atlantean architecture and decor. 'The walls and pillars and floor they coated with *orichalcum*'. To the Greeks *orichalcum* was an exotic, legendary reddish metal [33]. (See Chapter 1 for evidence of the identification of this mythical land with Crete.)

The Bull

Bull-leaping was an important feature of Cretan athletics but beyond this its significance may have been over-emphasised. The misconception at the root of the belief in the centrality of the bull as a Cretan religious symbol comes from the idea that this stage of belief on Crete included a male year godling.

> The male aspect of the Goddess, who was at this time still androgynous, uniting both male and female roles, was symbolised then by the crescent horns of the bull or by a male animal - the bull, ram or stag' [34]

Crete Reclaimed

In other words, because no image of a male god has been found on Crete scholars had to invent a male aspect of the Goddess. Baring and Cashford see the early neolithic Goddess of the Cretans as encompassing both male and female. These Jungian scholars, along with many others studying prehistory, are uncomfortable with this omnipotent female deity, who eschews male company, as an archetypal image. They start from the premise that a male principle is an essential element in this era of religious belief. As a consequence such theorists seize upon anything, the occasional male animal, the Horns of Consecration or male votaries whom they claim to be young godlings, to support their views. This theme is also present in the work of Neumann, another follower of Jung, writing many years earlier.

There is no evidence to support these claims. When we see the Goddess at her most powerful she is accompanied, guarded or counter balanced not by a 'male element' but by female animals. The year godling or male consort comes from a later stage of religious belief and is part of the transition to patriarchy. This phase was delayed on Crete, at least amongst the indigenous Cretans, probably until 1100 BC, the time of the invasion of the Dorians. Even following the demise of Crete, in the religious practice which was said to have been established by Cretan settlers at Eleusis, we see that the role of the vegetation deity was not assigned to a male but to Demeter's daughter, Persephone.

Blood sacrifice also appears to be associated with the Jungian archetype [35]. Anthropological evidence does indicate that the practice of sacrifice of the male element (human or animal) after the completion of his role as fertiliser, was widespread [36]. In some cultures this theme was treated literally with the young man being executed each year. In later developments the whole scenario is ritualistic and an animal (perhaps a bull) was sacrificed in lieu of a human consort. The association between bulls and fecundity may have derived from their role in farming. As Michael Dames has pointed out, oxen were used by neolithic peoples in agriculture. Diana of Ephesus (located on the west coast of what is now Turkey) is associated in the second century BC with a variation on the bull fertility cult. In one representation of her it appears, at first glance, as if the upper part of her body is a mass of breasts. Closer inspection reveals these 'breasts' to be a collection of bulls' testicles. There is no indication, however, that such ideas were current on Cretan during the bronze age.

What evidence is there to support the theory of the bull as a symbol central to Cretan religion, either in the role of vegetation godling or otherwise? Ox heads, complete with horns, are featured in the sacred rooms at Catal Huyuk (thought to be the ancestral homeland of the

The Goddess and Her Symbols

Fig. 69
Gold cup, Vaphio, south Peleponnese, 1600BC. Detail of cow decoy and bull. The two sets of horns are indistinguishable.

bronze age Cretans). It is not clear however whether these are bull's rather than cow's heads. The bronze age Cretans made *rhytha* in the form of bulls but these sacred jugs came in various shapes and forms and featured many different animals. The bull *rhytons* may have been used for the ritual of anointing the creatures used in bull-leaping sports.

If only the head or the horns are depicted there is no way of knowing whether an artefact is intended to represent a bull or a cow. One of the famous Vaphio cups shows three separate scenes in which a cow is used as a decoy to capture a bull [37]. Where the two animals are shown together both sets of horns are depicted in exactly the same way. In other words, we cannot decide that the Horns of Consecration or the exquisite Ox Head Rhyton are derived from bulls rather than cows, when there is clearly no difference in the size or shape of the horns in the Cretan artist's mind (fig. 69).

The ox was an important religious symbol in Egypt but, even though they were at a late stage of transition to patriarchy, it was the cow in the form of the Goddess Hathor that was considered sacred, not the bull. Peter Langrange has compared the rosettes which feature on the famous Ox Head Rhyton to the solar disc between the horns of the Egyptian Cow Goddess Hathor [38]. Isis as Hathor with the sun disc between the crescent moons of Her horns represents the Ruler of Heaven. The Egyptians also called the four cardinal points the Horns of the Earth and sacred cow horns were used as a symbol of the fertile earth [39]. In present day India, a land which barely clings onto the last remnants of its matriarchal past, it is the cow which is held sacred not the bull.

Blanche Williams, who points out the similarity between the position of the arms of Cretan Goddess figures and the form of the sacred Horns of Consecration, thinks it not impossible that in Crete as in Egypt, early worship of the Great Goddess as a cow was remembered in the raised

Crete Reclaimed

arms gesture [40]. As G. Rachel Levy points out, however, there is no evidence for cow (or bull) *worship* on Crete [41]. The Cretan Goddess, she argues, was never a cow as in Egypt and Babylon. She neither wears horns nor suckles a child. Nor is there any evidence for a bull king or a bull-masked man. If anything, she believes, the bull was merely an embodiment of the fertility of the earth to which it was sacrificed.

The faience reliefs from the Temple Repositories at Knossos show the tenderness that was felt for the wild cow with her suckling calf and the goat with her kid. Although these images incorporated the essence of the Goddess they were not intended to be seen as manifestations of Her in different forms. No image of a male godling or 'male aspect of the Goddess' or bull was contained in the sacred repositories.

The Horns of Consecration.

Marija Gimbutas stated that 'The schematised bull horn represents one of the basic philosophical ideas of old European religion. The symbol of the active power of the earth's motherly form traceable from the Neolithic period'. She sees the horns not as an object of worship associated with a male element but as a symbol associated with Goddess religion.

The Horns of Consecration predate the first settlers on Crete. They find parallels in Catal Huyuk (7000 BC) and Vinca in Old Europe (5000 BC). I have also identified this symbol in a 12,000 BC carving on the fragment of a mammoth tusk from Mezhirich in the Ukraine which is usually refered to as a 'map' [42]. The horns are clearly central to the symbolism of Cretan religion in the bronze age and are automatically assumed to represent bull's horns. As discussed above, it seems equally possible that they were cow's horns.

These stylised horns were used to symbolise the sacredness of an area and to compound and reinforce the sanctity of the *labyris* when it was placed into the socket that was frequently present between them. Also, as already noted, the schematised horns can be seen as representing the uplifted arms of the Goddess.

On gemstones from shrines at Knossos and Gournia the horns are depicted with a bough placed between them as part of a ritual scene. Evans believed that this is what the sockets in the Horns of Consecration found in the Shrine of the Double Axes would have been used for.

The Sacred Knot

This appears to be an insignia of theocratic office, equivalent to a combination of the modern crown and clerical 'dog collar'. It signified the highest office. The sacred knot often appears in association with the

The Goddess and Her Symbols

Figs 70, 71 and 72.
LEFT: Jug decorated with labrys and sacral knots. The lower toothed design is found on other objects and Mycenean hearths. Ayia Triada, 1500 BC.
MIDDLE: Jar decorated with labrys and sacral knots. Knossos, 1650–1500 BC.
RIGHT: Sacral knot. Knossos, 1500 BC.

labyris on sealstones and vase decorations. Some elegant examples of the latter are a Late Minoan I jug from Ayia Triada (fig. 73) and a Middle Minoan III vase from Knossos (fig. 74). We also see it worn by the Queen of Knossos known as La Parisienne. Sometimes the knot appears alone as in a 1500 representation from Knossos (fig. 75).

The snakes which writhe around the body of the tall-hatted snake Goddess form themselves into a knot on her belly. Perhaps it is this concentrated sacredness that the stylised sacral knot symbolised.

This important symbol has received little attention from scholars. In an uncharacteristic bout of ethnocentricism, however, Cameron, refers to it as possibly signifying 'possession by a male' [43]. This suggestion was part of his theory that the miniature Knossian frescoes depicted some kind of mass marriage/mating ceremony [44]. There is no indication anywhere in the archaeological evidence to suggest that men were 'possessed' by women or vice versa.

Castleden seems to be more on the right track when he suggests that it may indicate a bond between the wearer and the deity [45].

Baring and Cashford noted its resemblance to both the Isis knot or *menat* (worn as a headband by this goddess) and the reed bundle that was associated with the Sumerian goddess Inanna [46]. This may indicate that it was worn by the priestess or priestess queen as she took on the role of the Goddess in the ceremony of epiphany.

Boats

The boat, with an animal or bird head stern is encountered on sealstones and signet rings. Part of the scene depicted on the lost Ring of Minos shows a priestess, whose high status is indicated by the size of her breasts, steering a boat through the seas. The fantasy bird-prowed boat has two altars topped by Horns of Consecration (fig. 39). The Late Minoan I gold ring from Mochlos also features a boat. Its prow is formed by a horse's head and again we see a large-breasted priestess with an altar. A plant, resembling a cactus, has been placed into this one. Several enigmatic objects appear in the air above and something, which may be a small human figure or a second smaller altar, stands next to the first one.

Do these images represent the priestesses performing rituals at sea or are they associated with a journey of death and rebirth? There may be a link between the horse prows of this boat and the horse which was found interred with the remains of the queen in Phourni tholos tomb A.

Stages in the Development of Religious Ideas

There is overwhelming evidence from archaeology, anthropology and mythology of a pattern to the phases of religious development over the millennia [47]. As already noted, many of the cave paintings, carvings and statues which date from the Upper Paleolithic period of 35,000 to 10,000 BC include unequivocal representations of vulvas and figures whose femaleness has been emphasised. Stone age culture probably goes back to 65,000 BC but very little is known about this earlier period. However, in 1994 a roughly-carved stone figure was discovered in the Golan Heights. Its form has some similarities to paleolithic and neolithic Goddess figures and consequently it has become known as the Golan Venus. The most significant thing about it however is that it is a quarter of a million years older than the previously earliest known female figure, the Goddess of Willendorf. This puts its date at around 275,000 BC.

All the indications from early prehistoric finds (see page 45 and Chapter 2) are that the first phase of religious beliefs was monotheistic.

The Goddess and Her Symbols

The life force which created and nourished everything that was available to the paleolithic consciousness, was conceptualised as female because this was people's direct experience. The surviving Goddess figures and carvings and the burial practices from this time combine to give an unequivocal picture of our earliest ancestors' identification of the life force and the powers of the natural world as female. E. O. James, an authority on prehistoric religion, believes that these burial practices were 'in the nature of life giving ritual closely connected with the female figurines and other symbols of the Goddess cult' [48].

As the paleolithic age gave way to the neolithic, human social organisation and consequently religious ideas became more sophisticated and complex as did the way this sacred essence was seen and expressed. Many thousands of Goddess figures, massive earthworks and single standing stones (menhirs) found throughout Europe attest to the extent of these early beliefs. The reason why Crete is so important in the study of prehistoric religion and social organisation is that, just like Malta, its geographical isolation allowed its people to continue to celebrate the deity in Her traditional form far later than in many other areas whose location made them more vulnerable to assault from hostile cultures.

The source of the patriarchal ideology and religion that was superimposed onto the traditions of Old European culture seems to have been from the peoples inhabiting areas that had poorer climates. Such communities scratched out a survival in these arid areas while their contemporaries, living in more fertile regions, had to a large extent been freed from the burden of daily survival, enabling them to develop sophisticated artistic traditions and build great civilisations. The Indo-European stockbreeders, from northern peripheral regions would have had contact with some of these cultures through the mobility available to them from riding horses.

The evidence presented by Gimbutas of the Kurgan waves, excursions into the civilisations of Old Europe by marauding bands of patriarchally-organised men, supports this hypothesis. The waves were in three phases; 4300–4200, 3400–3200 and 3000–2380 BC. The timing of these waves may have been associated with particularly difficult climactic conditions, perhaps combined with population pressure, which called for drastic measures in order to continue the survival of the group.

In the traditional cultures that were invaded however, the power of the Goddess and Her legitimation of gynocentricity was not to be dislodged easily. In the first phase of the path towards patriarchy a male consort was introduced to the previously sexually independent and omnipotent female deity. In Egyptian religion, for example, Isis had been

Crete Reclaimed

Ruler of the Universe in her own right long before the year godling Osiris was invented to be her consort. As the transition evolved, the power of the Goddess was divided into various elements or persona which serving to further weaken Her overall dominion. It also allowed for some of these elements to be appropriated by the now well established year godling. [49] In the complex Greek pantheon deities of both sexes are constantly vying for ascendancy until Zeus is eventually established as supreme. A schematic representation of this process is:

Supreme Universal Monotheism (the Great Goddess)
::
Monotheism (the Great Goddess + the year godling consort)
::
Polytheism (majority Goddesses, some gods)
::
Polytheism (Goddesses diminishing in numbers and powers)
::
(Almost) Universal Patriarchal Monotheism

The timescale for these changes can be expressed as follows:

◄─────────────────────►◄────────►◄─────►
  Monotheism   Polytheism Mono.

The cultures the Kurgans invaded had never known anything other than the concept of a female god and the change was to be tortuous and bloody. The first phase of the above schema would have lasted into the end of the neolithic period around 3000 BC and in some areas, notably Crete, well into the bronze age (see page 11). In other cultures, like Japan, the concept of a supreme Goddess remains to the present day, though within a patriarchal structure. Similarly degraded remnants also remain in the Hindu and Roman Catholic religions and serve as a reminder of how religious symbolism can be manipulated by the ideology of the ruling group.

Elinor Gadon points out that the new monotheism of patriarchy is less that 4000 years old and that the idea of the exclusive authority of one universal male god goes back less than 1700 years to the conversion of the Roman Emperor Constantine in 320 AD and his imposition of christianity as a state religion [50].

The Goddess and Her Symbols

This religious picture is broadly mirrored by the organisation of society. The second phase of the schema corresponds to a human ruling queen and her consort. In Egypt and many other cultures, royalty had always been passed through the female line. In the transition to patriarchy endogamy (sister-brother marriage), was introduced to allow the heir's brother to make a genetic contribution to her royal offspring. In other cultues the human consort parallelled the year godling of mythology and the ruling queen would take a young lover annually. Marital customs among African queens caused them to treat these consorts as slaves whose death was seen as incidental in the ritual cycle of the society. The Shilluks of Sudan killed their kings in living memory. Their princesses enjoyed the right of free sex and in former days strangled the prince consort to death with their own hands [51].

While the Goddess remained independent, as we can see from Cretan artefacts, it was women who administered Her religion and performed accompanying civil duties. The Ayia Triada sarcophagus suggests that men appropriated these roles by first assisting in ritual. The next stage of the process can be traced in the practices of the Hittites and the Benin of Southern Nigeria. During the transitional phase from matriarchy to patriarchy in these cultures, the king was always accompanied by the queen and also, usually, her mother in order that he might be legitimated in important civil and religious roles.

We can imagine that the original arrangement would be a queen ruling alone, much as Elizabeth I of England did. Clan leadership had been a woman's birthright but eventually her brother husband came to rule in her stead. As men gradually took power from women, the male year godling grew in stature. Ultimately even the most sacred and previously exclusively female roles of priestess and leader were usurped by men. Monogamous marriage and powerful taboos against women's sexuality were established in order that inheritance could be determined through the male line. As we can see from the practice of stoning to death for adultery recorded in the Bible, these taboos were enforced with rigid and inhuman cruelty. Clitoral excision and infibulation is still perpetrated against girls in many countries.

Greek mythology is the story of the establishment of patriarchal power in the Aegean. The strength of the ideology that they had to overcome can be be deduced from the complex mythological manoeuvering that were necessary to establish Zeus at the head of the Helladic pantheon. His creators, the patriarchal ruling class, skilfully borrowed from the old tradition. The birthplace of the king of the new sky gods was set on Crete, in a sacred cave, where he was said to have been raised on milk and honey, foods which have powerful associations with the old Goddess tradition. Later, in imitation of the Goddess as creator of all life he even gives birth, albeit through his head (the source of ideology), to Athena who, as Jacquetta Hawkes points out, combines elements of the old Goddess religion with essential characteristics of patriarchy.

Before his metamorphosis to the most powerful god of the Greek pantheon, Zeus had been the humble year godling of the mainland's Great Goddess Hera. In earlier images she takes pride of place on the throne or is featured in a central position while he is displaced to one side. This godling's behaviour may indicate how his progenitors, the Greek patriarchate achieved their dominance in the Aegean. Zeus used deceit and rape to become consort to the previously independent representatives of the Goddess tradition. He then adopted their sacred symbols as a route to sharing, then appropriating their thrones. It was through such devious and violent endeavours that the patriarchs of the classical age undermined the last of the great European matriarchies which had existed on Crete.

The Role of the Godling in Cretan Religion.

The findings on Crete indicate a complete reversal of the present patriarchal situation where the female is invisible. Modern day children are bombarded with the image of the male as central and the female as marginal, with Father Christmas, Jack Frost, snowmen, Fireman Sam, Postman Pat and Spot. Almost the only females in most aspects of children's media are mothers, not of course powerful creators but passive servicers. On bronze age Crete and, to a large extent, in the Mycenaean world, the opposite was true. Even the animals depicted in association with the goddess - lions, griffons and goats - are almost exclusively female. The cornelian lentoid seal from Mycenae is an example of the popular theme of the Goddess flanked by female lions (fig. 73), the 1500 BC sealstone depicts a pregnant or recently whelped bitch (fig. 74) and jugs with breasts (fig. 75) were common. The contents of the Knossos Temple Repositories celebrated the female in all things - jugs with breasts to a cow and her calf, a goat and her kid, the Snake Goddesses and priestess robes.

Although it appears that the activity of bull leaping had a sacred sanction, the bull is never depicted in relation to the Goddess. Baring and Cashford claim the bull, ram and stag to be representative of a male religious principle but the artefacts do not support this. All the symbols of Goddess power are female. When male votaries are featured they are clearly there to emphasise Her omnipotence rather than share in it. They are often depicted shielding themselves or bent backwards because of the power and numinosity (awe and wonder) created by Her presence.

The Goddess and Her Symbols

Because this female centrality is anathema to modern patriarchal sensibilities, much is made of anything which could conceivably be interpreted as male. Even scholars who have made great efforts in their avoidance of ethnocentricism have problems in accepting the lack a male deity on bronze age Crete. Castleden notes that 'it is odd that we find so little in the Minoan religion about male deities'. He goes on to say that we could reasonably expect to find a father god, that such an absence suggests that the bull stands for the male creative force and aggression, that the bull was a surrogate god [52]. For the Cretans however, the creative force was associated absolutely with the female. Their culture had no need of aggression and the male role in reproduction is one of fertilisation rather than creation.

Castleden has done a remarkable job. He has presented the archaeological evidence that gives academic sanction to the true function of Knossos in a way which makes it comprehendible to the lay person. He also has the enviable ability to illustrate his own work. Unfortunately these illustrations can occasionally be somewhat misleading. He describes one signet ring scene as, 'Priestess praying, summoning up a male deity out of a pillar' [53]. His drawing suggests a small penis protruding towards the priestess. On examination of the original object however the protrusion is the top of the traditional broad belt which was worn by both sexes. The figure's flowing hair indicates descent and it also seems to be young but, given that both sexes wore this type of garb for athletic activity, there is nothing to suggest its sex. It also appears that the small figure's hair is knotted up on top in a similar fashion to that of the priestess. This figure could represent a godling but it could equally well represent the Goddess with a daughter.

TOP Fig. 73 *Goddess with stylised head seated on face-shaped stool flanked by lionesses. Cornelian lentoid seal from Mycenae.*

BOTTOM Fig. 74 *Bitch sealstone, 1500 BC.*

Crete Reclaimed

A much earlier commentator and acknowledged expert on Mycenaean and Cretan religion, Martin Nilsson, pointed out that the number of figures that could be claimed to be godlings can be counted on the fingers of one hand. He saw the possible candidates as:

* A small descending figure with a bow: gold ring, Ashmolean Museum.

* A small descending figure with a spear: gold ring, Knossos.

* Figure with, lion, shield and spear: seal, Knossos.

* Figure with bow: seal, Ayia Triada.

All these examples come from rings or sealstones which leaves them open to misinterpretation. Firstly because of the minuteness of the detail and secondly because the fresco painter's convention of distinguishing the sex of the figure by colour is lacking.

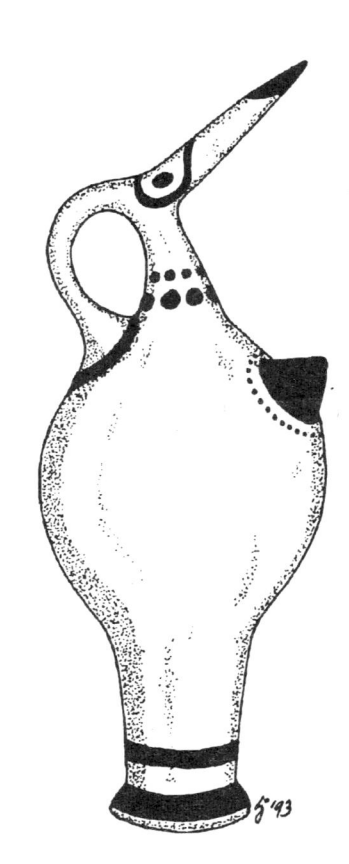

Fig. 75 Bird jar with breasts, Thera, 1500 BC.

As the list shows, these figures are usually descending holding a spear or bow or a shield and spear. Because of the later association of weapons and the hunt with men, Nilsson is drawn to the conclusion that the figure is male because it is holding a spear, bow or shield. Cretan figures which are clearly female (fig. 77) however can be seen holding what appear to be spears but may be some kind of ceremonial staff.

The second example on Nilsson's list refers to a Mycenaean seal, on which the Goddess is depicted seated beneath a tree as votaries approach Her. A figure which may represent Her daughter stands behind Her, and the tree, plucking fruit from it. A small shield-shaped figure holding a staff appears to be hovering in the air, only its arms and legs and head are visible. He compares this with the similar much

160

The Goddess and Her Symbols

larger limestone painting of the Goddess as Shield. Because the latter is a painting her sex is identified by the white skin colour. Nilsson concedes that the figure descending or manifesting in the sealstone scene could equally well be female.

He also points out that when such a figure is depicted, the attentions of the Goddess are devoted not to this figure but to Her approaching votaries. Even if one were to accept that these small descending figures are male, Nilsson believes that because they are shown 'armed', it is probable that the scenes depict a male intrusion on a sacred ritual. He concludes that:

> The male deity is, however, of rare occurrence and his position a distinctly inferior one. His advent is late, and he may indicate that already the northern influence of the Achaeans was causing their god to be accepted by the Minoans, though always subordinate to the indigenous Goddess. [54]

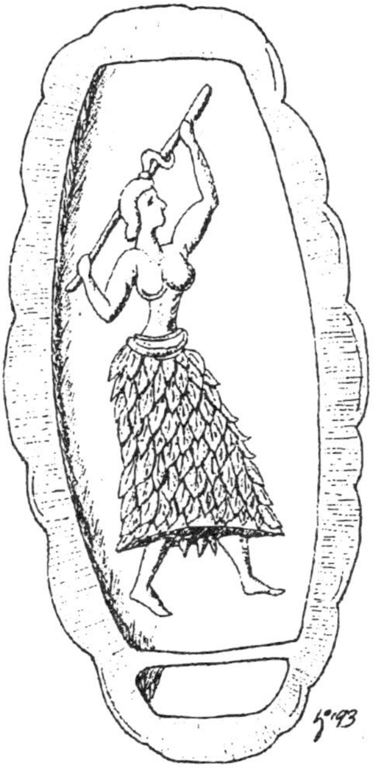

In other words, Nilsson accepted that the Goddess religion of the ancient Cretans did not encompass a male element. The appearance of a godling was not contemporary with the period on Crete that I refer to as matriarchal. It was introduced as part of the patriarchal take-over of this sacred island as it had been in many other cultures.

There are a number of artefacts that reveal that the Goddess was associated not with a male godling or son but with a daughter (figs 78–80) In the Cycladic figure the daughter is situated on her mother's head. In the Akkadian image she stands behind the enthroned Goddess, a position familiar from Cretan-Mycenaean artefacts (fig. 77 for example). Demeter and Persephone can be depicted as equals or as mother and daughter. These mother-daughter images have largely

Fig. 76   Priestess in leaf skirt with staff, Vaphio, South Peleppones, 1500 BC.

Fig. 77 Signet ring, Mycenae, 1500 BC. Goddess seated under sacred tree with female adorants. A small daughter(?) figure stands behind the tree touching its fruit. Sun and moon symbols are separated from the main scene by wavy lines and a small figure with a shield-like body and a staff hovers above. Other symolism includes heads, labyris and poppies.

been ignored and we are therefore missing what might be an important stage in the development of religious ideology because it is associated exclusively with the female principle.

Attitudes to Death and Burial Practices

Patriarchal societies, with their strong emphasis on war and, consequently, death, cannot afford to have a theology which does not include an afterlife. At the centre of Cretan religion there was the awareness that life is cyclical and that death regenerates the earth so that further growth is possible. As Henrietta Groenwegen Frankfort, whom Jaquetta Hawkes describes as being, 'a minutely analytical art historian', comments:

> . . . the human bid for timelessness was disregarded [by the Cretans] in the most complete acceptance of the grace of life the world ever known. [55]

The Goddess and Her Symbols

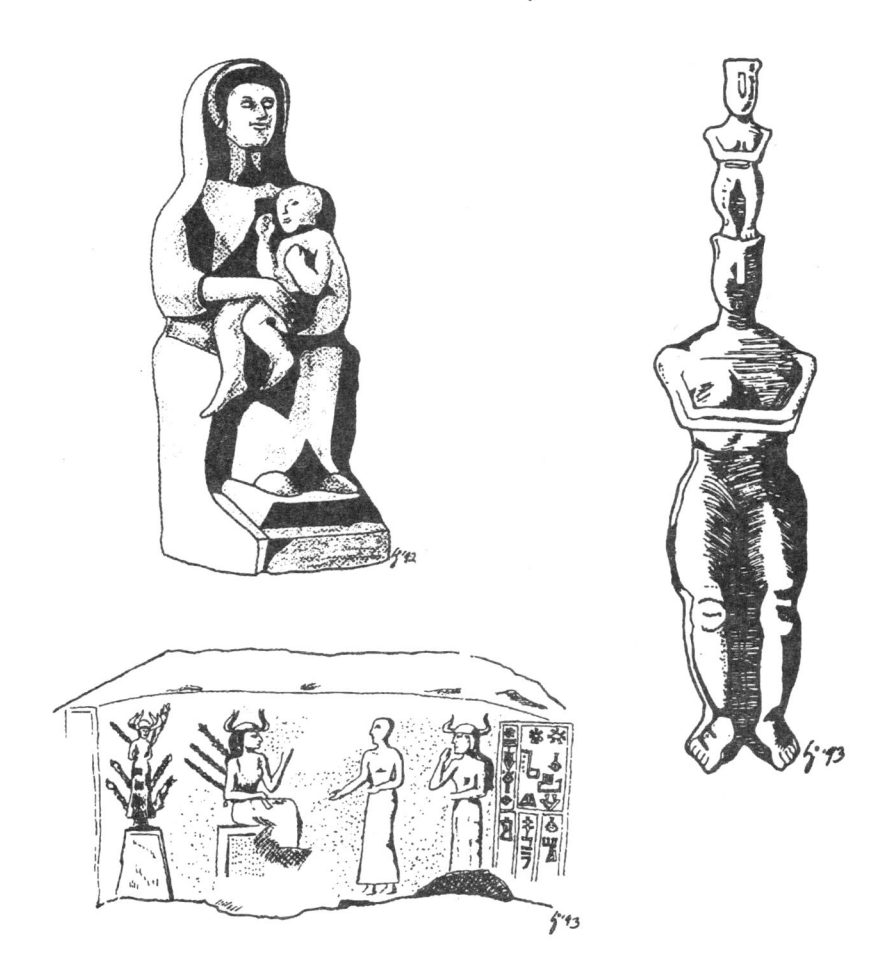

TOP LEFT Fig. 78 Demeter and Kore, stone, Thebes, Boeotia.
A blueprint for the virgin Mary?

RIGHT Fig. 79 Goddess with daughter on her head, Aegean Islands,
1700-1600 BC. This Aegean figure may represent the origins of the
Eleusian Demeter-Kore mysteries.

BOTTOM Fig. 80 Goddess with Daughter standing behind Her.
Akkadian cylinder seal, 3500 BC. Note the sprouting vegetation
coming from both sacred women.

Crete Reclaimed

Similarly, Platon prosaically notes that:

A hymn to nature as Goddess seems to be heard from everywhere, a hymn of joy and life. The agony of death so familiar in prehistoric civilisation is not perceptible here. [56]

Many of the burial traditions of the Cretans seem to have been brought from Anatolia by the first neolithic settlers. At Catal Huyuk it was the practice to truss corpses tightly in the foetal position, knees to chin, and leave them exposed until all the flesh had decayed or been eaten. In the case of foetuses the small body would be carefully boiled so that the flesh could be removed leaving the fragile embryonic skeleton intact. Once the flesh had gone the soul was deemed to have left the body and the remains were buried under the sleeping platforms of the houses. Children were buried under the much larger platforms of the women, never with the men and many more female remains were found buried than male ones.

On Crete burials were communal. Corpses, which had been contracted into the same foetal position, were laid on tomb floors or, in later times placed in twos or threes, into a *pithos* or *larnax* (clay casket). They were left with the goods needed for daily life until the flesh decayed. The remains were cleared away into heaps to make way for new burials once the flesh had gone. Sometimes these bones were then placed in a *larnax*. From around 1400 onwards, those who had commanded great respect in life were left as they had been buried.

Archaeologists have noted that the richest deposits of grave goods were found in the earliest tombs. Beehive-shaped *tholos* tombs on Crete predate the first equivalents on the mainland by a hundred years. Each town had one or more of these large circular tombs with its round domed wooden or stone roof and small entrance that had to be crawled through. They all faced east and were used for the clan of any one particular area for hundreds of years. Rectangular additions were made to them in the Early Minoan or Middle Minoan periods around 2000 BC when *pithoi* and *larnax* began to be used for burials.

The Temple Tomb to the south of Knossos, with its complexity and lavishness, is unusual for Crete. It is cut into rock and built on two floors with a porticoed court, vestibule, pillar crypt and sepulchre chamber. This type of complex is similar to the legendary Cretan tomb in Sicily which is associated with Aphrodite. It would have been here that some of the great Cretan queens were laid to rest. It was cleared out in the early 14th century BC when it may have been reused for the burial of an old man and a child, though very few skeletal remains were recovered.

Not all the burial practices of the bronze age Cretans are understood. Archaeologists have difficulty, for example, explaining the shortage of bones at some of the sites. In one *tholos* tomb which was used for generations, only eight skulls and few other bones were found. This could be explained by the practice of clearing away the remains into ossuaries. At Arkhanes two hundred skulls were discovered heaped together, suggesting that skulls may have been buried separately.

A rather gruesome and as yet unexplained find was made by British archaeologist Peter Warren in a building to the north-west of Knossos, beyond the Unexplored Mansion. Excavations revealed a collection of children's skeletons. Knife marks on the bones suggest that all 299 of them had been carefully dismembered. The implication is that the children had been killed and eaten. Although I refer to the matter here, Warren insists that this was not in any sense a burial; 'this was a town building with no burial, funerary or cemetery connections' [57].

Donald Tumasonis, a social anthropologist, proffers a less sensational explanation. He refers us to the observations of J.C. Lawson, a student of Greek religion and folklore, who described the Greek belief that the dissolution of the body is essential before proper burial can take place [58]. In modern Greece bodies are interred for three to seven years until they are clean of flesh, at which time they are ritually cleaned in a religious ceremony before being reinterred in the family vault. Lawson recorded his own eye witness account of people in Leonidi in the Peleponnese at the end of the 19th century. He saw them hacking the flesh off the remains and scouring the bones with soap and soda. They worked conscientiously for two days until all the bones were white and clean [59]. It seems reasonable to deduce from this that, fearing the small bodies of the children may have been removed and eaten by animals, they were not excarnated but instead had their flesh removed by human hand. Warren counters this view, however, by pointing out that there were no longtitudinal scraping marks on the bones, as would be expected if they had been cleaned for reburial.

The only other site associated with death with sinister overtones is the temple at Anemospilia. There is every indication that a boy was sacrificed here around 1700 BC, the time of the destruction of the old Temple Palaces. But there is evidence to suggest that the activities at this temple were conducted by people with ideas at variance with those of mainstream Cretan culture. One of the people involved in the proceedings was a man who, in contrast to the native Cretans, was

Crete Reclaimed

extremely tall (1.78 metres). He was also wearing a ring made from silver and iron, something unique on Crete at this time. If the group were visitors or residents from another culture, they may have felt that this sacrifice, perhaps of one of the servants or a family member, was an appropriate response of appeasement to the deity who was causing the earth to shake. It appears, however, that the Goddess was not impressed. Aside from the victim, who was already dead, the three other participants in the sacrifice ritual were killed in the earthquake. Other indications of the temple's alien provenance are its design and the fact that it was never reused.

Finds at Phourni, a large cemetery complex near to Anemospilia, are more in accord with the evidence from the rest of the island. What was discovered here in 1965 by Effie and John Sakellarakis reflects the tenor of life portrayed in the frescoes and other artefacts from Knossos. In the side chamber of a beehive tomb, Tholos Tomb A, the remains were discovered of a great queen who died in about 1400 BC. The body had been sealed in a lidded *larnax*. She was dressed in a robe trimmed with gold beads and decorated with over 140 pieces of fabulous jewellery. Many of these were gold and included five sacred signet rings and two seals. Two tiny amulet boxes had been placed on her breast. Jacquetta Hawkes describes the dress the Goddess is wearing on one of the rings, which depicts the uprooting of a tree or bough from a triple shrine, as 'much like her own'.

In 1975 the remains of a second queen were discovered in Tholos Tomb D in the same cemetery. She was arrayed in a gold diadem and lay on her left side, facing Mount Juktas, with a copper mirror in her left hand. One of the site workers believed the queen to have had green eyes for this is how she appeared in a dream [60].

These finds are the Cretan equivalent of the Mycenaean shaft graves or the tomb of Tutankhamun in Egypt. They are the most important burials found on Crete yet, predictably, they have been practically ignored by the scholarly establishment. They earn only a few lines in an edition of the *National Geographic.* Had these lines not been referred to by scholars like Gadon and Hawkes, who have remained committed to gender issues despite the limits that this must have place on their academic careers, they could easily be missed. The 1991 book *Archanes* by the excavators of the site, Professor John Sakellarakis and Dr Effie Sapouna-Sakellaraki, is an excellent source though unfortunately not easy to obtain in Britain.

Just as patriarchal influences have imposed selectivity on the recording and teaching of history, there has been an equivalent effect on archaeology in the form of the relative importance which it accords

The Goddess and Her Symbols

to the artefacts uncovered. As Riane Eisler points out, the work of James Mellaart at Catal Huyuk and Hacilar was so threatening to the patriarchal status quo that instructions were given for the excavations to be abandoned on the grounds that 'further work on the site would only yield repetitive results of no great scientific value'. At Hacilar and Catal Huyuk Mellaart had found overwhelming evidence for

> ... one great inspiring force, the old religion of Anatolia, the cult of the Great Goddess.' He also found clear evidence at both sites for matrifocal social organisation. He described the decision to abandon the excavations as 'one of the most tragic chapters in the history of archaeology. [61]

5
Not with a Whimper

The Fall

Perhaps one of the greatest puzzles surrounding bronze age Crete, which had thrived in peace for some 2000 years, is the nature of its end. Despite all the evidence from different disciplines, this phase in Crete's past cannot be explained satisfactorily.

All the great centres of celebration and the towns, including parts of Knossos town, and the Country House Shrines, were destroyed by fire in 1450 BC. Knossos, however, survived for at least a further 75 years. Recent radiocarbon dating evidence indicates that it may even have continued into the first millennium BC. Although the Temple Palace suffered some damage there was clearly nothing that could not be repaired. If this was the case at Knossos why not at the other great centres? It appears that the Temple-Palace sites at Hania and Arkhanes also continued in use after 1450 but I have not included them in this discussion as they have not yet been fully excavated.

The cause of this great wave of destruction is variously claimed to have been an earthquake, the eruption of nearby Thera (Santorini), the invasion of large numbers of Mycenaeans (from the Peleponnese), or a combination of all three. Hood for example, argued that natural disasters left Crete in a weakened state making the island vulnerable to attack by the Mycenaeans. Evans proposed, and many other scholars accepted, the theory that the Mycenaeans had control of Knossos following the generalised destruction on the island.

There are difficulties with all these theories. The opinions of archaeologists, vulcanologists and geologists are still at variance and the picture is confused. The different pieces of the puzzle can only be presented for consideration.

One argument is that since it was clearly an earthquake that caused the destruction of the first Temple Palaces in 1700 BC, this is a plausible explanation for the later waves of devastation. Wunderlich, a geologist

Not with a Whimper

by training, and many notable siesmologists argue that the effects of an earthquake are always so sudden that there is no time to salvage possessions or avoid loss of life. On Crete, however, there is no evidence for there being any loss of life in either the 1450 devastation or the subsequent fall of Knossos. With the exception of the island of Mochlos, no human remains were found in the debris of the sites of buildings that were destroyed. Perhaps the modern experts are unable to understand these events because they have not allowed for an ability, now lost in humans, to predict earthquakes, similar to the sixth sense that animals seem to have in relation to the weather.

If the Temple Palaces were not destroyed by an earthquake, could it have been a volcanic eruption? When Thera (Santorini) erupted, it did so with a force that is estimated as being three times that which fired Krakatoa in 1883 AD. The great Theran eruption was one of the most dramatic in history. Around 33 square miles of land were blown up and sunk. The island all but disappeared, being reduced from its original round shape to a mere crescent. When Krakatoa erupted 36,380 people were killed in one day in Java and Sumatra by 50 foot tidal waves. The lack of human remains in the Cretan settlements on Thera indicate that the residents here had sufficient warning to escape, taking with them only their most valuable possessions. But there are modern parallels for this too. Lyvia Morgan, a scholar with a particular interest in Theran frescoes, proffers the modern example of Sertsi, a volcanic island in the Icelandic archipelago which erupted from the sea in 1963. In this case all the inhabitants of neighbouring vulnerable islands were evacuated by sea in six hours. [1]

Experts argue that an inevitable accompaniment of the eruption and implosion of Thera would have been huge tidal waves along the shores of Crete together with earth tremors and a blanket of ash. This would have made agriculture difficult, if not impossible, for some time. A situation which, Sinclair Hood suggests, would have been an ideal time for invasion with the inhabitants in a weakened state suffering from economic and social problems. This theory, however, is also difficult to substantiate. There are no geological signs, claim Wunderlich and others, of any massive blanket of ash on Crete [2]. Nor, he believes, is there any clear evidence of the secondary effects that would have accompanied such an event. The fires, tidal waves and landslides would have resulted in untold fatalities. Moreover, if tidal waves had caused havoc on Crete, Wunderlich argues, they would have had the same effect on the Greek coast. It seems improbable then that while Crete was suffering from the effects of a volcanic eruption they were invaded by Mycenaean Greeks from an undisturbed mainland.

It was hoped that the 1970 excavations of the Cretan town of Akrotiri on Thera by Spyridon Marinatos would reveal clues as to what really happened. Marinatos, who was later killed in an accident on the site, found the remains of a sizable Cretan settlement with many well-preserved frescoes and other artefacts. His excavations also revealed that an earthquake had preceded the eruption and been responsible for significant structural damage to the city which had subsequently been buried under a blanket of pumice. It was this layer of pumice that was responsible for protecting the frescoes.

The insurmountable problem for scholars who see the fall of the Temple Palaces on Crete as a result of the eruption of Thera is the 50 year gap that is thought to separate the destruction of Akrotiri, usually cited as being around 1500 BC, and the demise of the majority of the Temple Palaces on mainland Crete around two generations later in 1450. Marinatos' dates for the destruction on both islands rely, to a large extent, on pottery finds. Only few pots at Akrotiri were in the local style but he believed that elements of their design identified them as distinctively Cretan from the 1600–1560 period. Only Late Minoan IA pottery was found in the latest deposits. He dated the eruption at 1525–20, suggesting a 70 year gap before the Cretan destructions in 1450.

One suggestion which tries to account for this discrepancy is that there were two eruptions – the first having little effect on Crete but destroying Akrotiri and the second destroying Crete. J.V. Luce is one of the proponents of this theory. The depth of his research and commitment to this subject appears to be unaffected by his being a formal scholar of Greek rather than geology. In 1969 he argued that Thera began erupting in 1500 but the first eruption was small and probably confined to Thera itself, the final tumultuous explosion coming 30 years later in 1470. Castleden, who finds this theory convincing, circumvents the problem of an equally-affected mainland by referring to a north-westerly wind which carried the fall-out from the eruption south-eastwards, away from the Peleponnese. Also the Greek mainland is over twice as far away from Thera as Crete and may therefore also have avoided the effects of tidal waves. This theory explains why the Temple Palaces to the east of Crete were abandoned but not the continuation of Knossos itself which, in Castleden's analysis, lies firmly within the fallout zone [3].

Another problem with this theory is that vulcanologists have difficulty with the proposal of two eruptions. They cannot accept that after lying dormant for so many years, Thera would erupt twice, in so short a space of time. They will only allow one eruption around that period which would have lasted no longer than a year. This, they say, is demonstrated by the lack of extensive erosion between the ash layers which would have been apparent had there been the gap the archaeologists claim.

Other recent suggestions are that the earthquake and eruption were separated by a 50 year gap. In his excavations of the Unexplored Mansion, Mervyn Popham noted the damage caused by an earthquake around 1500 which interrupted building work on this structure [4]. In this analysis the residents would have abandoned Akrotiri either prior to or following the earthquake. If we accept this theory, it is interesting that there was no attempt to return to the settlement following the earthquake, despite the lack of an eruption, for a further 50 years.

Clearly the scientists are at a loss to explain what happened. The link between the eruption of Thera and the laying to waste of the great Temple Palaces is at best tenuous. In 1977 Hans Pichler and Wolfgang Schiering made the dramatic statement that, 'There is no connection between the decline of Minoan civilisation and the Theran outburst' [5].

More recently, archaeologist Christos Doumas citing the works of S. Manning, published in 1988 and 1990, places the eruption of Thera much earlier: some decades before the end of the seventeenth century BC. As a consequence, he believes that the splendid Theran frescoes should be dated no later than 1759 BC, over 300 years before the mass destructions on Crete [6].

Natural Disaster or Human Hand?

As we have already noted, when all the great Temple Palaces were destroyed around 1450 there was no evident loss of life and the towns were in use again almost instantly following the destruction. All these factors, together with geological and other evidence, indicate that it may not have been natural catastrophe alone that overtook the island. One possibility is that natural disaster was augmented by human hand. The hand of the priestess rulers, with the power of the Goddess vested in them, who arranged for the return of the Temple Palaces to the earth, just as they had supervised the covering over of the sacred treasures in the Temple Repositories. An organised destruction and burial of the great sacred centres would have allowed the ruling Queens to maintain the sanctity of their most sacred religious treasures and buildings.

Much is made by Arthur Evans and others of the state in which the Throne Room and the Shrine of the Double Axes were found. Their condition suggested to these scholars the sense of an interrupted ceremony as if the participants were attempting to ward off some great catastrophe. This theory ignores the possibility that the ritual areas were in constant use and that, even had they not been in use, the ritual paraphernalia would have remained in situ. Even if a ritual had been in progress at the time of the destruction of Knossos and the Shrine of the Double Axes, it would not have been one designed to prevent the eruption of Thera. As we have already noted Evans believed that 75 years separated the eruption and Knossos' final demise and the Shrine is thought not to have been abandoned until around 1100 BC.

The evidence which has been interpreted as indicating that a ceremony to prevent an impeding disaster was in progress was not limited to Knossos. Perhaps the clearest indications come from Zakro. Thus we have consistent findings across a long period of time: 1450, around 1375 and 1100 BC. Could it be that if the evidence is indicative of rituals in progress, that they were intended to augment rather than prevent destruction? Such a theory would explain why no one was buried in the debris.

It might be argued that the priestesses used magical phenomena to harness the forces of nature, calling up a strong wind to fan the flames of their ritual fires. Or it could be claimed that they used spiritual practices to foretell the future in the oricular tradition that survived to classical Greece, the acclaimed age of rationality. Such theories would explain how the populations of Thera and the coastal and low lying areas of Crete escaped the devastation of the eruption. A more rational explanation is that the fires were planned to coincide with strong winds which the priestesses were able to predict by their understanding of physics and geography.

The reason for the destructions is evident in the political climate of the times. When the great Temple Palaces were destroyed Cretan influence was at its height in the Aegean but the menace of more aggressive cultures in the surrounding regions was growing. The Mycenaeans, who had acted as a buffer between the Cretans and other more hostile peoples, were eager pacifiers of both the Great Goddess and Her descendants that were later to make up part of the Greek pantheon. They were, however, also assigning increasing powers to the male godlings which gave ideological credence to their militaristic style of living. Their way of life was to become plunder and destruction, something hard to reconcile with the more peaceful attributes of the old Goddess tradition. Their growing greed for material wealth was alien to the Cretans for whom wealth abounded and was held in common. Dramatic changes were sweeping through the continent. That other great sacred island, Malta, was invaded around 1500 BC by warring peoples from mainland Europe who had copper daggers, axes and sharp obsidian arrowheads [7] and the whole of Greece, with the exception of Athens was soon to be overtaken by the barbaric Dorians.

Whatever caused the great disasters the result was that the Temple Palaces and most of their treasures would be buried under a protective covering of earth, unseen and unusable by the patriarchal tribes who were later to invade the island. When they became convinced of the inevitability of the strangle hold that patriarchy was placing around the rest of Europe it seems reasonable to suppose that Crete's leaders decided to take steps to preserve some of their most sacred icons. We know that select ritual articles were secreted in the Temple Repositories where they waited silently under the earth for three thousand years until they could be reclaimed, acknowledged, preserved and once again held as common, not private, wealth. The result of the mass destructions, perhaps not an accident, is that this culture is now as thoroughly and splendidly documented as any other in the world, except perhaps for that of Egypt where, though for quite different reasons, the rulers had also made a point of burying some of their greatest treasures.

Once the majority of the sacred centres had been buried (intentionally or otherwise), the activities of the island were to resume much as normal but with administration and large collective religious activities being concentrated more centrally at Knossos and, very probably, nearby Arkhanes and Hania in the west. Archaeologists are intrigued by the quality of the finds that have been collected from the Kastelli district of Hania and small areas of the remains, of what is clearly a Temple Palace, have been uncovered at Arkhanes. People on the rest of the island still celebrated the Goddess, but in small sanctuaries, in the open air and in caves.

Invasion or Immigration?
The Arrival of the Mycenaeans

The centuries between the fall of the great Temple Palaces in 1450 and the Dorian invasion in 1100 BC are poorly understood, though the presence of two parallel art forms, Linear B inscriptions, a change in burial customs and elements of militarism suggest a strong Mycenaean presence on the island. There is no reason to suppose, however, that the new settlers were in control.

There is a great deal of disagreement on this issue and theories are constantly revised with the discovery of new evidence. The date of the destruction of Knossos, for example, has recently been placed as late as 1150 BC, only fifty years before the devastating invasion of the Dorians.

It is now the predominant view that the Mycenaeans were not a hostile force on Crete. There is every indication that their presence on the island was a benign one, with their culture existing alongside that of

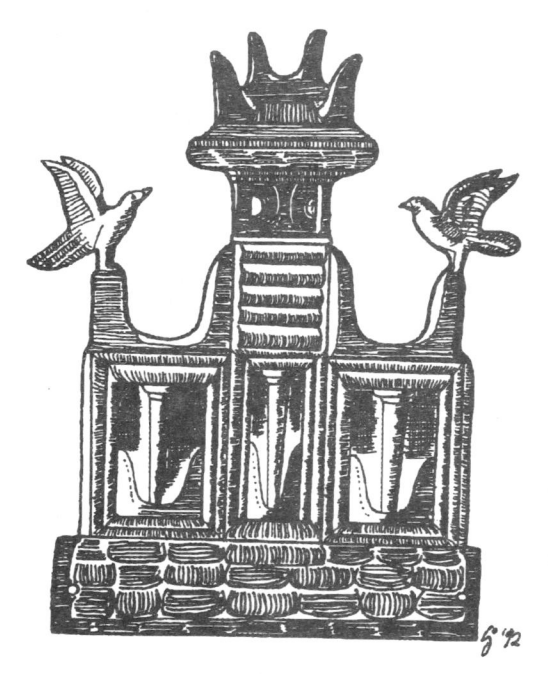

Fig. 81 Gold Ornament, Grave Circle A, Mycenae. This shrine's design includes many of the sacred features of Cretan religion and is interchangeable with a Cretan shrine. Its tripartite design can be seen in the miniature Temple or Grandstand fresco, on the Zakro rython and the remnants of the facade by the same name at Knossos. The Horns of Consecration, downward tapering pillars and perching birds are also common features of sacred Cretan architecture.

the native Cretans rather than overshadowing it. The Mycenaeans themselves were the product of a mixture of the middle Helladic mainland tradition and the civilising influence of the Cretans. Scholars highlight the dramatic effect their exchanges with the Cretans had on these once 'flint hearted' barbarians, in the centuries prior to their mass migration to the island. Even the most casual observers can appreciate the changes in the style of their art before and after their sustained contact with Crete. The Mycenaeans had been deeply affected by the religious imagery and beliefs of the Cretans (fig. 81) and had taken these ideas to mainland Greece and beyond. Wherever they settled they took with them their small bird-like Goddesses (fig. 50) which, according to Marija Gimbutas, express the deity in a way common throughout ancient matriarchal Europe. These small statues have been found as far afield as Syria and Italy.

Evidence from the Mycenaean's homeland in the Peleponnese indicates that the social status of women there mirrored that of women on Crete. The gold brooch of about 1600 BC (fig. 46) depicting the Goddess adorned with a fantastic headdress proclaims the high esteem in which women were held both through the splendour which is

Not with a Whimper

ABOVE Fig. 82 Mycenaean Fresco, Palace of Tiryns 1400–1100 BC. The importance of this woman (possibly a queen or priestess) is expressed by her exaggeratedly large breast.

TOP RIGHT Fig. 83 Mycenaean woman 1600–1400 BC. The naturalness of the figure, the jewellery and the excellence of design identify the painter of this fresco as Cretan. Her hair is shaped into a sacral knot.

RIGHT Fig. 84 Women's procession. Fragmentary fresco, Palace of Tiryns, 1400–1100 BC.

associated with the female deity and the importance of the woman who would wear such an object. Other indications are Mycenaean frescoes (figs 82–84 for example) and burials. It is difficult to know whether the many Cretan artifact found at Mycenaean sites belonged to Mycenaeans or whether, in some instances at least, these would have belonged to Cretan residents. Evidence of Cretan settlers is recorded in the Linear B texts from Pylos (see below).

Around 1200 BC there is evidence of a further peaceful settlement by newcomers from Mycenaean Greece whose principle towns and palaces on the mainland had been burned down by a new wave of barbarian invasions. This new Cretan-Mycenaean culture saw the beginning of a return to the prosperity of old, but any optimism for a restoration of ancient glory was dashed a century later with the invasion of the Dorians in great numbers bringing the bronze age on Crete to an end.

The Written Evidence

The linear A inscriptions that have survived on ritual objects indicate the script's sacred use, perhaps in the form of prayers, hymns or dedications. In contrast, Linear B was used to make lists of people, goods and offerings. One scholar described the Linear B tablets as the equivalent of the contents of several wastepaper baskets.

The change to the use of Linear B at Knossos was once taken as an indicator of Mycenaean rule there. Even Hood, however, who believed that the evidence points to a Mycenaean invasion, did not suppose that the Achaeans arrived in large numbers, took over Knossos and immediately started using their own written language to administer what was left of Cretan society. The Linear B listings are so sophisticated and in such minute detail that they could not have been made by an invading force. It would have taken the concerted efforts of a large section of the Cretan civil service to arrange and execute the task [8]. It seems that it was Cretan scribes who developed this proto-Greek script which was subsequently exported to the mainland.

The date of the tablets are a further source of scholarly contention. Evans estimate of 1400 BC was derived from the context in which they were found and his own theory of there being a decline at Knossos during this period following an invasion and take-over by the Mycenaeans. The validity of both these points has been questioned by subsequent scholars. Further excavations at Knossos, comparisons of pottery found at different levels and careful examination of McKenzie's (Evans' director of works) original excavation notes, have all cast doubt on Evans' dating of the tablets. L.R. Palmer, Professor of Comparative Philology at Oxford University in the 1960s [9] and, more recently,

Not with a Whimper

E. Hallager, one of the leaders of the Swedish-Greek excavation team at Hania [10], argue that the tablets should be dated much later, at 1150 and 1200 BC respectively. These revised dates relate to the time of the final fall of the labyrinth because the tablets were only preserved because of the fires which destroyed it.

One of the reasons given by scholars who believe that the Mycenaeans were in control at Knossos is the sense of a military presence thought to be conveyed by the tablets. While some do list spears and arrows these may, as Castleden argues, have been used for hunting. Professor John Chadwick, who has worked on the deciphering of the tablets for over 40 years [11], gets no impression of a military headquarters from his reading of them. He believes that some of the so-called 'military' tablets, which record chariot units, may have been practice pieces for scribes to learn the new script. He notes curious deletions and repetitions on some of them as if the symbols were being tried out. The tablets do not suggest a standing army. Many of the units have no horses or only one horse while others have horses but no chariots and a number have missing armour (courslets) [12]. Clearly these tablets cannot be taken as evidence of a military presence at Knossos.

Another important point is raised by Linda Baumbach's analysis of the personal names included in the tablets. She noted that not only were Greek names in a minority of 1:5 but also that there was no discernible status difference between Greek and native Cretan names. On tablet As 1516, for example 8 out of 31, 7 out of 23 and 2 of 12 or 13 names in the lists were Greek. Of the D series tablets only 5 of the 22 names were Greek [13].

Even at this late stage the tablets offer no evidence of a King Minos or any other king but the 'Potnia Mater' (Mother Goddess), 'Mistress of the Labyrinth', 'Leader of the People' or 'Leader of the Host' are repeatedly mentioned.

Tablets inscribed with a script which is closely related to Linear B were discovered at the Mycenaean palace of Pylos which was not destroyed until 1200 BC. Leonard Palmer believes that the Knossos tablets show later Greek forms than those from Pylos [14]. Non-Greek names (suggesting Cretan settlers) appear on the Pylos tablets that deal with land tenure [15]. This is also suggestive of a peaceful interchange of peoples rather than a relationship of dominance and submission.

So it appears that Knossian scribes (at least some of whom may have been priestesses who recorded the lists of offerings made) developed Linear B from their Linear A which Cretan settlers and then

Mycenaeans took over to the mainland where it grew into general use from its beginnings as a Cretan Temple Palace script. Or, perhaps Cretans developed the script on the mainland and they and/or the Mycenaeans brought it with them when they fled from the devastation caused there by the Dorians in 1200.

Other Evidence

Aside from the Linear B tablets; Mycenaean style *megarons, tholos* tombs and warrior graves have been cited as supporting the idea of Mycenaean domination on Crete at this time. *Tholos* tombs were, however, Cretan in origin. Their use on the island predates their appearance on the mainland.

The graves which contained warriors buried with their weapons and full armour were found in close groupings at Phaistos and Knossos. This in itself is suggestive of a small caste of foreigners rather than a major invasive force. German archaeologist Wolf Dietrich Niemeier, who has written widely on the subject of Knossos, notes that the separate Cretan burials in the grave circle at Pylos are a parallel case [16].

If we attempt to describe the period following 1450 in terms of Mycenaean domination on Crete, it is difficult to explain why they did not sack the great Temple Palaces, most of which would have been accessible to the casual thief? Zakro (the small Temple Palace in eastern Crete packed with treasures) was practically untouched. In later times the Mycenaeans were famed for their ransacking activities around the Aegean, the distance from Knossos to Zakro would have been no obstacle to them. A Mycenaean-style *megaron* (usually composed of a great hall, porch, vestibule and throne room) was built on the site of Ayia Triada yet great treasures were recovered from the underlying Temple Palace ruins there.

Nor does the theory of Mycenaean aggression address the issues raised by the Throne Room at Knossos. Following the case presented by Helga Reusch [17] and the excavations in the anteroom by Hutchinson and Platon in 1945 there is now enough evidence to suggest that the conception of the complex goes back to Middle Minoan times [18]. Its new layout, however, is thought to date from after the 1450 destructions and shows that the then rulers had a strong reason for rebuilding this suite of rooms during the enigmatic limbo period that followed the destruction of the other Temple Palaces. The Throne Room was undoubtedly designed for and used by the priestesses who were central to the sacred administration based at the Temple Palace. Even scholars who cannot entertain the possibility of a female sovereign at Knossos, and assign the royal women to the dark inner sanctum of the so-called

'Queen's Room', accept the Throne Room suite as the province of priestesses. This strengthens the case for it being indigenous Cretans who continued to be responsible for the affairs of the island.

Life after the Generalised Destruction

By about 1425 BC people had returned to the depopulated areas of central and eastern Crete but the majority of the great Temple Palaces were never to be rebuilt as whole units. Zakro was completely deserted but parts of the other Temple Palaces were brought into use again and some sections of the towns at Gournia, Mallia and Phaistos were rebuilt. Only on the sites of Ayia Triada and Arkhanes were new complexes, Mycenaean style *megarons*, to be constructed, though these occupied only a small part of the total area of the former Temple Palace. This general reuse of the towns but not the Temple Palaces is further confirmation of their sacred rather than secular identity. Even after the Dorian invasion the boundaries of the new Greek town which was built in the shadow of Knossos carefully avoided the vicinity of the, now buried, sacred remains [19].

For a time following the great destructions shoddy, mass-produced pottery was turned out on Crete which compares badly with earlier, quite exquisite, works, though this was soon to improve. Goblets and stirrup jars were the main products of this period. The separate exports of Mycenaean and Cretan wares continued and the religious tradition of the arts is evident in the production of clay Goddess figures. A new style of statue was introduced with a dome-shaped skirt thrown on the potters' wheel and softer gems like steatite were used for sealstones in contrast to the harder quartzes of earlier years.

People still lived in low lying areas and there is nothing to suggest that they were under any threat of attack. Cremation became popular around this time and other changes in burial customs indicate a reduction in the strength of clan ties in some areas. Typical tombs were now horizontal passage graves hollowed out of the soft rock of the hillside for three to four members of a family, suggesting a move from the clan group as a social unit to a smaller, more nuclear, family. A change of dress is indicated by the use of pins and *fibulae* (bone pins or stays) on clothing.

Some time after 1450 the Shrine of the Double Axes was built though it is difficult to say whether it was added to the existing structures at Knossos or rebuilt in an area which had been ruined. Other small shrines at Gournia and Ayia Triada were also established at this time. Both were situated on terraces overlooking the old towns, phoenixes in the ashes of the deserted Temple Palace environs. These shrines, together with others at, for example, Gazi, just to the west of Knossos, and Karphi, in the Lasithi region, were found to contain the traditional ritual trappings of Cretan religion: plaster benches, tripod stands and, in my opinion, some of the finest Goddess figures from the whole civilisation. The Great Goddess was venerated in these small sanctuaries until the last stages of indigenous culture on the island.

The Fall of Knossos

Evans favoured 1400 as the date for the final destruction of Knossos but, subsequent 'Minoan' specialists have proffered alternatives. Hood, Popham, Boardman and Warren all see 1375 or 1380 as more likely dates. Hallager and Palmer, however, estimate it to be as late as around 1200 and 1150 respectively [20]. Archaeologists can only speculate as to why Knossos was not destroyed at the same time as the other Temple Palaces. If we accept the theory that Cretan's religious centres were destroyed intentionally then Knossos may have continued because the queens retained some vestiges of hope, or decided that the eventual decomissioning of one (or perhaps two) centrally located complex(es) could be effected more easily than an island-wide programme of destruction once the final day came.

Evans believed that Knossos was destroyed by a fire fanned by a south facing wind. Wunderlich disagrees. He uses geological evidence to show that a normal fire would have reached 140 C whereas at Knossos (he calculated from the condition of the stone which has structural thermometers in the form of veins of bitumen built into it) the temperature reached was only 100-120 C. He concludes that the stones show evidence not of a destructive fire but fires which would have been deliberately lit and kept burning for illumination, warmth, burnt offerings or ritual purposes. My own view is that the queens and priestesses ritually dismantled this, the most precious of their sacred buildings, and then razed it to the ground. This may have been done in stages, which would have avoided the extreme of temperature eschewed by Wunderlich.

It is no accident that when Knossos was destroyed much of its structure was left intact and not carried away to form houses as happened with many great neolithic monuments like Avebury henge in England. It would make sense for the priestesses to demolish Knossos in order to preserve its sacredness. The great Temple Palaces might have had quite a different fate had they survived until the Dorian invasion.

It seems likely that the final, probably intentional, ritualised destruction of Knossos was accompanied by the end of the long line of priestess queens. All the greatest tombs at Knossos were built prior to its destruction and the queenly burials at Arkhanes are dated around 1400.

Whatever the reason, the period around 1450 BC saw the beginnings of the loss of one of the most advanced, most genial, most sophisticated, and artistically original civilization in European history. Some 340 years later, at the end of Late Minoan IIIC, one of the greatest cultures in the known and catalogued prehistory of the world drew to a close. Fortunately it left us, stored away in the sacred confines of the earth, a great wealth of buildings, frescoes, carvings, ceramics and other artefacts.

The accompaniment to the beginning of the crossing of this great matriarchal culture from the present into the past, became associated with the stupendous implosion of an island. Its passing marked not with a whimper but with a phenomenal bang that reverberated throughout the whole Aegean, a cry from the soul of the earth to mourn her lost glory, the prelude to the end of an era of peace, joy and plenty.

The Final Loss: The Dorian Invasion

The destruction of the old culture and religion of Crete was not brought about by natural disaster or an invasion by the Goddess loving Mycenaeans but with the iron swords of the Dorians who sacked the wealth of matriarchal and Mycenaean cities alike. As Thompson asserts:

> Rude and vigorous invaders subjugate and assimilate a superior culture, thereby bringing about an economic and social upheaval marked by the accumulation of wealth in the hands of an energetic military caste, which, torn by internecine conflicts of succession and inheritance, breaks loose from its tribal bonds into a career of violent, self-assertive individualism - a career as brief as it is brilliant, because their gains have been won by the sword and not by any development of the productive forces. [21]

This invasion fulfilled the worst expectations of the great priestess queens who had begun their preparations some 350 years earlier so that the Temple Palace sites were hidden and protected not only by the earth but by the mists of time.

The Dorians brought with them patrilineal succession, the disenfranchisement of women and monogamy. They had no plans to live as a parallel culture with the indigenous population as the Cretans had done in their colonies and the Mycenaeans on Crete. Though they were clearly influenced by the Cretans, they were also keen to establish

Crete Reclaimed

control. The land, which had once been the responsibility of whole clans, was now taken by Dorian families and apportioned into country estates which only they were allowed to own. The Cretans, with their skills in agriculture, still worked the land but were forced to pay a fixed portion of their product to the Dorian family.

It is easy to image that this gentle people were subjected to barbarity and even genocide. We could reasonably accept this given the archaeological and historical record of the behaviour of peripheral invaders elsewhere. Gimbutas noted that the majority of the female population in Kurgan settlements in Old Europe were not Kurgan but Old European. This suggests that the Kurgans had slaughtered the indigenous male population and had forced the women, or at least the girls, into marital slavery. This practice accords with the advice given by Yewah in the Old Testament to the patriarchal Hebrews [22]. Sites in other parts of Old Europe revealed evidence of human sacrifice and suttee and we know from Herodotus that the Sythians made sacrifices to their sacred dagger, Akenakes [23]. But to assume that such atrocities were committed on Crete is to ignore the evidence of the Gortyns Code.

Gortyns succeeded Phaistos as the chief Greek city of the Messera plain and was later to become the Roman capital of the island. The (amended) legal code that was discovered here on stone tablets must have been the result of the civilising influence of the Cretans on the Dorians. Although these laws were designed to facilitate the introduction of patriarchy and took many liberties and powers away from the old matrilineal clans, it was by later standards quite liberal. It took western civilisation over two thousand years to return to this level of freedom and justice. If the indigenous Cretans had such an influence on this nation that Hesiod describes as a 'filthy race' for whom 'right shall depend on might and piety shall cease to be', it is clear that they had not been almost entirely wiped out or completely subjugated.

The ideology contained in the Greek myths also suggests that the suppression of the matriarchal spirit of the Aegean was a long and difficult process, particularly on Crete. If women were taken in marital slavery they would potentially have been in a position of great influence. In other parts of the Aegean, as we have already noted, there is evidence that Greek clans settling among an alien matrilineal people rose to power by conforming to the indigenous rule of succession. The later Romans could also attribute their success in empire building to their great sense of parallelism in social and religious matters. When Alexander and his legions invaded Egypt they had the same 'hearts of flint' and the same ambitions for their empire as the early Kurgans but it is impossible to say that they were not greatly influenced by what they encountered in the culture that was epitomised by that great Queen Cleopatra, despite her own foreign origins.

The Dorians would certainly have had a much better quality of life on Crete with the cooperation of the indigenous population than without it. The Cretans were extremely skilled, their fingers were both green and golden. They could charm the fruits from the earth to feed the new invaders and spin and weave to clothe them and their ceramic skills could provide them with the trappings of everyday life. Another indicator of the gradualness of this process is the continuation of the old Goddess tradition long after the Doric influx.

Gazi and Karphi

Following the destruction of Knossos there seems to have been an increased reliance on simple rustic sanctuaries as the focus of religious activities for the whole community. There is evidence that over 30 grottos were used for religious purposes in the period between 1380-1200. One of the greatest of these, the remote sacred cave at Psychro, however, continued to be in use until 970 AD.

The two post-Knossos, Late Minoan III (twelfth century BC) settlements at Karphi and Gazi are examples of this move to outlying centres of celebration and provide important evidence for what happened after the destruction of the last Temple Palace and in the 50 years following the Dorian invasion.

The statues found in these sanctuaries show the Goddess with a crown or tiara depicting Her different attributes though, significantly, no snake symbols were found at either site. Among them was the famous Poppy Goddess (fig. 10). Another's crown is replete with Horns of Consecration and singing birds (fig. 42). Many of the scenes on contemporary rings and gemstones show the Goddess seated with Her attendants in a sacred grove, bareheaded with long tresses blowing in the wind.

The rectangular shaped sanctuary at Gazi, a few miles west of Knossos, was discovered in the middle of a vineyard. Although the site was damaged by local villagers when they found it in 1936 and only one room of the sanctuary could be excavated, five Goddess figures were retrieved together with vases and other sacred objects. All have skirts thrown on the potter's wheel and express the traditional gesture of epiphany. Three were large (about 760 mm high) and one was headless. This same style of figure continued to be made by mainland artists until the seventh century BC.

Karphi (its name means 'the nail') was a settlement of 150 rooms, situated on a hilltop rising from the Lasithi plain over 1200 metres above

Fig. 85 Decorated model of sanctuary with detachable door. The Goddess is seated inside in the pose of benediction and viewed by adorants. Painted terracotta, Arkhanes, 1150-1000 BC.

sea level. Arthur Evans was aware of its existence in 1896 but it was not excavated until 1938–9 by Pendlebury. A temple and the house of a priestess leading out of it were discovered and two sealstones found. The house was large and had been complicated by the addition of a Mycenaean-style *megaron*. The temple had an altar and it was on a ledge here that nine bell-shaped terracotta Goddesses, similar to those from Gazi, were discovered. Their arms were raised in the standard position, but the style of the base had altered with the feet being modelled separately to protrude from the skirt. The crown of one of these figures is also adorned with Horns of Consecration. The inhabitants of this settlement buried their dead in beehive-style tombs indicating their adherence to the clan-based lifestyle of matriarchal tradition.

Gazi and Karphi were inhabited from approximately 1150–1050 when they appear to have been quietly deserted leaving, as was the custom in other sanctuaries, most of their sacred goods *in situ*. Thus it is clear that groups of people whose social base was the matriarchal clan celebrated the Goddess in the traditional manner in these remote and inaccessible regions for around 100 years after the Dorian invasion.

Other Goddess figures in this late style have been recovered from Pankalochori near Rethymnon and a sanctuary at Koumasa. The little Temple from Arkhanes with the Goddess sitting inside and votaries on top (fig. 85) also dates from this period. The model has a detachable door expressing the probable feeling of the time, when the traditional Cretan Goddess became hidden from the view of all but Her most persistent followers.

These sites, and there may have been many more than those already identified, were perhaps the last refuges of the indigenous population who were still faithful to the Goddess for many generations after the invasion of the Dorians.

Not with a Whimper

Escape and Emigration

While some of the Cretans unable to accept the new ways of the invaders stayed on to continue their old way of life in remote areas, others fled taking their traditions with them. There is a myth which tells of the Cretan Goddess (She is unmistakable as Her attributes are listed as the snake, trees, poppies and small animals) sending Her people far and wide as messengers with seed corn and a plough, to teach agriculture and a love of the land throughout the world. Thomson details a number of communities which seem to have been descended from Cretan emigrants. One, focussed around the cult of Demeter Europa, was established at Lebadeia near Thebes by the Kadmeioi. A branch of the same clan seems to have settled in Athens where, in the fifth century, a seat was reserved for the Priestess of Demeter Achania in the front row of the theatre of Dionysus [24].

Other evidence of Cretan settlements, dating from this time, exists in Tunisia, Palastine and England. In Tunisia history tells of a tribe known as the Atlantes who were present in the classical period and are thought to have been Cretan in origin. The Philistines mentioned in the Bible (Jeremiah 47:4) as the 'remnants of the country of Caphtor', are also thought to have been Cretans who travelled east settling in the coastal strip of southern Palestine.

Fig. 86 The Goddess Ashera, ivory box lid, Ugarit 1300-1200 BC. The Goddess, holding vegetation, sits atop a rock flanked by goats, demonstrating the influence of Cretans along the Syrio-Palestinian coast. The design has strong similarities with a fresco from the Citadel House, Mycenae, of a woman holding vegetation.

A 13th century BC box lid from Ugarit (fig. 86) depicts the Goddess Ashera. The position of the Goddess on a rock and between two animals standing on their hind legs; Her bared breasts and the design of Her skirt are all derivatives from Cretan sacred art. The way that the Goddess is holding what appear to be pieces of vegetation in Her hands is a common theme in representations of later Aegean goddesses, only the face and hair style of the figure is unfamiliar.

The Canaanite Goddess is associated with upright posts or living trees. It is thought possible that the Cretans had a settlement at Ugarit which developed from an earlier trading post. It may be that some groups of Cretans fleeing from their homeland in response to the Dorian invasion, chose areas like Ugarit on the Syrio-Palastinian coast where there were existing Cretan settlements.

In Margate, England, cut into the soft rock there is an underground temple cave dating from around 1500 BC. It is formed in the shape of a serpent. This enigmatic structure has been painstakingly decorated with many thousands of shells. The panels that the shells form have obvious sacred significance though they show no direct relation to the symbolism of Cretan religion. The overall plan of the temple, however, does. Perhaps the structure, plan and decoration of the Temple were originally of Cretan design but subsequent users of the temple changed the decoration to suit a later and different tradition. The basic structure of a 'pregnant' serpent, however, remained unchanged (fig. 87).

Also in England Jacquetta Hawkes describes a patterned rod that was found in one of the ancient burials discovered around Stonehenge. It has an equivalent in an almost contemporary grave in the lower circle at Mycenae. She also argues that the shape of a dagger carved on one of this monumental temple's huge sarcens is foreign to this part of Europe and similar to one carved on the gravestone of a Mycenaean

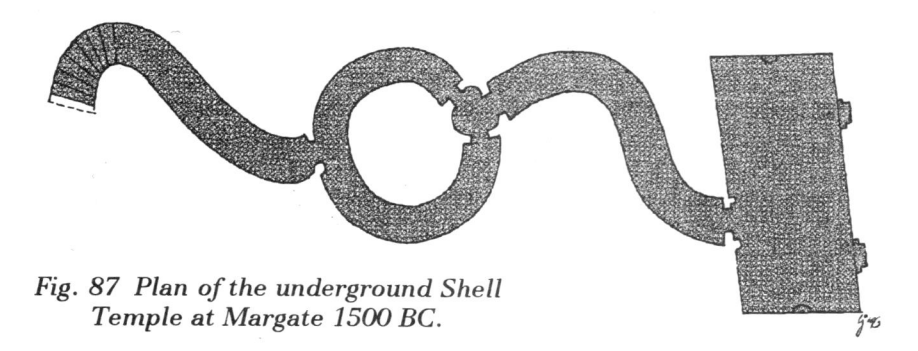

Fig. 87 Plan of the underground Shell Temple at Margate 1500 BC.

dignitary [25]. This evidence at least indicates that the communities of the bronze age were rather more mobile than might be expected.

The Jewel in the Empire Builder's Crown

The triumph of the Dorians was short lived. They were succeeded by the Romans in 67 BC and, when the dominions were divided, Crete was allocated to the Eastern Section becoming part of the Byzantine Empire. In 823 AD Arabs became the new masters of what was left of Crete. Their reign lasted less than 100 years until 961 when the island was recaptured for the Byzantines. In 1204 Crete fell again to Crusaders who sold it off to the Venetians in 1347. Between 1645 and 1898 a new invader, the Turks, controlled Crete and it was not until May 1913 that the island finally became part of Greece. From which time it has retained its own integrity, apart from a brief occupation by the Nazis in 1941-5. These hostile occupations and the Cretans' struggles against them took their toll. After the withdrawal of the Turks, for example, the indigenous population had been reduced by half.

6
The New Religion

Behind the work of the humane poets who composed the *Iliad* and *Odyssey* lies an age of brutality and violence, in which the bold pioneers of private property had ransacked the opulent, hieratic (sacred), sophisticated civilisation of the Minoan matriarchate. [1]

The Overthrow of the Great Goddess

Eventually the religion of the new Greek invaders could be summed up in one word: Zeus, but it took many generations for this refinement to take place. On the mainland the Mycenaeans had adopted the Great Goddess both in Her original form and through the many goddesses of the Greek pantheon. Their religious world included male deities which were clearly subordinate to the Goddess (fig. 88), but their principal god was not Zeus but Poseidon. Following the deposing and demotion of the Great Goddess, the battle between the old and

Fig. 88 Signet Ring, gold, Mycenae, 1500 BC. The relative size of the two figures leaves no doubt about the power relationship between them. The female figure, seated on a throne with vegetation behind, would be more than twice the size of the male were she to stand.

The New Religion

new ideas of social organisations represented by the Mycenaean and indigenous Aegean religions on the one hand and the new ways of the Dorians on the other, was mirrored by the struggle for ascendancy on the heavenly plain – Poseidon versus Zeus and later, Poseidon versus Athena. Even when Athena won the position of supreme deity of Athens (for which she was awarded the Parthanon) her victory, which should have legitimised female power, was used to disenfranchise and subjugate women.

When the Indo-European invaders arrived in the Aegean with their patriarchal sky gods they encountered entrenched and formidable commitment to Hera, the name by which the Great Goddess was known on the Aegean mainland. Rituals and celebrations were firmly established around this Goddess. Her emblems were the cuckoo, to denote spring (her youth) and the pomegranate (symbolic of her fecundity and maturity).

In order to facilitate the disintegration of matriarchal society and to dissipate the power of the old tradition, the new patriarchs decided that the Goddess, who had always been identified as completely independent of any male partner, was to have a consort. The story of Hera exemplifies the practice recorded in the myths associated with many other matriarchal peoples that the Aryans subjugated. Because Hera's following was too strong to destroy, the new deity had to acquire some of Her power by sharing Her throne. As the Goddess would not willingly be divested of Her power, She had to be forced. The rape of the Aegean cultures by Aryan invaders is recorded in the mythological defilement of this virginal Goddess. As the omnipotent creator and provider, the Goddess had no need of a male consort. Unable to win Her over by reason, Zeus disguised himself as Her cuckoo, in order to gain access to Her lap. He raped Her and by this means became Her husband. The fact that no children were born to this union may attest to its rejection by the indigenous community. Each did however have many children in their own right. Hera, for example, gave birth to Ares (god of war) after touching a flower [2].

The ideology of the invaders extended beyond a partnership between the two deities. In an attempt to completely usurp the Goddess' role as creator, Zeus gave birth to a new patriarchal version of the goddess, Athena (fig. 92). The plurality that resulted from the disintegration of the omnipotence of the Great Goddess was the beginning of the transition from a monotheistic to a polytheistic religion. Different goddesses came to represent the many different aspects previously associated with the one Great Goddess. She had previously been known by many names in different areas but these names had essentially represented one entity. This division allowed new, alien, male godlings to represent some of these elements. This dissipation of the Goddess' ascendancy eventually culminated in a return to monotheism, but this time, a patriarchal one. In the Greek pantheon, God the mother is ultimately replaced by Zeus the father (and mother). The move to complete monotheism was not of course achieved with Zeus but the idea was there and the way prepared for acceptance of the later deity of the Judeo-Christian and Islamic traditions whose holy books insist that 'you shall have no other God but me'. Accepting the authority of this patriarchal god became a condition of 'salvation' which promised the irresistible caveat of 'everlasting life'. The christian crusaders, explorers and colonisers offered no alternative. Unlike the Greek and Roman empire builders, who tolerated the worship of indigenous deities alongside their own, Christianity tolerated no deviation from a belief in 'the one true God'. Refusal to accept this 'God of love' was met with slaughter.

Fig. 89 The Three Wisewomen approach a shrine, their differing status is represented by their breasts.

The adaptation of the old tradition to the new religious imagery is not confined to the Greeks. Christian imagery draws heavily from Goddess symbolism. Demeter and Persephone, mother and daughter goddess (fig. 78), become a blueprint for Mary and Jesus and in the scene on a gold-plated silver ring from Mycenae (fig. 89), three important women approach a shrine. There is more than a suggestion here of the wise men *en route* to a stable.

Zeus' alien origins are apparent from his name which is Indo-European and, therefore, a product of the Greek-speaking invaders. The converse is true of Eileithyia, for example, whose name is of non-Indo-European origin. Zeus first appeared as a subordinate in the Goddess religion. As Zeus Wellchanos, the Cretan Greek youth godling associated with a festival to celebrate fertility at which he was eaten as a bull (a practice later adapted by the christians in their ritual of communion). By the classical era he was known on Crete as a boy, the son of the Great Goddess Rhea, deriving his importance from his mother with none in his own right.

In a hymn dating from the third century AD which contains some ancient material, the godling is invoked not by name but as 'the greatest

The New Religion

Kouros', by the other Kouretes, who implore him to remember how they protected him from his father Kronos. As Jacquetta Hawkes points out, the power of the Great Goddess was so strong that the Greeks had to pull their great sky god down, 'from self-created majesty on Olympus to wailing infancy in a Cretan cave' [3].

To the post-Dorian Cretans, Zeus was the bull, the dying year godling who was buried in Mount Juktas. The mainland Greeks saw him as no mortal year godling but a mighty sky god, beyond death. They found this suggestion that he could die deeply offensive. This schism of belief is at the root of the mainland Greek's claim, said to persist to the present day, that all Cretans are liars.

Coin engravings, from the fourth century BC, which originated in Phaistos and Gortyns, give an indication of the contemporary mythology of the Dorian age. Europa is shown riding on a bull which represents Zeus, clearly demonstrating her superiority over him.

This imagery is turned on its head by Homer, who is thought to have lived around 800 BC. He describes part of the legend of Zeus where, in the form of a bull, he abducts Europa from the mainland and takes her to Crete where he rapes her. She is then said to have given birth to Minos who becomes the new ruler of Crete. This may be a mythological record of the invasion of the Dorians which produced the Cretan Greeks, represented by the term Minos. A race born of rape. R.F. Willets, however, notes that Minos was remembered more as the consort of Queen Pasiphae, claimed as another of Zeus' many offspring, rather than in his own right.

In one strand of Greek myth Minos asks for a gift from the sea god Poseidon and is given a magnificent bull whom he then refuses to sacrifice to the gods because of its great beauty. To punish this disobedience Poseidon causes Pasiphae (originally a goddess, the daughter of the sun and the moon whose name means 'She who shines for all'), Queen of Crete and now daughter of Zeus, to fall in love with the bull. Cretan ingenuity (Daedalus) then assists her to mate with the bull by constructing a hollow cow for her to hide in. Thus two generations of Cretan Queens are forced to copulate with bulls, a literary record of the Greeks' enforcement of the concept of the bull as the male year godling. On the mainland, in the ritual enactment of the marriage of Hera and Zeus, the male priest dressed as a bull to represent the new deity.

These legends record the Cretan rulers' (the queens), reluctance to adopt the religious ideology of the year godling (bull) necessitating its repeated enforcement from the mainland. As the conflict passed into legend it became embellished with sea gods and artificial cows.

Crete Reclaimed

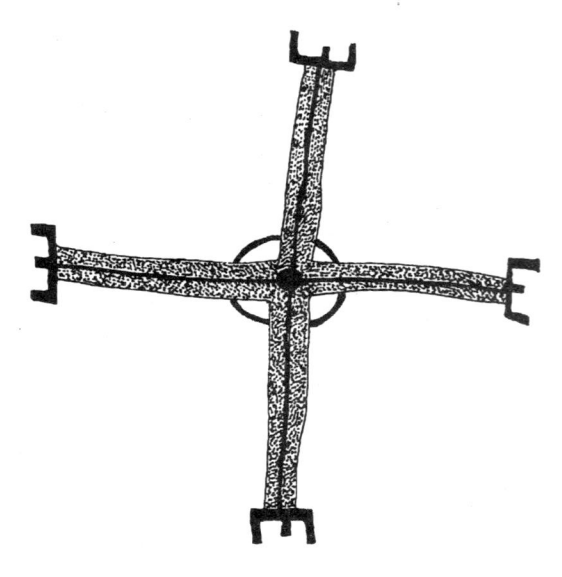

Fig. 90 Wall Painting, Catal Huyuk shrine 5800 BC, illustrating the ancient origins of the trident as a sacred symbol. Along with the trident it was carved on sacred Cretan pillars.

There is another serious undercurrent to the legend. Already, in the most influential area of ideology, religious imagery, we have the position of women established in the patriarchal hierarchy. The Greeks demonstrate their contempt for, and pornographic degradation of women by transforming them into male chattel. In order to punish Minos, Poseidon afflicts, not the disobedient king, but the innocent, though more ideologically important, Queen. Through force and trickery the Goddess (in the form of Europa) and Her representative on earth the great Queen of Knossos (Pasiphae) are degraded by the Greek bull. The first because a god desires power (control of what was to become Europe?) and the second because one male wishes to punish another.

Following her liaison with the bull, Pasiphae gives birth to the minotaur, half-man, half-bull, with a hearty appetite for the youth of the Greek mainland.

These myths have no place in bronze age Cretan tradition. They are later Greek aberrations designed to transform the island's religious beliefs. In this way the new patriarchate used their gods to subjugate the indigenous peoples of the Aegean and undermine its symbolic centre, the sacred labyrinth. Homeric poetry is devoted to remembering the deeds of famous men – such as Theseus, Heracles, Perseus and Jason – in myths which are individualistic, aristocratic, patriarchal and martial. They were written by and for the ruling male elite and it is their glory that they created. They misrepresent the story of the backward who conquered and plundered the civilised.

These legendary records are supported by artefacts. Representations of the new order, as epitomised by the illustration on an Attic vase

The New Religion

(fig. 52) offer a condensed version of the process of patriarchalisation. Zeus, the aspiring principal god squats on the usurped throne as he gives birth to the new order through his head, the source of ideology. He is accompanied by Hephaistos holding the sacred *labyris* and Poseidon who grasps what is now known as the trident spear but was once a symbolic replication of the image of the Goddess with arms upraised in benediction (fig. 90).

Rather like a retreating army destroying or burning anything that might be useful to the new occupying force, Cretan priestesses made sure that their sacred legacy was safely stowed away. The myths and stories concerning ancient Crete were written in historical times over a thousand years after the period they claim to describe. What the story of Zeus, as an example of mythology, demonstrates is how religious ideology is used to facilitate change to a new social order. There was no King Minos and no notion of Zeus or a minotaur on Crete in bronze age times yet many popular books on ancient Crete refer to King Minos, the Palace of Minos at Knossos, his brother's palace at Phaistos and his chief architect and artist Daedalus, *ad nauseam*. Arthur Evans has to take some of the responsibility for this. He succeeded in imposing an identity on bronze age Cretan culture that led to its being confused with the classical era.

Fortunately the ancients left us a mass of evidence which attests to their achievements. The tone, beauty, serenity, creativity and absolute peace of this culture evoked by the archaeological evidence, all give the impression of an ancient civilisation totally alien to these later, discrediting, patriarchal myths of rape, brutality, bestiality and human sacrifice. What the myth of the minotaur and the Athenian tribute does tell us is that the mainland Greeks had a folk memory of a once great power across the sea on Crete.

The New Goddesses

In Linear B texts references are made to the Lady of the Labyrinth, to Hera, Hermes, Athena, Artemis and Eileithyia. Although Poseidon and Zeus are mentioned only as of minor importance, their very presence signals the beginning of the end for the old Goddess religion.

Some scholars have suggested that Athena was worshipped in Knossos around 1400 and that there was also a Demeter cult there. As we have seen, however, the Knossian tablets may be dated as late as 1150 BC. These deities along with other new and developing goddesses gradually replaced the omnipotence of the Great Goddess. As the power of the Goddess was divided up and thus weakened the Cretan bull began to acquire inflated religious significance and the new

Goddesses gradually became associated with the role previously allotted to the male, fertility. The Goddess' role in regeneration and as provider of the fruits of the earth was adapted to an association with fecundity.

Crete was used as a centre for the action of many of the classical myths because it was on Crete that the greatest power of the Goddess continued for longest. The goddesses that were the descendants of the Great Goddess on Crete inherited many of Her aspects. They were all virginal in the original meaning of the word, that is they lived without men. The Great Goddess needed no male partner for She was the creator in Her own right and the originator of all things. Thus Her descendants, in one way or another, are described in these terms. Ariadne's name means 'very pure maid' and Britomartis means 'sweet maid', demonstrating their 'virginal' nature. But part of the role of the myths attached to these goddesses was to violate their independence and power. In one way or another most of them became, through the ideological propaganda of the Greek patriarchate, associated with male figures. Only Demeter managed to survive with her independence intact, wherever she was worshipped it was clear that she maintained her ban on the other sex.

The invading Greeks would have encountered the reverence in which the Goddess was held by the indigenous Cretan population. The stories that were attached, to Her descendants served to reduce them from the once omnipotent status of the deity whom they all represent, to heroines in male dramas. Although, as we have already noted, Goddess religion was the norm throughout the Aegean prior to the invasion of the Dorians, I have concentrated here only on the new goddesses associated with Crete. The one exception is Athena whom I have included because of her central role in the new Greek pantheon.

Ariadne and the Transition to Patriarchy

The discovery of Knossos, Troy, Amnissos and many other places mentioned in classical mythology confirms that these legends were based on factual places. The actual events, though they have clearly become adapted and embellished to suit the propaganda requirements of their authors, may be derived from factual situations.

According to mythic sources Ariadne was celebrated as a late Cretan goddess in whose honour sacred dances were performed. Patricia Monaghan says of her that:

The New Religion

In her original Minoan form Ariadne was apparently a goddess worshipped exclusively by women, a goddess of the underworld and of germination, a vegetation-goddess much like the Greek Persephone. [4]

For the commissioners and consumers of classical mythology, the Greek patriarchate, she was reduced to the dancing princess who played a supporting role in the story of a Greek hero, Theseus. This prince of Greece, travelled to Crete with the tribute of mainland youth in order to put an end to the sacrifice of his country people to the Cretan Minotaur. Ariadne, cast as one of the daughters of Queen Pasiphae and King Minos, assisted him by revealing the secret of the labyrinth. He killed the minotaur and Ariadne helped him to escape. He then abandoned her on the island of Naxos (Dia), though other versions tell of her abduction there by Dionysus.

The story of Ariadne and Theseus is a truncated version of the overthrow of the Cretan matriarchate. By revealing the secret of the labyrinth (or the ancient mysteries) to a Greek man, She (the Goddess) loses Her immortality. By giving Theseus the spool of thread for his escape from the Labyrinth she gave life to him, helping him to return from the underworld (labyrinth). Inherent in this tale are elements of the thread of life associated with Eileithyia and Persephone's descent into the underworld. Ariadne's gift of life to Theseus results in the loss of her own immortality

Though once an aspect of the omnipotent, eternal, immortal Goddess, Ariadne is thus reduced to mortal proportions and like Britomartis and Persephone becomes associated with vegetation. In a complete reversal of roles with the male year godling she is killed. As Nilsson pointed out, there is no other goddess who has met her death in so many different ways as Ariadne. Following her abandonment, different versions of the legend tell of her being raped by or joining forces with Dionysus and becoming leader of the Dionysian women, the Maenads; or being killed by Artemis (in one legend she is said to have died in child birth which was in the classical pantheon ruled by Artemis); or hanging herself; or She was then raised to (the patriarchal Greek) heaven.

As Ariadne is allotted the male (vegetation) role, Theseus assumes hers. Whereas dances were once held in her honour, when Theseus arrived on Delos he set up an image of Ariadne, 'the work of Daedalus', and the *keraton* altar with horns and led the girls and boys he had rescued around it to 'the inward and outward windings of the labyrinth' [5].

Crete Reclaimed

Arthur Evans notes the significance of the transfer of Ariadne's role in the dance, to Theseus, pointing out that she became a passive bystander [6].

In order to reinforce this message of the usurpation of the power of the Cretan Goddess and Her earthly representatives, the myth writers have Theseus return to the island for Ariadne's sister, Phaedra who is to become the subject of further degradation at their hands.

The reverberations of the Theseus legend do not end with Ariadne's betrayal and death and Phaedra's humiliation. Following the assistance Daedalus gave to Ariadne in divulging the secret of the labyrinth, he (the apportionment of gender to present and future generations of Cretan genius, reflects the character of Greek rather than Cretan society), escaped from the island in the flight which ended so tragically for his son Icarus.

It is useful to break down what we have already seen of this myth and what follows into its component stages in order to explore its symbolism, which I have placed in parenthesis.

1. Pasiphae, the daughter of the sun and moon whose name means 'She who shines for all' (representing the power of the Cretan Queens which the Greeks needed to deconstruct) is tricked by a Greek god (representing the new order) into copulating with a bull (a combination of the symbolism of the Cretan bull games and the much later Greek ritual marriage ceremony where the priest wears a bull's head mask) and the minotaur results.

2. Theseus (representing the new order) comes to Crete.

3. Ariadne, Pasiphae's daughter (symbol of the old Cretan order) betrays Crete (the old tradition) by assisting Theseus and is then abandoned by him. (Clearly there was to be no happy joining of the old order with the new).

4. Daedalus and Icarus (symbols of the original and future generations of the creative genius of Crete also abandon the island). Icarus dies (there will be no future Cretan genius) and Daedalus arrives on the far shores of Sicily.

5. Minos (symbol of the new order imposed on Crete) pursues Daedalus to Sicily and tries to retrive (revive) the

The New Religion

creative genius of Crete and fails (we are again reminded that the old and new orders cannot cooperatively co-exist).

6. The women of the Sicilian court then kill Minos to protect Daedalus. (Women as heads of the matriarchal clans were obliged to avenge clan members. Could the Sicilian princesses be Cretan immigrants who dispatched Minos in revenge for the devastation that had been wrecked on their homeland?)

Thomson gives evidence of the matriarchal tribes that fled to Sicily in order to escape the regressive changes that were taking place in the Aegean at the time of the move towards patriarchy.

It seems that this legend tells the story of how Cretan glory was lost when subjected to alien rule and of how some of the people of Crete fled and were welcomed in other lands, not least for their ingenious skills in design and engineering.

There were two festivals in Athena's name on Naxos. Both reinforce the message of the myths. One celebrates her as the bride of Dionysus and the other mourns her abandonment and death. The idea of the death of a Goddess in this way is most un Greek and would certainly have been anathema to Cretan religious beliefs. It represents a drastic attempt on the part of the new patriarchy to disclaim the Goddess as immortal.

The theme of a Goddess' or priestess' betrayal of the old order is a consistent one throughout Greek mythology. In Jason's great adventures and heroic deeds, the story makes it clear that none of his actions would have been possible without the help of the magic of Medea, a priestess of the goddess Hecate. The significance of Medea's act is reinforced by the plethora of Goddess symbolism inherent in her story. She uses her powers to take the Golden Fleece from the sacred grove where it is guarded by a great serpent whom she calms with a branch onto which she has poured sacred fluids.

The most famous Greek myths, which are now being revived in English schools, tell of the heroes Perseus and Heracles, both sired by Zeus through rape, establishing supremacy over powerful female figures. Heracles strangled two serpents before his first birthday, outwitted old hags (wise women?), decapitated the serpent woman Medusa, killed the hydra (a many-headed snake), captured the Cretan bull, (which he offered to Hera but she refused), and had a battle with the Harpies (half-woman, half-bird).

Britomartis

This goddess, whose name is closely associated with Artemis, also dates from the post matriarchal phase on Crete. Her name and worship survived into Hellenistic times. There are the remains of temples to her in Hersonissos (once the centre for her worship) at the port of Lyttos and at Olous. A festival is also held in her honour. According to legend a wooden statue of Britomartis was made by Daedalus.

One of the stories attached to Britomartis tells of her pursual by Minos for nine months. She eluded capture by leaping from a mountain and plunging into the sea and was saved by the fish nets which had been her gift to humanity. This tale records another attempt to establish the mortality of the Goddess. The ending of the story suggest that it was reworked by the indigenous Cretans who would not have accepted the death of a goddess who was, by definition, immortal. The use of the fishing net to establish her power or immortality has parallels in other legends. Athena, for example, is said to have won her contest against Poseidon (for Attica and the Parthanon) because of her gift, to the people, of the olive tree.

The story of Britomartis in this adapted form also reflects the traditional beliefs of the indigenous Cretans with regard to the cycle of birth, death and rebirth. The pursual is for the duration of a human pregnancy followed by what is thought to be death in the sea and rebirth.

Dictynna

This Goddess' name, which can clearly be linked with Mount Dikte, is pre-Greek and may therefore be the name by which the Great Goddess was known in this area. Dictynna is closely associated with Britomartis and Artemis (Diana), indeed Monaghan notes that her name, which means 'netted one', indicates that she was the persona of the goddess Britomartis after she was saved by the fish net [7]. Or it could be that both these names and that of Artemis, referred to the same goddess but in different parts of the island. She was associated with the wild countryside and mountains and is often depicted as a huntress. In classical times she had sacred dogs in her service who protected her from the unwanted attentions of men. According to one myth Apollonius of Tyana met his death after visiting her sanctuary late at night.

Dictynna is said to have hunted with Artemis and to have been exceedingly loved by her. There is a temple to her in the city of Lisos and a more famous one in Hania. Her cult is especially Cretan and is associated with the northern coast from Knossos to the gulf of Mirabello. Her most important temple was situated on the cape of Mount

Dictynnaion between Kydonia and Phalasarna in the Polyrrhenium district.

Eileithyia

Because Eileithyia's name is pre-Greek we can assume that she represented an aspect of the ancient Cretan Goddess. She was the creator who spun the thread of life.

Under the new order Eileithyia became the women's goddess designated as responsible for childbirth and the protection of women. The herb dittany, which still grows wild on the mountain slopes of Crete, was used in her name to ease childbirth and was woven into chaplets dedicated to her.

She was celebrated at the sacred cave of Amnissos. Linear B inscriptions record that the Mycenaeans brought pithoi filled with honey to the cave as offerings. Roman fragments and christian lamps were found there suggesting that the veneration of Eileithyia continued well into historical times.

Athena

Although not associated with Crete this goddess is important because of the way in which she was used by the new patriarchate in their ideological battle against the power of the old tradition. An effective way of neutralising the identity of the Great Goddess was to carry Her symbols over to the new goddesses (and gods). Many features of the old Goddess were too deeply ingrained to be eradicated so they were overlaid and reinterpreted. Consequently Athena was associated with the snake (fig. 91), the pillar, the olive grove, the dove and the owl. The owl was sometimes depicted, in her stead, as representing her. Also in keeping with earlier tradition she never married.

This primal goddess of the new patriarchy was born, fully armed, from the head of Zeus [8]. By this deftly conceived move Zeus, the minor godling with immortal ambitions, becomes the originator, the mother, of the great Mother Goddess Herself while she is reduced to the position of his favoured daughter.

Athena was patron of weaving, pottery and the arts, indicating the association of these skills with the women of the Aegean. In addition She took on a martial element and in direct contrast to Her predecessor became the Goddess of War. She wore an elaborate helmet and was often depicted holding a shield and a spear (fig. 92). She combines the old order with the new, as goddess of valour, eloquence and judgement.

Through Athena the Great Goddess is transformed, Her old powers and attributes now having come from Zeus, the new mighty father of all

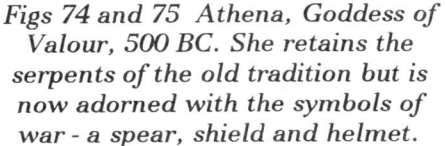

Figs 74 and 75 Athena, Goddess of Valour, 500 BC. She retains the serpents of the old tradition but is now adorned with the symbols of war - a spear, shield and helmet.

the gods of which she is only one. Just as is the case with the christian's Mary, because her status is derived through the male deity all the religious fervour and energy that had once been channelled into celebrating the old Goddess could be now be lavished on this female demi-deity in a patriarchal context. To the people, the forty feet high statue of Athena encrusted with gold and ivory, built in the facade of the Parthanon which was dedicated to her, was a means of celebrating the female element. The patriarchate could claim all this reverence for themselves, however, because Athena's status was derived from Zeus, just as Mary's is from her son. Thus the capital of Greece was named after Athena and her original power may be reflected in the order of the Greek alphabet where 'A' comes first.

The New Religion

Thompson reports the telling mythical account of how Athena retained the Acropolis: She and Poseidon, the sea god, struggled for the control of this temple. In the Athenian assembly all the women voted for Athena and the men for Poseidon. The women succeeded by a majority of one and Athena retained the temple. As a punishment however the men then excluded women from all future assemblies and instituted a prohibition on matrilineal succession. Thomson notes that the men in this story are a symbol for the patriarchal immigrants to the Aegean and the women are the indigenous people, perhaps the Pelasgoi, one of the matriarchal tribes known to have inhabited this area of the mainland. Thus the conflict ends with the institution of patrilineal succession, the disenfranchisement of women and a move from free, exogamous, sexual association to monogamy [9].

Clearly the power given to Athena through the people's love of her was a source of concern to the Greek patriarchate, despite the careful choice of her origins. There are a myriad of stories associated with Athena which show how the Greeks edged their way to power using mythology to consolidate and legitimate their rule. Erechtheius, for example, was a Greek hero who had originally been given a place in the temple and cult of Athena. Later we read in Homer that Erechtheius has become the owner of the house in which Athena has her abode. Another instance of this practice was confirmed by French excavations at Delphi. Some time after the neolithic period the temple here was known as the home of the Great Mother Goddess. It was later dedicated to Athena but then became known as the Temple of Apollo who is recorded in classical works as having won the oracle of Delphi from older deities. Its original possessor was the Goddess Ge who was known as a great serpent. Apollo destroyed Her by firing an arrow charged with the new authority of the patriarchate, into Her serpent or dragon belly, causing Her to rot away.

6
Conclusion

Our journey through the history of this sacred island began with a legend of paradise, a golden age, a time of peace and plenty. The island's first inhabitants had been neolithic peoples, probably from Anatolia, whose cultural focus was a female deity. They brought with them their skills in textiles, ceramics and horticulture and a philosophy of collectivism and pacifism.

Through either indigenous development or as the result of later immigration the great Temple centres were planned, designed and constructed. The next 350 years, which cover the Old and New Temple Palace phases was a time of peace and plenty when cultural development continued rapidly throughout the Aegean. The remnants of Cretans settlements have been discovered all around the area and there is evidence of trading links between Crete and the whole of the Mediterranean and north Africa.

The fresco evidence from Knossos and the Cretan settlement on Thera, which is supported by finds from many other sites, reveals two central and consistent cornerstones in the culture of the ancient Cretans; their dedication to Goddess religion and the importance allotted to its arbiters, the priestess queens.

During this Golden Age the Cretan's were world leaders in design and construction, art, horticulture, seafaring, textiles and ceramics. Although they developed their own written language and printing systems, we have no comprehensible written records of their culture. Later evidence in the form of the Gortyns code and Greek mythology however, tell us that these practical skill were matched by liberal laws and systems of philosophy, mathematics and astronomy. Furthermore, archaeologists have found no evidence to suggest that the great material wealth of the Cretans was not spread equitably throughout all levels of society. Reviewing the evidence of the buildings around the Arkhanes Temple Palace, the Sakellarakis' noted that, '. . . gaping social divisions probably did not exist.'

The great learning of the Classical era is synonymous with the development of European civilisation but, as we have seen, the settlers who became the Greeks were barbarians when they invaded the Aegean. Their systems of learning were appropriated from the sophisticated Aegean tribes whom they subjugated.

The eruption of Thera cannot be successfully associated with the date of 1450. Some theorists place it in the early part of the seventeenth century. The enigmatic mass destructions in 1450 BC brought about the abandonment of all the known Temple Palace centres apart from Knossos, neighbouring Arkhanes and Hania, all close to the northern coast. In the centres that were deserted at this time there was no loss of life, the surrounding towns were immediately reinhabited and many of the great religious treasures were buried in the debris, all of which suggests that the priestesses had a hand in the destruction or ceremonial firing and burial of these great religious centres.

An influx of Mycenaeans followed the 1450 destructions but there is no real evidence that they represented a hostile presence on the island at this or indeed any other time. The Goddess continued to be celebrated at Knossos and in hill top sanctuaries, caves and in small shrines that were built on the edges of the old Temple Palace sites. In remote communities new shrines were built which continued in use well into the period of the Dorian invasion in 1150 BC.

Following the invasion, evidence is sketchy but we do know that the Temple Palaces were not desecrated or built over to any great extent. The Greek town at Knossos for example carefully avoided the boundaries of the Temple Palace. We also know that the transition to the new patriarchal ways of the Indo Europeans was a gradual one. This is clear from the legends of the Greeks, in particular those associated with Zeus; and the written evidence of the Gortyns code.

The legacy of Crete was preserved for us by the great regal priestess queens of the many surviving frescoes: La Parisienne, the Ladies in Blue, the Processional Queen, the Ladies in the Temple fresco, the Queen in the garden at Ayia Triada, the many regal women of Thera, Tiryns and Mycenae and those whose remains were discovered in the splendid queenly burials at Phourni and Ayia Triada. Their legacy is the vision of a way of life now lost to us, a vision of an island paradise that has been equated with the Garden of Eden and the idyll of Atlantis.

Glossary

Biblos
In bronze age Cretan times, a major port on the coast of Lebanon, north of Beruit, where, after 2000 BC, Astarte was worshipped. Also known for the early alphabetic inscription that was discovered on a sarcophagus there.

Chthonic
Relating to the regenerative power of the earth or the underworld; associated with Rhea the name under which some vestiges of the Great Goddess survived.

Epiphany
Traditionally seen as the occasion on which the Deity manifests Herself to Her people.

Ethnocentricity
The process by which other cultures are viewed by the standards of a culture whose values may be completely alien to it.

Faience
A type of glaze for decorating pottery. A core of crushed quartz grains coated with glass and coloured by the addition of copper compounds to produce a rich finish. It was not developed (re-invented) in England until 1570 AD.

Horns of Consecration
Assumed to be stylised bovine (cow or bull) horns, they could, perhaps more feasibly, be seen as reflecting the crescent moon. They were used to designate or consecrate an area or object as sacred.

Libations
The pouring of wine, oil etc. in honour of a deity, or that which is used for such purposes.

Light Well
An area similar to a stair well where either the area has been left open to the outside light or windows have been placed to illuminate the adjacent rooms or staircases.

Linear A
This system of writing originated on Crete between 1900 and 1500 BC and is as yet undeciphered. What has survived is thought to constitute records or accounts; religious dedications and graffiti, but a great deal more, that would have been written on more perishable materials has been lost.

Linear B
This script was first found at Knossos and later became widespread on the Greek mainland and was the language of Mycenaean Greece.

Decipherment is thought to show a form of Greek written in syllables, consisting mainly of accounts dealing with foodstuffs and supplies, though a group of tablets from Pylos (a Mycenaean palace in the Peleponnese) speaks of defensive preparations against an unnamed attacker.

Megaron
A Greek word for a type of hall, found on the mainland and elsewhere, which usually has a central hearth and only one entrance, through a porch to the side.

Neolithic
The name comes from the Greek meaning new or later stone age and is so called because the only tools that have survived from this period were made from stone. Metal-work was unknown. By their very definition pre-historic dates cannot be firmly fixed. The neolithic period is said to date from 2500 in Britain and Germany whereas in Egypt, Mesopotamia and Crete it ended 1000 years earlier. The Maoris of New Zealand were still living in a neolithic way when Captain Cook arrived.

Rhyton
A vase used in sacred rituals for pouring liquids (libations) with a wide hole at the top and a small one at the bottom.

Sacral Knot
The knot of material shown in artistic representations at the back of the head of a priestess, queen or other important woman which designates her or her activity as sacred. It usually has a fringe at each end and may have developed as a symbolic representation of a knot of coiled snakes. It is similar to the Egyptian *ankh* or Isis Knot and the Sumarian reed bundle of Innana.

The Levant
The old name for the Eastern Mediterranean now Lebanon, Syria and Israel.

Seals
A seal or seal stone is the carved object, usually a gemstone, with, most commonly, a religious scene from which sealings are made.

Sealings
These are impressions that result from a seal stone being pressed into clay (wax would also have been used but any resulting impressions would not have survived) to set a seal on something to leave a record of that person or to secure, for example, the contents of a bottle, jug or casket.

Abbreviations

The abbreviations used for Greek and Latin authors are those used by the *Greek-English Lexicon* of Liddell and Scott (new edition) and the *Latin-English Dictiornary* of Lewis and Short.

Sources and further reading

Andersson, W. *Holy Places of the British Isles.* Edbury Press, 1983.
Bachofen, J.J. *Myth, Religion and Mother Right.* Trans by Ralph Manheim. Princeton University Press, 1967.
Bahn, P.G. and Vertut, J. *Images of the Ice Age*, Windward, 1988.
Baring, A. and Cashford, J. *The Myth of the Goddess: Evolution of an Image.* Penguin, 1993.
Bord, J. and C. *A Guide to Ancient Sites in Britain.* Paladin, 1984.
Beard, M. *Woman as a Force in History.* McMillan, 1946.
Boserup, E. *Women's Role in Economic Development.* Allen and Unwin, 1970.
Boulding, E. *The Underside of the Universe.* Boulder and Co: Westview Press, 1976.
Bowman, J. *Crete, The Travellers' Guide.* Jonothan Cape, 1981.
Branigan, K. *The Foundations of Palatial Crete: A Survey of Crete in the Early Bronze Age.* 1970.
Briffult, F. *The Mothers* (abridged version). Allen and Unwin, 1959.
Brindenthall & Koonz (eds), *Becoming Visible, Women in European History.* Houghton Mifflin, 1977.
Brown, A. *Arthur Evans and the Palace of Minos.* University of Oxford, Ashmolean Museum, 1989.
Budge, E.A.W. *The God of the Egyptians* Vol.2, London, 1904.
Butterworth, E.A. *Some Traces of the Pre-Olympian World.* De Gruyter, 1966.
Cadogan, G. *The Palaces of Minoan Crete.* Routledge, 1976.
[The best guide to the Temple-Palaces and some other sites though it needs concentrated efforts to follow sometimes.]
Campbell, J. *The Masks of God: Primitive Mythology*, Secker and Warburg 1959-68.
Castleden, R. *Knossos Labyrinth: A View of the Palace of Minos at Knossos.* Routledge, 1990(a).
— *The Minoans, Life in Bronze Age Crete.* Routledge, 1990(b).
— *The Making of Stonehenge.* Routledge, 1993.
Chadwick, J. *The Decipherment of Linear B.* Cambridge U.P., 1967.
Clayton, P.A. and Price, M.J. (eds) *The Seven Wonders of the Ancient World.* Routledge, 1988.

Coldstream, J.N. *The Sanctuary of Demeter.* Thames and Hudson, 1973.
Cotterell, L. *The Minoan World.* Michael Joseph, 1979.
— *The Bull of Minos - The story of the excavations.* Pan, 1955.
Dames, M. *The Avebury Cycle.* Thames and Hudson, 1977.
Davaras, C. *Phaistos, Ayia-Triada, Gortyns.* Athens
Doumas, C. *The Wall Paintings of Thera.* The Thera Foundation, 1992.
Eisler, R. *The Chalice and the Blade.* Harper and Row, 1987.
Ekdotike Athenon, S.A.(ed) *History of the Hellenic World: Prehistory and Protohistory.* Athens, 1974.
Ehrenreich, B. and English, D. *Witches, Midwives and Nurses - a History of Women Healers.* Compendium, 1974.
Engles, F. *The Origins of Family, Private Property and the State.* London, 1940.
Evans, A.J. *The Palace of Minos.* MacMillan, 1921-35.
Gadon, E.W. *The Once and Future Goddess.* Aquarian Press, 1989.
Gero, J.M. and Conkey M.W., (eds) *Engendering Archaeology: Women and Prehistory.* Blackwell, 1991.
Gimbutas, M. *Goddesses and Gods of Old Europe 7000-3500 BC.* Thames and Hudson, 1974.
— *The Language of the Goddess.* Thames and Hudson, 1990.
— 'The Beginning of the Bronze Age in Europe and the Indo-Europeans: 3500-2500 B.C.' *Journal of Indo European Studies* Vol.1 (1973) p166.
Goodison, L. *Moving Heaven and Earth: Sexuality, Spirituality and Social Change.* The Womens Press, 1990.
Glotz, G. *The Aegean Civilisation.* Routledge and Kegan Paul, 1925.
Groenewegen-Frankfort, H.A. *Arrest and Movement.* London 1951.
Gould Davis, E. *The First Sex.* Penguin, 1975.
Hagg, R and Marinatos, N. (eds) *The Function of the Minoan Palaces. Proceedings of the Forth International Symposium at the Swedish Institute in Athens 1984.* Stockholm 1987.
Hallager, E. *The Mycenaean Palace at Knossos,* Stockholm, Medelhavsmuseet Memoir 1, 1977.
Harrison, J. *Prologomena to the Study of Greek Religion.* 1905 (reprinted Merlin Press 1980).
Harper-Cory, G. *The Goddess at Margate,* mentioned in *The Grotto* by Howard Bridgewater, available from The Grotto, Grotto Hill, Margate, Kent.
Hawkes, J. *The Dawn of the Gods.* Random House, 1968.
Higgins, R.A. *Minoan and Mycenaean Art.* London, 1967.
— *The Archaeology of Minoan Crete.* Bodley Head, 1973.

— *The Aegina Treasure*. British Museum, 1979.
Hood, S. *The Home of the Heroes: The Aegean before the Greeks*. London, 1967.
— *The Minoans, Crete in the Bronze Age*. Thames and Hudson, 1971.
Hopkins, C. *The Early History of Greece*. Yale Classical Studies Vol.2 (1928) p115
Horowitz, S.L. *The Find of a Lifetime*. Weidenfeld and Nicholson, 1981.
Hutchinson, R.W. *Prehistoric Crete*. Harmondsworth, 1962.
— *The First Great Civilisations.* Hutchinson, 1973.
James, E.O., *Prehistoric Religion*. Barnes and Noble, 1957.
— *The Cult of the Mother Goddess.* Thames and Hudson, 1959.
Judge, J. 'Minoans and Mycenaeans: Greece's Brilliant Bronze Age'. *National Geographical*, Vol 153, part II, 1978.
Krzyszkowska, O. and Nixon, L. (eds). *Minoan Society: Proceedings of the Cambridge Colloquium, 1981*. Bristol Classical Press, 1984.
Lawson, J.C. *Modern Greek Folklore and Ancient Greek Religion*. Cambridge, 1910.
Levy, G.R. *The Gate of Horn: A Study of the ReligiousConceptions of the Stone Age and their Influences on European Thought*. Harper and Row, 1963.
Luce, J.V. *The End of Atlantis*. Thames and Hudson, 1973.
Mantegazza, P. *The Sexual Relations of Mankind*. Eugenics Publishing Co., 1935.
Marinatos, N. *Art and Religion in Thera: Reconstructing a Bronze Age Society*. Mathioulakis, 1984.
Marinatos, S. *Crete and Mycenae*. Thames and Hudson, 1960.
Matz, F. *Crete and Early Greece*. Methuen, 1962.
Mead, M. *Male and Female*. Morrow, 1949.
Mead, R. *Crete*. Batsford, 1980.
Mellaart, J. *Catal Huyuk: A Neolithic Town in Anatolia*. McGraw Hill, 1967.
— *The Neolithic of the Near East*. Schribner, 1975.
— *Excavations at Hacilar*. Edinburgh U.P., 1977.
Mellerish, H.E.L. *The Destruction of Knossos.* Hamish Hamilton, 1970.
— *Prehistory.* Mentor, 1965.
Michailidou, A. *A Complete Guide to the Palace of Knossos.* Ekdotike Athenon S.A., 1982.
Michelmore, S. *Sexual Reproduction.* New York National History Press, 1964.
Monaghan, P. *Women in Myth and Legend*. Junction Books, 1981.

Morgan, L. *The Miniature Wall Paintings of Thera.* Cambridge U.P. 1988.
Neumann, E. *The Great Mother, An Analysis of the Archetype.* Routledge and Kegan Paul, revised edition 1963.
New Internationalist Publications. *The State of the World's Women.* Compiled for the United Nations Organisation, 1985.
Nilsson, M.P. *The Minoan-Mycenaean Religion and its survival in Greek Religion.* Gleerup, Lund, second edition, 1952.
Palmer, L.R. *A New Guide to the Palace of Knossos.* London, 1969.
— *Mycenaeans and Minoans.* London, 1965.
Pendlebury, J.D.S. *The Archaeology of Crete.* Methuen and Co, 1979.
Persson, A.W. *The Religion of Greece in Prehistoric Times.* University of California Press, 1942.
Platon, N. *Crete.* London, 1975.
Popham, M.R. *The Minoan Unexplored Mansion at Knossos.* Thames and Hudson for British School of Archaeology at Athens, 1984.
Powell, D. *The Villa Ariadne (a study of Evans et al).* M. Haag, 1985.
Ridgeway, W. *The Early Age of Greece.* Cambridge 1901-3.
Robinson, J.M. *An Introduction to Early Greek Philosophy.* Houghton Mifflin, 1968.
Rogers, B. *The Domestication of Women: Discrimination in Developing Societies.* St Martins, 1979.
Rohrlich-Leavitt, R. 'Women in Transition: Crete and Sumer', in *Becoming Visible.* R. Bridenthal and C. Koonz (eds), Houghton Mifflin, 1987.
Rossiter, S. *Blue Guide, Crete.* Ernest Benn, 1974.
Rostovtzeff, M. *History of the Ancient World.* Oxford, 1927.
Rutkowske, B. *The decline of the Minoan Palace Sanctuaries,* 1967.
Scully, V. 'The Great Goddess and the Palace Architecture of Crete' in *Feminism and Art History: Questioning the Litany.* Braude, N and Garrard, M.D. (eds) Harper and Row, 1982.
Seltman, C. *Women in Antiquity.* Pan, 1956.
Shanks, M. and Tilley C. *Reconstructing Archaeology: Theory and Practice.* Routledge, 2nd edition 1992.
Sjoo, M. and Mor, B. *The Great Cosmic Mother.* Harper and Row, 1987.
Smith, E.W. and Dale, M. *The Ila-Speaking Peoples of Northern Rhodesia.* London, 1920.
Stuckley, W. *Abury Described.* London, 1743.
Stone, M. *The Paradise Papers.* Virago, 1979.
Tacitus. *Agriculture and the Germania.* Penguin, 1971.
Thomas, C.G. 'Matriarchy in Early Greece: The Bronze and Dark Ages'

in *Arethusa* Vol.6, Autumn 1973.
Thomas, J. *Rethinking the Neolithic*, Cambridge U.P., 1991.
Thomson, G. *The Prehistoric Aegean*. Lawrence and Wishart, 1978.
Ucko, P J. *Anthropomorphic Figurines*. Royal Anthropological Institue Occasional Paper No 24, 1968
Von Daniken, K. *Chariot of the Gods* (trans. M Heron) Souvenir Press, 1989.
Warren, P. *Myrtos*. Thames and Hudson for The British School in Athens, 1972.
Willets, R.F. *Everyday Life in Ancient Crete*. Batsford, 1969.
— *The Civilisation of Ancient Crete*. Batsford, 1977.
— *Cretan Cults and Festivals*. London/New York, 1962.
Wilson, H.H. *The Great Mother*. Oriental Translation Fund, 1840.
Woolstonecraft, M. *A Vindication of the rights of Women*
— and Stuart Mill, J. *On the Subjection of Women*. Everyman, Dent Dutton, 1970.
Wunderlich, H.G. *The Secret of Crete*. (trans. R Winston) Souvenir Press, 1976.

Notes

Preface
1. Inevitably the attitudes of most scholars are ethnocentric or reflect their own culture. Because most academics, by virtue of the privileges awarded to males in our society, are men, however, their views are more than ethnocentric they are andro (male) centric. The female equivalent of this term is gynocentric.

Introduction
1. Matriarchy: literally female rule, usually associated with matriliny, the inheritance of identity, name, land and property, through the female line. There is growing evidence that this mode of social organisation was widespread in neolithic and bronze age times. There are many examples of cultures which have retained elements of matriarchal organisation because for some reason, usually geographical, they have been isolated from the mainstream. Among the cultures that still conform to a sub-matriarchal mode in the 20th century are the people of Galicia in the west of Spain, the Cheju islanders in Korea and the Meningkaban of Sumatra. In a matriarchal culture (sometimes referred to as a 'gynarchy') the focus and orientation of society is around women. The clan, tribe or family group is identified through its female ancestry. Women (possibly priestesses), acting as representatives of the female deity, would have determined the rules or laws of the culture. Crete shows overwhelming evidence of interdependence between the state, the economy and religion. Its religion was very clearly administered by women. All the evidence suggests that matriarchy was not the mirror image of patriarchy. There seems to have been much less inequality in matriarchal societies combined with a strong sense of social and public welfare. I hope these issues will be clarified in the text.
2. Much of the work of classical historians was destroyed by those in power who did not agree with its political tenets. Aristotle, for example, ordered many works to be burned. See page 80 for further information.
3. One such surviving group is the Meningkaban of Sumatra where land is still inherited by daughters through their mothers.
4. Ehrenreich and English 1974.

Chapter 1: Daily Life on bronze age Crete
1. Gould Davis 1975, p78, referring to the findings of Mellaart 1967.
2. The Hittites were Indo-European invaders who swept down from the Caucasus with their horse-drawn chariots around 2200 BC. They established themselves in Anatolia, north west of Babylonia by

suppressing the indigenous peace-loving matrilineal Hattians who were probably related to the peoples of Catal Huyuk, 125 miles to the south of the Hittite capital Hattusa.
3. For discussion of this see Thompson 1978.
4. Mellaart 1975, p280.
5. Gimbutas 1974.
6. Castleden 1990, p42.
7. Mead 1980.
8. See Luce 1973 and Castleden 1990 for a discussion of the association of Crete with Atlantis.
9. See Morgan 1988 and Luce 1973 for a discussion of this.
10. Luce 1973, p47.
11. Strictly speaking the term should be exo-*andry* as it is the women who select *men* from outside the clan. Patriarchal language, however always assumes male centrality.
12. Branigan 1975, quoted in Castleden 1990b.
13. B. Todd Whitelaw 1983, quoted in Castleden 1990.
14. See Mellaart 1967 chapter 9; Eisler 1987; and Gimbutas 1974.
15. Brown 1989.
16. Bachofen 1967 translation. The original was published 100 years before the discovery of Catal Huyuk. Quoted in Gould Davis 1975, p78.
17. This culture flourished from 700–200 BC. Herodotus thought they originated in Lydia moving to Italy in about 1200 BC.
18. This painting is too fragmentary to be illustrated here but can be seen in Neumann 1963, p131.25.
19. Mellaart 1967 quoted in Gould Davis 1975, p78.
20. Ucko 1968.
21. Doumas 1992.
22. N. Platon 'Minoan Colonisation', in *Ekdotike Athenon* 1974, p219.
23. Morgan 1988.
24. N. Platon, *The Development of Minoan Writing: Linear Hieroglyphs*, in Ekdotike Athenon 1974, p159.
25. Evans 1921-35 Vol I, p587.
26. Castleden 1990b, p145 quoting Alexiou p108.
27. Referred to in a discussion at the Swedish Institue Symposium, reported in Hagg and Marinatos (eds) 1987, p320.
28. Chadwick 1976.
29. Boserup 1970 and Rogers 1979.
30. Thompson 1978, p150.
31. Eisler 1990, p69.
32. Ehrenreich and English 1974.
33. Gould Davis 1975, pp78-80.

Chapter 2: The Meaning of Sacred Art

1. Mellaart 1967, Ch VI p225; Ch.IX-XI, p60, 202 & 207; quoted in Gould Davis 1975.
2. James 1957, p148 and 1959, p16, quoted in Eisler 1990, p2.
3. Gimbutas 1974.
4. As note 1 above.
5. Stuckley, 1743, p102.
6. Hopkins 1928.
7. Platon 1975.
8. Higgins 1967.
9. Scully 1982, p11 quoted in Gadon 1989, p90.
10. Marinatos, N and Hagg, R. Anthropomorphic Cult Images in Minoan Crete 1981. In Krzyszkowska and Nixon (eds) 1983. The Mallia feet were discovered in an obviously religious context, together with an altar, tripods and other sacred objects. Any other clay feet were found either singly or in contexts that were clearly practical. They were, for example used as lasts for shoe making at Gournia. Outsized locks of hair were also recovered from Juktas, these were destroyed before their find spot could be accurately charted.
11. See also MacGowan K and Hester Jnr. J.A., *Early Man in the New World*, Revised Edition, Doubleday, 1962, pp 37-38.
12. Evans 1921-35, Volume I, p434.
13. Evans 1921-35, Volume I p124-5.
14. Different conjectural restorations of the complete frescoes can be seen in Hagg and Marinatos (eds) 1987.
15. Hood, mentioned in the discussions reported in Hagg and Marinatos (eds) 1987, p268.

Chapter 3: Gender Roles

1. Thompson, 1978.
2. Ibid. p206, refering to Briffault 2, p389, 410; Schoolcraft 5.10; Pliny NH 28.78; Colum. R.R. 11.3.64. and Krige J.J. *Social System of the Zulus* London 1936, p200.
3. Gould Davis 1975, pp37-8.
4. Mantegazza 1935, p133.
5. Mead 1949, p98.
6. Briffault 2, 1959, p407, quoted in Thompson 1978, p205.
7. Michelmore 1964, p145 quoted in Gould Davis 1975, p93.
8. In the classical legend Atlanta, a woman athlete, won all the events in the mixed Olympics.
9. Tacitus 1971, p66, 108, quoted in Brindenthall & Koonz (eds) 1977, p26. There is no contradiction here between the early matriarchal

cultures whom Briffault and Bachofen found to be vegetarian. This was a warlike and therefore transitional culture where women had refused to be subjugated as with Budicca in Britain and the legendary Amazons.
10. Evans 1921-35.
11. Ridgeway 1901-3.
12. Harrison 1905.
13. Glotz 1925, quoted in Stone 1979, p65.
14. Briffault 1927 (abridged 1959).
15. Rostovtzeff, 1927.
16. Hobhouse L.T. p150-4, quoted in Thompson 1978.
17. Eisler 1987, p68.
18. Leacock E, 'Women in Egalitarian Societies', in Brindenthall & Koonz (eds), 1977.
19. Engels 1940.
20. Feature article in *The Guardian* by S.J. Yoon.
21. Lesko B, in Brindenthall & Koonz (eds), 1977.
22. Quoted in Eisler 1987, Introduction.
23. Gimbutas, 1974, p18.
24. Mellaart, 1975, p280.
25. Eisler's information is taken from Gimbutas 'The First Wave of Eurasian Steppe Pastoralists into Copper Age Europe', *Journal of Indo-European Studies* Vol.5 (Winter 1977).
26. Thompson, 1978.
27. Briffault Ib 2 407, as quoted in Thompson 1968.
28. Address given to La Leche League Conference, Ilkley, West Yorkshire, 1989.
29. The high maternal mortality suffered when male medical practitioners began to take over childbirth was in inverse relation to social class. Working class mothers who were still being delivered by midwives had a much lower mortality rate.
30. Gould Davis 1975, pp158-176.
31. Eisler 1987, p81.
32. Hesiod, *Works and Days and Theogony* in Robinson 1968, p12-13, quoted in Eisler 1987.
33. Herodotus 1 173.5. The same rule also held in ancient China, see Wittfogel quoted in Thompson 1978.
34. Eusibuis, quoted in Thompson 1978.
35. AC 631-4, quoted in Thompson 1978.
36. Arr. Ind 1 23.7. Arrian (native) from Thompson 1978.
37. Hawkes 1968, p43 and Smith and Dale 1920, 1, p292, both quoted in Thompson 1978.
38. Hesiod as note 33 above, pp12-13.

39. Ibid. pp13-14.
40. Meskell, L. 'Goddesses, Gimbutas and New Age Archaeolgy'. *Antiquity* 69, (1995) 74-86.
41. Hesiod, ibid pp15-16.
42. Clearch 49, Charax 10, Uli.Ant. 13, cf Varr. ap Aug. CD 18.9. note given in Thompson 1978.
43. Eisler 1987, p106 and Gould Davis 1975, p193.
44. Harrison 1905, p646.
45. Beard 1946, p46, quoted in Eisler 1987.
46. Boulding 1976 p262-3 quoted in Eisler 1987, p115.
47. Bachofen op cit p104-5 quoted in Gould Davis 1975, p113.
48. Strabo, 503-4 quoted in Thompson, 1978. Thus in at least one part of the Caucuses there was an agriculturally based matriarchal people, though it seems that they were also militarily minded, perhaps because of the hostile groups surrounding them.
49. Herodotus 4, 110-3, quoted in Thompson, 1978.
50. Diodoros Siculus 3. 52, quoted in Thompson, 1978.
51. Arrianus fr 58, Markwart 29, quoted in Thompson, 1978.
52. Letharby, W.R. 'The Earlier Temple of Artemis at Ephesus' (*Journal of Hellenic Studies*, 37.1), quoted in Thompson, 1978.
53. Diodoros Siculus 3, 52-4, quoted in Thompson, 1978.
54. Themistag 3F HG, 4 512, quoted in Thompson, 1978.
55. Gould Davis 1975, p60. See also Spence 1968, p112.
56. Hood 1971, p117. For the discussion of Crete as a matriarchy see Hawkes 1968, Thompson 1978, Evans 1921-35 and H. Reusch, *Zum Wandschmuck des Thronsaales in Knossos*, in *Minoica: Festschrift zum 80 Geburtstag von J. Sundwall*, Berlin 1958, pp334-58.
57. Willets 1969.
58. Seltman 1956, quoted in Stone 1979, p64.
59. Butterworth 1966, quoted in Stone 1979, p68.
60. Platon, N. 'Minoan Palaces as Centres of Organisation of a Theocratic and Political System', in Krzyszkowska and Nixon (eds), 1981.
61. Ibid.
62. Hood 1971, p117.
63. Glotz 1925, p143.
64. Nilsson 1952.
65. Evans 1921-35.
66. Mellaart 1967, p128.
67. Ibid.
68. Shanks and Tilley, 1992.
69. Thomas, 1991.

70. Shanks and Tilley, 1992.
71. Cameron's paper reconstructions of this fresco can be seen in Hagg and Marinatos (eds), Stockholm, 1987, p326.
72. Evans 1921-35, Vol III p66.
73. Hagg and Marinatos (eds), Stockholm, 1987, p233 (discussion).
74. Evans 1921-35 Vol III, pp497-509.
75. cf Kaiser, B. *Untersuchungen zum Minoischen Relief*, Bonn 1976 p280 fig 445. noted in Immerwahr, S. 'The People in the Frescoes', in Krzyszkowska and Nixon (eds), 1981.
76. Platon, N. 'The Development of Minoan Writing: Pictorial Hieroglyphs', in Ekdotike Athenon S.A. (ed) 1974, p157
77. Hawkes 1968, p153.
78. Tzedakis, Y and Hallager, E. 'A Clay Sealing from the Greek-Swedish Excavations at Khania', in Hagg and Marinatos (eds), Stockholm 1987, p119.
79. Cameron, M. 'An Addition to La Parisienne', *Kritika Chronika*, 1964, 38-53.
80. From the discussion held at the Swedish Institute Symposium, published in Hagg and Marinatos (eds)1987, p328.
81. The Etruscan section of the British Museum, plate 324A.49.
82. Mellaart, 1967. p207,225.
83. Gimbutas, 1974, quoted in Eisler 1987, p14.

Chapter 4: The Goddess and Her Symbols
1. The Irish people's reluctance to accept the new patriarchal religion was due to their dedication to Brid/Bride/ Bridget, Goddess of smithcraft, poetry and inspiration, healing and medicine. Monaghan 1981, notes that in the effort to overcome Her worship She was adopted by the new patriarchal church as a saint. Brid was invoked and celebrated in this role for more than a thousand years. Brid's earlier identity as an independent omnipotent Goddess is recalled by the tradition which forbade men to pass beyond the hedge which surrounded Her sanctuary.
2. Stone 1979, p52.
3. This suggestion comes from Angela Solstice, wisewoman, teacher and artist.
4. Wilson 1840, quoted in Nilsson 1952.
5. Ucko, P 1968.
6. Stone 1979.
7. Ibid, Introduction.
8. Marinatos, S. 1960, p34.
9. Nilsson 1952.

10. Neumann 1963 p118.
11. Nilsson 1952.
12. Baring and Cashford 1991, p113.
13. Ibid p114.
14. Ibid p140.
15. Ibid fig 49, p139.
16. Baring and Cashford 1991, p23 figs 20 and 21.
17. Budge 1904, quoted in Thompson 1978.
18. Campbell 1959 (reprinted 1968).
19. Eisler 1987, p86.
20. Ibid p88.
21. Ibid p89.
22. Stuckley 1743, p102 quoted in Dames 1977, p82.
23. Dames 1977, p90.
24. Castleden 1990, p141, quoting Trell in Clayton and Price (eds) 1988 & Marinatos 1984.
25. Evans 1921-35, Vol III p181.
26. Evans 1921-35, Vol III p182.
27. Evans 1921-35, Vol III p182.
28. Eisler 1987, p7.
29. Evans 1921-35 Vol III p485-92 contains illustrations of a wide range of examples.
30. Graves 1961 p316.
31. Ibid. p192.
32. This can also be seen as representing the Goddess Herself; see Chapter 2.
33. Plato *Critias* quoted in Castleden 1990, p149.
34. Baring and Cashford 1991, p131.
35. Ibid p140; Neumann 1963, p279.
36. For examples of ritual regicide see Stone 1979, p158 and Thompson 1978.
37. Evans believed that these three scenes would have been painted on the three separate sections in the triple bastions underlying the two porticoes at Knossos.
38. Peter Langrange quoted in Nilsson 1952; see also illustration of Hathor from 300 BC in L. Durdin-Robertson, *The Year of the Goddess*, Aquarian, 1990, p152.
39. Professor Kristensen quoted in Nilsson 1952.
40. Blanche Williams, *Gournia* p84
41. Levy 1963.
42. Can be seen in Bahn and Vertut 1988, p181.
43. Hagg and Marinatos (eds) 1987, p324.

44. This may be doing an injustice to Cameron who died before his paper on the frescoes was completed and his manuscript and illustrations were mysteriously lost.
45. Castleden, 1990.
46. Baring and Cashford 1991, p121.
47. See Gould Davis 1975; Stone 1979; Gadon 1989 and many others.
48. James 1959, p16.
49. That this consort was ever called a god is due to the ethnocentricism of the religious chroniclers.
50. Gadon 1989, pxiv
51. See note 36 above.
52. Castleden 1990, p 110.
53. Ibid, fig 51.
54. Nilsson 1952.
55. Groenewegen-Frankfort 1951.
56. Platon 1975.
57. Personal correspondence with Peter Warren 1995.
58. Lawson 1910, p540-1.
59. Tumasonis, D. 'Some aspects of Minoan Society: A View from Social Anthropology' in Krzyszkowska and Nixon (eds) 1983 p307.
60. Judge 1978, p166.
61. Mellaart 1977, 2:VI, quoted in Eisler 1987, p76.

Chapter 5: Not with a Whimper

1. Morgan 1988.
2. An ash layer of 780mm was discovered in a core taken from the sea bed 120 kilometres south east of Thera, but the level of ash on Crete can only be estimated. Castleden, 1990, p146 suggests that Knossos, which is equidistant from Thera compared to where the core was taken from, would have had an ashfall of between 200 and 300 mm thick.
3. Castleden 1990 p144-6.
4. Popham 1984
5. Quoted in Morgan 1988.
6. Doumas 1992, p30 referring to the work of Manning, S. 'The Bronze Age Eruption of Thera, Absolute Dating, Aegean Chronology and Mediterranean Cultural Interactions'. *Journal of Mediterranean Archaeology*, 17-82, 1988,(p47) and Manning, S. 'The Eruption of Thera. Date and Implications'. TAW III, 1, 29-40, 1990, (p30-33).
7. Gadon, 1989.
8. Hood 1971.
9. Palmer 1969.
10. Hallager 1977.

11. Chadwick 1976.
12. Castleden 1990, p168.
13. Baumbach, L. 'An examination of the Personal Names in the Knossos Tablets', in Krzyszkowska and Nixon (eds) 1983.
14. Palmer 1969.
15. as note 13.
16. Niemeier, W.D. 'The Character of Knossosian Palace Society in the Second Half of the Fifteenth Century BC, Mycenaean or Minoan?', in Krzyszkowska and Nixon (eds) 1983.
17. Reusch, H. *Zum wandschmuck des thronsaales in Knossos in Minoica* (supra n 14) 334-358, 1961 refered to in Hagg and Marinatos (eds) 1987.
18. Niemeier 1981 (as note 16 above), p226.
19. Castleden 1990a, p67 fig 11.
20. Ibid. p159.
21. Thompson 1978, p413.
22. Eisler 1987, p95.
23. Gimbutas 1973, p202-3.
24. IG 3, 373 cf Isaeus 5,47. quoted in Thompson 1978,
25. Hawkes 1968, p183.

Chapter 6: The New Religion
1. Thompson 1978, p430.
2. Ov, f5, 229-56 quoted in Thompson 1978.
3. Hawkes 1968, p134.
4. Monaghan 1981, p25-6.
5. *Pausanias* IX.4.3; Plutarch, *Theseus* quoted in Evans 1921-35.
6. Evans 1921-35 Vol III, p74.
7. Monaghan 1981, p51.
8. Hesiod, *Theogonia* 929 k-m quoted in Thompson 1978, p267.
9. Varr ap Aug quoted in Thompson 1978, p267.

Index

Spelling of place-names

Because of differences in the Greek and Roman alphabets some of the place-names mentioned in the book can have alternative spellings. Examples are Hania (Chania, Khania), Iraklion (Heraclion), Ayia (Aghia, Ahia, Ayia, Hagia).

Indexing of place-names

All places in Crete and Greece are indexed under the place-name. Places in other countries are indexed under the name of the country; for example - Egpyt: Thebes.

Adonis 110
adyton 120, 138–9, 140
Aegean Islands 163
Aeschylus 79, 90
Agamemnon 90
Akkadia 161, 163
Akrotiri 26–7, 29, 63, 96, 101, 103, 170–1
Albania 128
Alexander the Great 83, 182
Alpnu 107
altar rituals 139–140
Amazons 68, 89–92
Amelthae 109, 145
Amnissos 17, 37, 142–3, 194, 199; see also Eileithyia
Anatolia 26, 81–82, 136
Anderson, William 69
Andros 26
Anemospilia 53, 133, 166
Aphrodite 27, 82, 165
Apodoulou 17
Apollo 128–9, 201
Apolonius of Tyana 198
Archolochori 23, 34. 62, 131
Ares 189

Arete of Cyrene 87
Ariadne 134, 194–8
Arignote 87
Arinna 119
Aristaeus 144
Aristophanes 87
Aristotle 80, 87
Arkhanes 2, 16, 39, 62, 96, 136, 149, 165, 168, 173, 179, 181, 184, 202–3
Artemis 136, 193, 195, 198
Ashera 185–6
Asine 98
Assyrians 54
Äström, Paul 41
Atlanta 213
Athena 54, 57, 93, 116, 125, 137, 157, 189, 193–4, 197
Athens 86, 128, 185, 189
Atlantis 11–13, 203
Ayia Irini 26–7
Ayia Triada 14, 16, 33, 35, 96–7, 99, 103, 106, 114, 117, 121, 138–40, 153, 157, 160, 178–9, 203
Ayios Nikolais 145

Index

Bachofen, J.J. 22, 69, 83, 90
Baring, Ann 126, 145, 150, 154, 158
Basilea 92
Baumbach, Linda 177
beehive tombs – see tholos tombs
bees 122, 143–5
Benton, Sylvia 27
Biblos 204
birds 145–6
bird–like figurines 174
bird–like jars 146–7, 160
Boardman, J. 180
boats 107, 154
Boudicca 90
Boulding, Elise 88
Boulotis, Christos 106
Boxer's Vase 104
breasted jugs 145, 158
breasts and breastfeeding 78, 101
Bride or Bridgit 128
Briffault, Robert 39, 57, 66, 67, 69, 77
Britomaris 194–5, 198
Brown, Ann 20
Bull Leaper figurine 60
bulls and bull–leaping 7, 149–152, 137–8, 158, 193, 196–7
burial traditions 164
butterflies 121–2, 142
Butterworth, E.A. 94

Cadogan, Gerald 97
Cameron, Mark 95, 101, 106, 133, 153
Campbell, Joseph 128
Cashford, Jules 126, 145, 150, 154, 158
Castleden, Rodney 11, 18–21, 35–36, 41, 60, 133, 154, 159, 170

Catal Huyuk 2, 7, 8, 10, 20, 24, 40, 42, 48–49, 62, 64, 106, 111, 120, 150, 152, 164, 167
cave shrines 131–2
Cerridwen 40
Chadwick, John 36, 177
chariots 23
Chieftain Cup 104
childbirth 78, 149
Cleopatra 183
Clymemnestra 90
cod–pieces 8, 104
Conkey, Margaret 99
consciousness, altered levels of 135
Corinna of Boeotia 87
Corinth 131
cowries 46
crocus 27
cuckoo 189
Cup Bearer fresco 113
Cybele 144
Cyclades 25, 26, 84, 161

Daedalus 134, 191, 193, 195–8
Dames, Michael 49, 128, 150
dance 134–5
Davis, Elizabeth Gould 42, 66–68, 83, 88, 92, 111, 118
Delos 26, 129, 145, 195, 201
Delphi 27, 87
Demeter 40, 65, 109, 150, 161, 163, 185, 194
Demokritis 66, 87
Dia 195
diamonds 146–7
Diana of Ephesus 150
Dictynna 198–9
diet 42–3
Diktian Cave 113
Diodorus 91–92
Dionysus 195, 197

221

Index

Diotema 87
dittany 199
Dorian Greeks 88
Dorian invasion of Crete 25, 173–6, 181–3
Doumas, Christos 27, 171
doves 7, 199

earthquakes 168–171
Egypt 54, 73, 136
Egypt, Cretan pottery in, 31
— Alexandria 88
— Hawara labyrinth 18
— Medinet Habu labyrinth 20
— Raquote 88
— Thebes 32
— Tutankhamum's tomb 166
Eileithyia 128, 142, 145, 190, 193, 195, 199
Eisler, Riane 25, 40, 57, 74, 79, 87–88, 111, 128, 167
Elephsus 135
Eleusian mysteries 135
Eleusis 27, 109, 133, 150
Elizabeth I 157
endogamy 80
Engels, Fredrich 72
England: Avebury 49–52, 130, 138
— Grimes Graves figurine 47
— Guernsey 52
— Jersey 52
— Margate 186
— Saffron Walden 134
Epeiros 128
Epicurus 87
Erechtheius 201
Etruscan religion 107
Europa 191–2
Eusebuis 82
Evans, Arthur 1, 4, 8, 19, 21, 33–34, 37,41, 52, 61, 64, 69, 97–8, 106, 126, 137, 168, 171, 176, 180, 183, 193, 196

faience 52, 59–60, 152, 204
figs 141
figurines ('goddess') 46–47, 50, 53, 84, 103–4, 116, 124–5, 139, 154, 174, 179, 183–4
'flame ware' 58
Fournou Korifi 16, 58
France: Laussel 47
France: Niaux 121
Frankfort, Henrietta Groenwegen 162
frescoes 23, 29, 32, 54, 63–64, 95–96, 99–103, 113
Fromm, Erich 65
Furumark 36

Gadon, Elinor 156, 167
'galopetrai' 38
Gazi 42, 139, 180, 183–4
genital mutilation 66
Gero, Joan 99
Gimbutas, Marija 16, 25, 33–34, 39, 48, 57, 74, 86, 121, 122, 152, 155, 182
'goddess' figurines – see figurines
Golan figurine 120, 154
Goodison, Lucy 79, 104
Gortyns 127, 182, 191
Gournia 16, 18, 121, 139, 152, 179
Glotz, Gustave 69, 97, 115
Graves, Robert 144
groves 133, 141
'guardrooms' 23
Guernsey 52

Hacilar 2, 111, 167
Hagg, Robin 53
hairstyles 102, 113

Index

Hallager, Eric 177, 180
Hania 2, 105, 168, 173, 177, 198, 203
Harpies 197
Harrison, Jane 69
Harvesters Vase 55, 104, 135,
Hathor 109, 151
Hawkes, Jacquetta 24, 31, 53–55, 57, 68, 85, 88, 103, 110, 112, 118, 131, 157, 162, 166–7, 186, 191
Hecate 109, 197
Hephaistos 125–6
Hera 40, 157, 189, 191, 193, 197
Heracles (Hercules) 126, 129, 192, 197
Hermes 193
Herodotus 82, 90, 182
Hersonissos 198
Hesiod 43, 79, 85, 62, 182
Higgins, Reynold 52
Hobhouse 71
Homer 12, 24, 83, 87, 134, 137, 188, 191–2, 201
Hood, Sinclair 18, 32, 64, 92, 96, 168–9, 176, 180,
Hopkins, C. 52
Horns of Consecration 7, 117, 152
hunting 97
Hutchinson, R.W. 178
Hyakinthos 131
hydra 197

Iasos 27
Icarus 196
Iceland: Sertsi 169
Inanna 154
Iraklion 42
Iraq: Halaf culture 121
Ishtar 8, 40, 119
Isis 39–40, 119, 151, 154

Isopata 61
Israel: Goddess figure from Golan Heights 154
Italy: Cretan tombs in Sicily 165
ivory 59–60
ivy 142

James, E.O. 46, 155
Japan 156
Jason (and the Arganauts) 82, 192, 197
Jersey 52
jewellery 52

Kamares Cave 131
Kamares pottery 57–58
Kamilari 57, 104, 134
Karphi 53, 180, 183–4
Kastri 26–7
Katamba, tombs of 137
Kato Pervolakia 132
Kea 26–7, 29
Kekrops 86
Kephala Hill 10
kernos 120, 135
Knossos 2, 10, 14, 16–18, 20–23, 29–30, 33–37, 39, 53, 56–57, 60–61, 63, 96–97, 102, 106, 107, 116, 121, 125, 132, 134–9, 143–5, 147, 149, 152–3, 158–60, 164–5, 168, 172–3, 177, 179, 183, 193–4, 202
Kober, Alice 36
Kore 163
Korea: Cheju 72–73
Kos 85
Koumasa 184
Kourete 134
Kronos 134, 191
Kurgans 74
Kydonia 199
Kyrene 32

Index

Kythera 26–7, 29

La Parisienne fresco 54, 96, 99, 103, 106, 153, 203
labyrinths 14, 18, 20, 131
 — Egyptian 18, 20
labyris 7, 18, 29, 62, 78, 96, 103, 116–7, 120–6, 131, 133, 135, 139–141, 143, 145, 152–3, 162, 193,
Langrange, Peter 151
larnax 149, 164, 166
Lausel figurine 46–47
Lawson, J.C. 165
Leacock 72
Leacock, Eleanor 41
leadership 67
Lebadeia 185
Lemnos 85
Leonidi 165
Lesbos 85
Lesko, Barbara 73
Lespugue figurine 46
Lethaby 91
Levy, G. Rachel 152
Liedloff, Jean 41
Lily Prince(ss) fresco 95
Linear a and B - *see* scripts
Lioness Rhyton 55
Lisos 198
Luce, J.V. 170
Lustral basins – *see* adyton
Lyttos 198

Maat 40
Maenads 195
'magazines' 14
Mallia 14, 17–18, 20–21, 23, 31, 34, 53, 61, 121, 139, 179,
Mallia pendant 143
Malta 49–52, 155, 172
 — Ggantija Temple 51

Manning, S. 171
Mantinea 87
Marinatos, Spyridon 36, 53, 62, 63, 119, 170
Marinatos, Nanno 135
mazes 134, 146–7
Mead, Margaret 66
Medusa 197
medicine 42
Medua 197
megarons 178–9, 184, 205
Melissa 109, 145
Mellaart, James 2, 7, 10, 20, 25, 42, 44, 48, 62, 74, 98, 109, 111, 145, 167,
Melos 26, 29, 145
menstruation 66, 78
Meskell, Lynn 86
Mesopotamia 136
metalwork 61–62
Michelmore, S. 67
Miletos 26–27
'milk stones' 38
Minos (Cretan title) 1, 191–2, 196–8
Minos, King 193, 195
minotaur 192–3, 195
Mirabello, Gulf of 141
Mochlos 122, 124, 169
Monaghan, Patricia 92, 194, 198
monotheism 156
Morgan, Lyvia 29, 101, 169
Mount Dictynnaion 198–9
Mount Dikte 198
Mount Juktas 132, 166, 191
Mycenae 105, 133, 158
Mycenaean art 122, 142
 — bird–like Goddess 124
 — shaft graves 166
 — seal 56
 — 23, 32, 36, 54, 97, 100, 107–8, 145, 162, 172–3, 203

Index

Mykonos 26

Nana 119
Nathor 117, 146
Naxos 26, 85, 195, 197
Nepthys 109
Neumann, Erich 39, 57, 150
Niemeier, Wolf Dietrich 178
Nigeria 157
Nilsson, Martin 97, 116, 121, 140–1, 160–1, 195
Ninlil 39
Nirou Hani 121

ochre 148–9
Octopus chalice 144
Odent, Michel 78
Odyssey 83
Old European culture 155
olive trees 198–9
Olous 198
Olympia 27, 128
Olympic Games 88
opium 135
oracles 40, 129, 145
Osiris 109, 156
owls 199
Ox Head Rhyton 55, 151

pairs 147–8
pairs, women depicted in 107
Palaikastro 134
Palestine 185
Palmer, L.R. 176–7, 180
Pankalochori 184
papyrus stalks 122–3
Paros 26
Pasiphae 80, 191–2, 195–6
Peak sanctuaries 132–3
Pendlebury, J.D.S. 184
Persephone 40, 109, 129, 150, 161, 195

Perseus 192, 197
Phaedra 196
Phaistos 14, 17–21, 23, 33, 35, 37, 116, 121, 133–4, 147, 149, 179, 182, 191, 193
Phaistos pottery 57
Phalasarna 199
Phourni 63, 95–96, 149, 154, 166, 203
Phylakopi 26
physiology of gender 67–68
Pichler, Hans 171
pillars (as symbol for Goddess) 7, 100, 142–3, 145, 199
pillar crypts 7, 132
pillar libation rituals 139
Piskokephalo 133
pithoi 17, 19, 58–59, 117, 121, 141, 164
Plato 12–13, 87, 149
Platon, Nicholas 11, 52, 95, 164, 178
Pliny 66
Plutarch 84
polytheism 156
pomegranates 141, 189
Popham, Mervyn 171, 180
Poseiden 107, 112, 125–6, 188–9, 191–3, 198, 200
pottery 57–59
Prasa, country house shrine 17
Processional fresco 113, 122
Proximal 87
Psili Korfi 132
Psychro 132, 183
Pylos 32, 36, 176–8
Pythagurus 87–88
Pythia 145

Rethymnon 17, 184
Reusch, Helga 178
Rhea 134, 190

Index

rhytha 55, 59, 139–40, 151, 205
Ridgeway, W. 69
Ring of Nestor 121
rituals 139–40
Robinson, J.M. 85
Rostovtzeff, M. 69

sacral knots 28, 120, 152–4, 205
Sakellarakis, Effie and John 166–7, 202
Samos 110
Santorini – see Thera
Sappho 87, 110
Schiering, Wolfgang 171
Schliemann, H. 107
scripts – see writing
Scully, Vincent 53
seafaring (Cretan) 24
sealstones 33, 52, 55–56, 105–6, 140, 153, 159, 205
Seltman, C. 94
Serbia: Vinca 33, 111, 152
serpents 7, 116, 119, 126–131; see also Snake Goddess
Setlund, Gosta 102
Shanks, Michael 98–99
sheela–na–gigs 65
shields 8, 23, 148
Skandeia 27
Sklavokampos 17
'slave troops' 24
Snake Goddess 54, 60, 96, 103, 113, 153
snake venom 135
snakes – see serpents
Socrates 87–88
Sophia 40
Spain: Menorca 118
spinning – see textiles
spirals 146–7
splitting cell 147–8

Stone, Merlin 79, 88, 118
Stukley, William 130
Sudan 157
Sumer 73, 154
swords 23
Syria 136

Tacitus 68, 72
Telesila of Argos 87
textiles 39, 63–64
Thanner 107
Thebes 163, 185
Themistoclea 87
Thera (now Santorini) 13, 23, 26–7, 29, 58, 96, 100–1, 122, 136–7, 146, 160, 168–72, 202–3
Theseus 192, 195–6
tholos tombs 7, 15, 140, 145, 154, 164, 166, 178
Thomas, Julian 22, 98
Thompson, George 8, 15, 26, 33, 39, 57, 65, 66, 69–71, 74, 78, 82, 86, 88, 90, 109, 111, 181, 201
Tilley, Christopher 98–99
Tiryns 97,–98, 175, 203
trade (Cretan exports) 30–33
trees – see groves
Trianda 26
Troy 194
Tumasonis, Donald 165
Tunisia 185
Tutankhamum 166
twins 147–8 (see also pairs)
Tylissos 17, 37
Tzedaskis, Yannis 105

Ucko, Peter 24, 46, 118
Ugarit 27, 185–6
Ukraine: Mezhirich 152
Vaphio 161

Index

Vaphio cups 137, 151
Vaphio Ring 121
Vasiliki 11
Vasiliki pottery 58
Vathypetro 17
Ventris, Michael 36
Vernofereto cave 132
Vestonice figurine 46
volcanic eruption (Thera) 168–171, 203

Warren, Peter 16, 165, 180
waz, lily-shaped 122–3
weaving – see textiles
Willendorf figurine 46–47, 120, 154

Willets, R.F. 72, 94, 191
Williams, Blanche 151
Wilson, Horace H. 118
windows, women at 136
writing (early scripts) 8, 12, 33, 36, 176–7
Wunderlich, Hans 19–23, 102, 117, 132, 168–9, 180

Zakro 17–18, 34, 55, 121, 172, 178–9
Zeus 80, 107, 109, 112, 116, 125–6, 129, 132, 134, 145, 156–7, 188–91, 193, 199–200
Zominthos 37, 131